Employee Ownership, Participation and Governance

This volume is an examination of the origins, characteristics and performance of employee-owned firms. Representing the first in-depth study of Employee Share Ownership Plans (ESOP), it focuses on firms which have converted to either partial or full employee ownership using recent institutional, fiscal and legal innovations. Key questions addressed include:

- under what circumstances do firms convert to employee ownership?
- what are the main organisational and institutional features of firms with ESOPs?
- are ESOPs an effective method of stakeholder capitalism?

Based upon five years of empirical research, this is an important and topical contribution to recent debates on the changing nature of employment.

Andrew Pendleton is Professor of HRM at Manchester Metropolitan University.

Routledge Research in Employment Relations

1 Social Partnership at Work
Carola M. Frege

2 Human Resource Management in the Hotel Industry
Kim Hoque

3 Redefining Public Sector Unionism
UNISON and the Future of Trade Unions
Edited by Mike Terry

4 Employee Ownership, Participation and Governance
A Study of ESOPs in the UK
Andrew Pendleton

Also available from Routledge:

Rethinking Industrial Relations: Mobilisation, Collectivism and Long Waves
John Kelly

Employee Relations in the Public Services: Themes and Issues
Edited by Susan Corby and Geoff White

The Insecure Workforce
Edited by Edmund Heery and John Salmon

Public Service Employment Relations in Europe: Transformation, Modernization or Inertia?
Edited by Stephen Bach, Lorenzo Bordogna, Giuseppe Della Rocca and David Winchester

Employee Ownership, Participation and Governance

A study of ESOPs in the UK

Andrew Pendleton

London and New York

First published 2001
by Routledge
11 New Fetter Lane, London EC4P 4EE

Simultaneously published in the USA and Canada
by Routledge
29 West 35th Street, New York, NY 10001

Routledge is an imprint of the Taylor & Francis Group

Typeset in Baskerville by Exe Valley Dataset Ltd, Exeter
Printed and bound in Great Britain by
Biddles Ltd, Guildford and King's Lynn

British Library Cataloguing in Publication Data
A catalogue record for this book is available
from the British Library

Library of Congress Cataloguing-in-Publication Data
Pendleton, Andrew, 1957–
Employee ownership, participation, and governance: a study of ESOPs in the UK / Andrew Pendleton.
p. cm.
Includes index.
1. Employee ownership—Great Britain.
2. Management—Employee participation—Great Britain.
3. Stock ownership—Great Britain. I. Title.

HD5660.G7 P419 2000
331.2'164—dc21 00–04263

ISBN 0–415–20424–0

To Amy, Eileen, and Leah

Contents

Tables and figures

Tables

Figures

Acknowledgements

This book has been a long time in the making. I first developed an interest in employee ownership at the beginning of the 1990s. Nick Wilson, then a colleague at Bradford University, was mainly responsible for introducing me to this field. We spent an enjoyable few months travelling the length and breadth of Britain collecting information on the early ESOPs. He was mainly responsible for assembling the questionnaire used to collect data on employee attitudes (see Chapter 8). Nick's research interests later shifted from profit sharing and share ownership to credit management, but I continued to find ESOPs and employee share ownership fascinating. My main interest has been in the interface of employee share ownership, industrial democracy, and corporate governance. Hence the title and subject matter of this book.

It is inevitable that many colleagues have contributed to this research. Keith Walley, and later John McDonald, provided able research assistance. Also at Bradford, Maria Gonzalez-Menendez and Andrew Robinson provided invaluable help with the research, and contributed to a broader programme of work on employee financial participation. The role of financial support cannot be underestimated. Nick Wilson's initial investigations were assisted by the Centre for Economic Performance at the London School of Economics, whilst later the research was supported by the Nuffield Foundation, the Economic and Social Research Council (grant R000234936), and the Bradford University Research Fund.

A very large number of people in organisations with ESOPs and employee share ownership have contributed to the project. It is invidious, of course, to name individuals but mention should be made of Dave Wheatcroft and Norman Watson of the Centre for Employee Ownership and Participation. It was at a CEOP conference in the Mainline social club in Rotherham that I first really appreciated the importance of the ideas that are the central themes of this book, namely that the interests, philosophies, and objectives of the key actors in ESOPs determine the structures and character of employee participation and governance. More recently, I must acknowledge the stimulating debates on employee share ownership held with colleagues on the Inland Revenue Advisory Group on Employee Share Ownership, and in the Inland Revenue itself.

Many others have contributed to the development of ideas presented in this book. Many a discussion has been held with Neil Carter on workers' co-operatives and employee ownership. Howard Gospel has provided invaluable advice and help. As the book was being written, we started to work together on the labour effects of corporate governance systems, and this helped to broaden the disciplinary boundaries of the book to include some engagement with the Financial Economics literature on governance. I have also enjoyed working with Mike Wright on employee share ownership in newly industrialising countries and on employee attitudes to share ownership. Colleagues at the University of Sydney (where I spent some study leave in 1997) provided a most welcoming and stimulating atmosphere in which to start writing the book. Mention should also be made of stimulating discussions with Lisa Trewhitt and Erik Poutsma.

I must also thank colleagues in the Department of Management and the Human Resource Management Research Group at Manchester Metropolitan University for their forbearance and support during the final stages of writing the book. In particular, I am grateful to Sue Shaw for understanding the demands that writing a book entails, and to Pat Walker for her unfailing help and enthusiasm.

Last but not least, I must record my deepest gratitude to Amy, Eileen, and Leah. They put up with a distracted father and partner without complaint, and displayed an interest in the progress of the book that was beyond the call of duty.

Abbreviations

ABI	Association of British Insurers
AESP	All-Employee Share Plan
AEU	Amalgamated Engineering Union
AGM	Annual General Meeting
APS	Approved Profit Sharing
BALPA	British Air Line Pilot's Association
BIFU	Banking, Insurance and Finance Union
CBI	Confederation of British Industry
CEC	Commission of the European Communities
CGT	Capital Gains Tax
CSOP	Company Share Option Plan
DTI	Department of Trade and Industry
EBO	Employee Buy-Out
EBT	Employee Benefits Trust
ECOP	Employee Common Ownership Plan
EMA	Engineers and Managers' Association
EMI	Enterprise Management Incentives
EPEA	Electrical and Power Engineers' Association
EPS	Earnings Per Share
ERISA	Employee Retirement Income Security Act
ESOP	Employee Share Ownership Plan
ESOT	Employee Share Ownership Trust
GAO	General Accounting Office
ICA	International Co-operative Alliance
ICI	Imperial Chemical Industries
ICOM	Industrial Common Ownership Movement
IOD	Institute of Directors
LA	Local Authority
LT	London Transport
MBO	Management Buy-Out
MEBO	Management-Employee Buy-Out
MMC	Monopolies and Mergers Commission

NALGO	National Association of Local Government Officers
NBC	National Bus Company
NFC	National Freight Consortium
NI	National Insurance
OECD	Organisation for Economic Co-operation and Development
PLC	Public Limited Company
PRP	Profit-Related Pay
PST	Profit Sharing Trust
PTE	Passenger Transport Executive
QUEST	Qualifying Employee Share Trust
SAYE	Save As You Earn
SBG	Scottish Bus Group
TGWU	Transport and General Workers' Union
TRASOP	Tax Reduction Act Stock Ownership Plan
TUC	Trades Union Congress
TWA	Trans-World Airlines

1 Introduction

In April 1990 the 350 bus drivers, administrators, maintenance and garage staff of Chesterfield Transport bought the company that employed them from Chesterfield Borough Council. They paid £2.45 million, having raised £215,00 from amongst themselves, and most of the rest from bank loans.[1] The employees acquired 15 per cent of the equity of the new company directly, whilst 85 per cent was purchased by an Employee Benefits Trust (EBT), using a loan from the trade union bank Unity Trust. The employee buy-out team comprised senior managers and representatives from the Transport and General Workers' Union (TGWU), the Amalgamated Engineering Union (AEU), and the National Association of Local Government Offices (NALGO) (now part of UNISON). The Employee Benefits Trust, which was composed of elected employee trustees and outside experts, became the supreme governance body of the new company. It oversaw the activities of the Board of Directors, upon which there was an elected employee director.

The conversion to employee ownership facilitated a package of productivity improvements in the company, thought to be necessary in the intensified competitive environment of the bus industry post deregulation in the mid-1980s. Initially the company progressed well, with scheduled repayments of the loans leading to steep increases in the value of the shares held by the workers. By 1992, however, the company was facing a financial crisis and the top management decided to impose pay cuts on the workforce. Virtually all of the TWGU membership voted for a strike. Although the dispute was resolved before industrial action was to take place, the long-term outlook for the company was not good. By the mid-1990s the company was making an operating loss and had to reschedule its bank loans. It had an ageing bus fleet and was unable to generate the investment funds to buy new vehicles. By 1995 it was clear that Chesterfield had no long-term future as an independent company (Monopolies and Mergers Commission 1996). Stagecoach submitted a bid to buy the company in that year. Ninety-five per cent of the employees voted in favour of the bid and each received around £15,000 for their shares. This was 300 times their initial investment in equity shares.[2]

This book is about companies like Chesterfield Transport. It examines the birth, life, and demise of employee ownership of firms. The type of employee ownership examined in this book is where employees acquire some or all of the share capital of the firms that employ them. In the UK this is mainly a recent phenomenon, though there are isolated examples of firms where employees have held or benefited from share ownership for many years. The significance of the new forms of ownership is that ownership, governance, and internal company organisation are not necessarily closely interrelated in the same way as in the more traditional form of employee ownership in the UK, the workers' co-operative. There, a philosophy of equality bound these dimensions together: employees held equal shares and, in many cases, all employees were actively involved in governance and the management of the firm. Hierarchies were eschewed, and the process of management was exercised collectively. A division of roles between workers and managers and between employees and owners was not to be found, at least in theory.[3] By contrast, in firms like Chesterfield Transport, employee ownership typically co-exists with conventional forms of management organisation, and may be shared with external, non-employee owners. The two roles of employee and owner may be kept distinct so that employees' ownership of stock does not impact directly upon their day-to-day conduct of work tasks. Usually, a cadre of professional managers is responsible for co-ordinating and directing the production of goods and services.

Two sets of issues arise from this new configuration of ownership and management. The first is concerned with how employee share ownership affects the governance of the firm. Do employees acquire control rights commensurate with their ownership rights? Are there specific institutional innovations, such as co-determination on company boards, and do these give effective 'voice' to employee owners? How do employee owners monitor the actions of the professional managers? The second set of issues concerns the involvement of employees in the management of the firm, defined as the direction and co-ordination of the inputs to production. Does employee ownership confer greater rights on employees to influence these processes? Are there any specific innovations in what is normally termed 'employee participation'? To distinguish these two sets of questions, it could be said that one is concerned with employees as owners, whilst the other is more concerned with employees as employees. A further question concerns how far these two are interconnected in practice. For example, do employees seek greater rights to decide how their daily work tasks are undertaken as a result of their ownership of the firm, and if so, how successful are they in achieving this?

Our focus in the book is a small group of organisations where employees acquired a substantial portion of equity from the latter half of the 1990s onwards. In most, but not all, cases an ESOP – Employee Share Ownership Plan – was used to transfer equity to employees. The distinguishing feature of ESOPs is the presence of one or more trusts to acquire, hold, and distribute equity to employees. These trusts normally have powers to borrow money to finance acquisition of shares for eventual allocation to employees. There are other mechanisms used to bring about employee ownership, not all using the ESOP mechanism strictly defined. Employees may purchase shares outright, though it is common in organisations where substantial ownership passes to employees to create trusts to repurchase shares from departing employees (so that ownership does not pass to outsiders). In other cases, shares are acquired by employee trusts but are held in trust in perpetuity rather than distributed to employees. Some firms use a combination of these mechanisms, so it is difficult to draw sharp demarcation lines between methods of creating employee ownership.

However, we do distinguish the employee ownership firms under scrutiny here from the much larger group of firms with employee share schemes. There are currently about 1,750 firms with broadly based share ownership schemes operated in accordance with government legislation (Treasury 1998). We refer to these as 'conventional' share schemes as these are clearly the dominant form of employee share ownership and because these rarely involve attempts to reshape corporate governance or employee participation.[4] Instead, the primary objective of these share ownership schemes is to provide additional remuneration to employees. Typically, only a small proportion of total equity (2–3 per cent) passes to employees, compared with 10 per cent and above in the most of the employee ownership firms we focus on. However, the distinction that we make is inevitably a fuzzy one, for two reasons. The first is that the employee share ownership firms make use of elements of schemes (such as approved profit sharing trusts) used by firms with 'conventional' share schemes. The second is that many large firms with 'conventional' share schemes have started to use ESOP-specific institutions, such as statutory employee benefits trusts, to resource their share schemes and to take advantage of a recently created tax 'loophole' (see Chapter 4).

Our concern then is with a sub-set of share ownership schemes where employee share ownership is at high levels and where share ownership is intertwined with considerations of governance and participation. This is not to say that revolutions in either governance or participation necessarily occur alongside conversions to partial or full employee ownership. In some firms little change in either appears to have taken place. However, these issues tend to loom large either during or after the conversion process, to an extent that does not normally occur in the case of 'conventional' share schemes. Furthermore, share ownership is explicitly focused on transferring ownership, not just on providing additional share-based remuneration.

It is difficult to determine the population size of these firms with employee ownership as they tend to be subsumed within official statistics for the various statute-based forms of profit sharing and share ownership, and no specific statistics exist for firms with substantial employee ownership.

Estimates in the mid-1990s suggested that there might be up to 100 such firms but this was based on little more than inspired guesswork.[5] However, ESOPs attracted more interest, support and publicity than their small numbers might appear to warrant. As we show in Chapter 3, the major political parties, employers, and trade unions proclaimed there to be significant benefits in the ESOP form. From the mid-1990s a large proportion of ESOPs have been sold on to other firms (especially in the bus industry) and the number of employee ownership firms appears to be smaller than in the mid-1990s. However, there are now very many more firms with ESOP structures, but most of these are using them in conjunction with 'conventional' share schemes and to secure a tax benefit rather than transforming ownership, governance, and participation.

In the main the employee ownership firms we focus on came about in two ways. One was where management and employees mounted buy-outs of public sector firms undergoing privatisation. Most of these occurred in the late 1980s and early 1990s, and were found especially in the bus industry. Most were highly leveraged buy-outs whereby large loans were taken out against the firm to enable employees to purchase their firms from central or local government bodies. In many cases, these firms were highly unionised, and both the manner of the conversion and the governance/participation structures created were powerfully influenced by this feature. The second arena for employee ownership conversions was the private company sector where the owner(s) wished to divest or exit. In many cases these were owner-managed firms. The motives for conversion typically involved a concern to protect the firm from take-over and dismemberment on the exit of the owner and also 'paternalist' sentiment that employees should share in the cake they had helped to make. Some of these firms were highly unionised, but on the whole the departing owners were the prime or sole movers in the conversion, and the governance/participation structures reflected this.

Perspectives on employee ownership

In recent years employee share ownership (as broadly defined) has become widespread in some advanced industrialised countries, and its nature and impact has become an important issue for policy-makers, managers, and employees. Employee ownership is most widely found in the United States where in 1999 it was estimated that there were 11,500 ESOPs and stock bonus plans, supplemented by 3,000 broadly based stock option plans and 4,000 stock purchase plans. When the employee shares held in 401(k) pension plans[6] are included, it is estimated that around 8 per cent of US corporate equity is held by employees (National Center for Employee Ownership 1999). Employee share ownership is less common in Europe but is also widespread in the UK where it is estimated that about five million employees have acquired shares through the various approved share schemes and privatisation initiatives (Inland Revenue 1999c). Other European countries have a lower incidence of employee share schemes and a greater emphasis instead on employee savings plans (e.g. Germany, Sweden) or profit sharing, defined as payments to employees financed out of company profits (e.g. France) (see Poutsma *et al.* 1999; Poutsma 2000). There have also been some attempts to promote employee share ownership in privatisation initiatives in Latin America, Africa, and Asia but in most instances employee ownership levels have not been sustained over time (see Wright *et al.* 2000).

There are several important perspectives on employee share ownership in both the academic literature and in policy discussions. The ESOP concept itself dates from the 1950s, and is associated with the American investment expert Louis Kelso. He argued that capitalism would benefit from much wider ownership of productive assets, and saw employee ownership as a means of overcoming fundamental divisions between capital and labour. By spreading ownership, capitalism would become a stronger economic system (an argument recently echoed by Jeffrey Gates in *The Ownership Solution* (1998)). It was suggested that if workers received a greater share of profits they would be less likely to join unions or to seek wage increases (Kelso and Adler 1958; see also Kaufman and Russell 1995).

In the 1960s Kelso devised the core mechanisms of the ESOP. Firms would sell shares to an ESOP, which had raised the finance to purchase them using a loan. The firm would acquire the proceeds of the loan from the ESOP but would then make contributions over time to the ESOP. These would be used to pay off the loan and to release shares to employee accounts. This concept appealed to several major conservative politicians such as Richard Nixon and Ronald Reagan. Reagan enquired 'could there be any better answer to the stupidity of Karl Marx than millions of workers sharing in the ownership of the means of production?' (quoted in Russell 1984). Most important, Kelso attracted the support of Senator Russell Long who was involved in the drafting of the landmark Employee Retirement Income Security Act (ERISA). This legislation introduced a set of tax benefits for ESOPs (corporation tax relief on the full cost of ESOP loans, i.e. both the principal loan and the interest payments) which led to substantial growth in this type of employee ownership.

A similar perspective on financial participation more generally is found in some currents of academic literature. It has been argued that profit sharing and employee share ownership have been used as measures to weaken employee attachment to unions and to mitigate wage pressures during periods of tight labour markets. Harvey Ramsay demonstrated that employer use of sharing schemes in the UK tended to be concentrated in periods when labour militancy was high or the power of organised labour was strong (usually in the upswing of the business cycle or in wartime) (Ramsay 1977, 1983). Once the crisis passed, schemes tended to fall into decay. The past evidence is certainly very supportive of this interpretation, but it is widely thought that it has weaker explanatory power for the growth of share ownership schemes from the 1970s. The decline of union membership in countries such as the USA and the UK has coincided with expansion rather than contraction of sharing schemes. An alternative view, advanced by Michael Poole (1989), is that of 'favourable conjunctures'. In his view, organisational democracy has advanced over time but unevenly and with considerable variation both between and within nations. Whilst the type of factors identified by Ramsay can be important, there are also counter-cyclical factors such as the tendency for some distressed firms to convert to employee ownership during recessions. From the late 1970s the 'favourable conjuncture' encouraging sharing schemes in the UK was the succession of right-wing governments subscribing to views about 'popular capitalism' and the emergence of Human Resource Management as a more strategic form of Personnel Management.

More recently there are a number of strands of literature which suggest that employee share ownership has to be seen in the context of fundamental restructuring of economies and firms. Blasi and colleagues have recently argued that the growth of employee share schemes in the US can only be understood in the context of a collapse in the 'fixed wage' system. They point out that over two decades growth in average real wages has been nearly flat, compared with average real stock price increases of around 8 per cent. Real growth in pension contributions has also been more or less flat over the same period. They suggest that companies prefer contingent forms of compensation such as profit sharing, share schemes and defined contribution pension schemes[7] so that remuneration can be tied to company performance. At the same time, employees have sought these kinds of benefits to compensate for the lack of growth in 'fixed' or core wage benefits (Blasi *et al.* 1999).

Blasi and his colleagues do not discuss why this phenomenon is occurring but there are several explanations elsewhere in the literature. One suggestion is that intensification in product market competition lies behind the shift to contingent compensation systems generally and to employee ownership in particular. Many firms aspire to transfer risk to employees in the form of contingent compensation so that pay and benefits can be adjusted to meet the market circumstances and performance of the firm. There is a certain amount of evidence from surveys in the United States (Kruse 1996), the UK (Gonzalez-Menendez *et al.* 2000), and Australia (Drago and Heywood 1995) to support this. An alternative approach draws on theories of optimal labour contracts to explain why employee ownership conversions are widespread in industries facing growing competition, such as airlines. It is suggested that the offer of employee ownership assists firms in renegotiating labour contracts (usually to achieve wage concessions) in circumstances where low-cost entrants are threatening their viability (Gordon 1998). In these industries, union bargaining power is such that managements cannot usually impose wage or employment reductions unilaterally, at least not without the possibility of seriously damaging conflict. The offer of stock to employees signals to employees that the competitive threat is a real one, whilst at the same time indicating that post-contract opportunism on management's part will be precluded (because workers will share in any future gains). Although this line of argument is clearly not appropriate to explain the very high incidence of share schemes in the United States, it does have powerful explanatory value in accounting for major conversions to employee ownership in a number of industries, such as steel and airlines.

An alternative set of arguments links the rise of share ownership to major changes in the ownership and management of the American corporation since the 1970s. Broadly speaking, comparisons are made with an era of 'managerial capitalism' when the managers of large companies had a substantial degree of autonomy from its diffuse and widely dispersed owners. To use Berle and Means' (1932) words, there was a separation of ownership and control. Managers exploited their autonomy to develop internal labour markets, long job tenure, and seniority wage systems (Donaldson 1994). This system can be contrasted with 'investor capitalism' in the 1980s and 1990s. Growing concentration of ownership, coupled with greater assertiveness of investors, placed much greater constraints on management activity. These circumstances favoured employee ownership in several ways. The major financial restructuring of American corporations that occurred in the 1980s included highly leveraged buy-outs (Jensen 1993) which in some cases involved employees. More generally, the growing demands and scrutiny of firm behaviour by investors tended to encourage the use of performance devices, such as share schemes, which aligned the interests of employees with those of investors. To use the language of principal–agent approaches, principals (i.e. owners) could reduce monitoring costs by linking the remuneration of agents (i.e. employees) to corporate performance. Employee ownership would promote information sharing, thereby reducing asymmetries of information between managers and workers, and also monitoring of workers by each other.[8] However, the danger of employee ownership is that it dilutes incentives and control rights (cf. Jensen and Meckling 1979), and for this reason institutional investors usually place limits on the amount of equity that they are willing to share with employees.

An alternative perspective suggests, on the basis that most broadly based share schemes are initiated by managers, that share schemes are used to provide protection for incumbent managers from the market for corporate control (Useem and Gager 1996). Given the stringent restrictions on take-over activity in most US states, an employee-owned portion of equity can block take-overs since employees are likely to side with managements in a contested bid. The most well-known case is that of the Polaroid Corporation which managed to resist a hostile take-over by Shamrock in 1988 by establishing an ESOP. The presence of the ESOP prevented Shamrock from acquiring the 85 per cent of equity or two-thirds of the votes necessary under Delaware law to permit immediate take-over (see Blair 1995: 310). Useem and Gager suggest that investors find it politically difficult to contest the establishment of an ESOP since promotion of share ownership is widely viewed in the USA as a good thing and, furthermore, is seen as desirable for investors because of its apparent interest-alignment properties.

Recently a new literature has emerged which gives some insights into the spread of employee share ownership but which is mainly prescriptive in character. Margaret Blair in *Ownership and Control* (1995) has presented a case for employee involvement in ownership and corporate governance based not on notions of social responsiveness or idealistic views about stakeholding but on core principles of corporate governance found in the Financial Economics literature. Drawing on Williamson's views on asset specificity and relationship-specific investments (1979), she argues that in many instances employees make firm-specific investments in human capital. There is a risk to employees in that managerial opportunism may prevent employees from securing the full benefits of this investment. Furthermore, there are opportunity costs to employees in so far as they could have invested their human capital in more remunerative ways elsewhere. In situations where employee knowledge and skills are central to wealth creation, employees bear risk as well as financial investors. On the established corporate governance principle that those with firm-specific investments at risk should have rights to residual incomes and to control (i.e. the power to make decisions not specified in explicit contracts) (Grossman and Hart 1986; Hart and Moore 1990; Hart 1995b), employees should share in profits and control. Blair writes that 'employee-owned companies are the ultimate examples of governance structures that empower employees and protect investments in firm-specific human capital' (Blair 1995: 298).

The contemporary significance of this interpretation resides in the shift that is thought to be occurring in advanced economies towards a 'knowledge economy'. Increasingly, wealth creation involves the application of human knowledge to the provision of services rather than the production of goods using physical capital. The critical investments therefore are those made in human capital. In these circumstances, the appropriate mode of governance is one involving employees in ownership and control. This line of argument is now filtering through into reformulations of the theory of the firm, and it has been proposed recently that the modern firm should be conceptualised as a 'nexus of specific investments' (Rajan and Zingales 1998). The other side of the coin is that firms need to find ways of binding employees with highly developed firm-specific knowledge to the firm so as to protect investments the firm has made in training and development. Employee ownership, both as remuneration and as a governance device, provides a way of doing this. A further relevance of employee ownership is that products and services requiring the application of extensive and specialised human capital may have long development times, and it may be some time before the firm can generate an income stream. In these circumstances the provision of stock, which pays future dividends based essentially on current human capital investments, can substitute for wages (see Leadbetter 1997). For this reason, employee share ownership is widespread in software development companies in areas like Silicon Valley.[9]

It is possible to identify individual cases which exemplify these developments and possibilities but in the main these types of argument tend to be speculative and prescriptive. As yet they are not firmly based on specific empirical research but, since they are recent in origin, this is inevitable. That said, they are highly plausible interpretations of recent developments. Furthermore, these arguments are of immense conceptual importance as they are contributing to a reformulation of contract-based and property rights-based theories of the firm that is currently underway in US Financial Economics.[10] In addition, they provide a rationale for employee involvement in ownership and governance based on 'hard' economic and financial rather than 'soft' idealistic principles.

Ownership, governance, and participation

An extensive literature on employee ownership has developed over the last 25 years, mainly reflecting the growth of ESOPs in the USA after the passing of the ERISA legislation in 1974. Not surprisingly most of this literature is American. There is a moderately sizeable UK literature on 'conventional' share schemes and profit sharing, but as yet very little on ESOPs as such. This is not surprising either given that so far there have been few ESOPs in the UK. The purpose of this book is to go some way towards remedying this gap in the literature by providing an empirically based analysis of the development of UK ESOPs and of the interrelationships between ownership, governance, and participation within them. Before outlining the themes that will emerge in the book, an overview of the employee share ownership literature is provided so that the book can be located in the various disciplinary traditions.

The central theme and finding that has pervaded virtually all of the literature on employee ownership is that of employee participation in decisions. Ultimately this is based on fundamental principles of ownership. As Ben-Ner and Jones put it:

> ownership of an asset consists of the right to control its use and to enjoy its returns. In an organization, control entails the determination of the objectives of the organization, the positions that individuals occupy, what are the functions of these positions, who occupies them and how their occupants are induced to carry out their functions. Returns include the financial and physical payoffs generated from the operation of the organization.
>
> (1995: 532–3)

A critical feature of ESOPs, as indeed of other forms of ownership, is that in practice these two formal rights (control rights especially) may give rise to complex sets of institutions and procedures which may vary between firms and contexts. Varying configurations of control rights and return rights are possible. It is common to represent these two sets of rights emanating from ownership as two separate dimensions, with the possibility that a large number of combinations of the two can be plotted (see also Gordon 1998). A common finding in much of the employee ownership literature is that control rights are less substantial than return rights. This is interesting and perplexing given the 'conventional wisdom' in writing on corporate governance. Property rights theory, for instance, would suggest that, as owners, employees should have residual control rights (i.e. all rights not explicitly stated in a prior contract).

In Labour Economics most attention has been paid to the performance of firms with employee ownership, and in particular whether the productivity performance of employee ownership firms is superior to that of others. The intellectual origins of this literature can be located in landmark studies in the theory of the firm (Alchian and Demsetz 1972; Jensen and Meckling 1976). Alchian and Demsetz viewed the firm as a system of team production in which the firm co-ordinates a set of labour inputs internally rather than acquiring these externally on each occasion a good is to be produced. It is necessary to provide a set of incentives and performance measures to guide the performance of team members (i.e. employees), and to appoint a monitor to oversee the work of the team. However, in many circumstances, the complexity of the production processes is such that it is difficult to monitor and measure the performance of each employee, and hence standard incentive payment systems cannot be readily used. In these circumstances collective incentive systems are necessary to provide incentives and to prevent shirking.[11]

To these insights were added those of Jensen and Meckling a few years later. They also applied principal–agent theory to the theory of the firm, and analysed the problems of incentives and control based on asymmetrical distribution of information between principals and agents. They emphasised the monitoring costs for principals given that employees have superior information about many aspects of the production process, and the bonding costs to employees arising from the possibility that employers will in the future take most of the gains arising from long-term employment and the development of human capital. Although these authors were not sympathetic to employee ownership and co-determination (because it diluted the monitoring incentives of principals, and discouraged hierarchical co-ordination) (see Jensen and Meckling 1979), it has been widely argued that financial participation will reduce agency and bonding costs by providing employees with incentives to share information and to give commitment to the objectives of the firm (e.g. Conte and Svejnar 1990). The performance of employee ownership firms is therefore predicted to be superior to that of other firms. Equally, it can also be argued on the basis of the Jensen and Meckling approach that firms with employee ownership will have inferior performance because of the dilution of principals' returns and control rights, thereby weakening incentives to monitor employees

There has been a succession of studies of the performance of employee ownership firms to test these predictions. The main findings (summarised in Conte and Svenjar 1990, Cotton 1993, and Kruse and Blasi 1997) from these studies are the following. Contrary to one set of predictions, employee ownership does not appear to have negative effects on productivity. In fact there is some evidence of positive effects. However, the extent and character of employee participation in decisions tends to have a substantial bearing on productivity effects in many instances. This finding emerged most clearly in a major study of employee ownership by the US General Accounting Office in the mid-1980s (General Accounting Office 1987). Employee ownership by itself appeared to have no productivity effects, but when it was combined with participation positive effects were observed. The reasoning for this finding is that, without participation, the capacity for reducing agency costs via information sharing is underdeveloped. Conte and Svejnar (1990) note that employee participation in work decisions rather than employee participation in governance (i.e. by representation on corporate boards) tends to be associated with productivity enhancements. This is consistent with the notion that task-level participation provides a forum for sharing information about production whilst co-determination rights may dilute the monitoring incentives of other owners and their agents.

Whilst the emphasis in this literature on the importance of participation is valuable, there are limitations with this approach. One problem, as Ben-Ner and Jones (1995) point out, is that writers in this tradition tend not to incorporate the reasons for adopting employee ownership. As the literature has shown (e.g. Blasi and Kruse 1991), ESOPs and other forms of employee ownership are introduced for a variety of reasons, such as preventing take-overs or taking advantage of tax breaks, and are not necessarily focused on improving productivity. Any performance effects associated with ESOP seem likely to be strongly influenced by the circumstances in which employee ownership is introduced and the motives for it. The rationale, type, and effects of participation may well vary between these different contexts. In an adequately performing firm, the most appropriate type of participation (from a performance perspective) to accompany a modest employee ownership scheme may well be task-level participation, so as to promote information sharing and commitment. By contrast, where an ESOP is introduced in a distressed firm alongside a package of wage concessions, participation in corporate governance may well be appropriate to protect employees against post-contract managerial opportunism. This configuration of ownership and governance may well lead to substantial performance improvements but these may not be picked up by comparisons of employee-ownership and non-employee-ownership firms as the performance of the firm in question may well still be below average.

The other main body of literature is mainly located in Industrial Relations and Human Resource Management, and to a certain extent in Psychology and Sociology. Once again participation and governance are critical issues. There are several strands in this literature. One has been concerned with providing in-depth information on conversions to employee ownership and the characteristics of participation and governance subsequently. Raymond Russell's case studies of San Francisco refuse collectors and taxi firms are a good example of this (1985a), as are Hammer and Stern's analyses of the Rath Packing Company and other conversions (1980; 1986). This type of study tends to highlight the objectives of the various groups involved in the transfer to employee ownership, especially in relation to the design of participation and governance institutions, and how the institutions adopted are bargained outcomes.

A second strand of literature has been concerned with identifying the incidence of various forms of participation (for example Russell 1988; Blasi and Kruse 1991; Rooney 1988; Logue and Yates 1999). The main finding in this literature is that participation in task decisions and in corporate governance tends to be limited to a minority of firms with ESOPs. As ESOPs in these studies include both majority worker-owned firms and companies with low levels of employee share ownership (most companies), this set of findings is not surprising. They differ somewhat from studies of 'conventional' share schemes in the UK which tend to find that firms with these schemes have a higher incidence of task-level participation mechanisms than firms without schemes (Poole 1988).

A third, and substantial, strand of literature has focused on employee attitudes. Here, the premise is that participation in ownership should lead employees to develop more favourable attitudes to the firm, to show more commitment to it, and to derive greater satisfaction from their work and employment. There is a rich diversity of findings from this literature (which is considered in more depth in Chapter 8) but a unifying theme has been that participation in decisions is essential if attitudinal change is to be realised (Klein 1987). Equally, there are powerful indications too that the financial rewards from ownership are a significant determinant of employee attitudes (Klein 1987; French 1987), and the two findings mirror the conceptualisation of ownership mentioned earlier which sees it as (potentially) conferring rights to control and rights to returns.

Finally, there is small strand of literature concerned with the involvement of unions in conversions to employee ownership and the impact of ownership on union role and functions. Here, the starting point is the conflict of roles for unions that employee ownership appears to generate, with unions potentially representing both employees and owners. This appears to have the potential to undermine unions' traditional representational role, especially if they become involved in governance institutions

(McElrath and Rowan 1992; Stern *et al.* 1983). A further problem for unions is that once employees become owners they may perceive less need for institutions designed to protect them against the employer (Bradley and Nejad 1989; Kruse 1984; Toscano 1984). This literature explores whether these potential conflicts of function materialise and whether employee attachment to unions does in fact weaken (see Pendleton *et al.* 1995b for a summary of this literature).

Issues of participation and governance, then, have been central to the literature on employee ownership. Much more has been written on this aspect, and much greater importance has been attached to it than to return rights. Yet whilst the coverage of the various literatures has been comprehensive, further work could be done on participation and governance in a number of respects. First, greater attention could be paid to the circumstances in which employee ownership takes place. The context of conversion seems likely to influence the objectives of the various parties involved (owners, managers, workers etc.) and hence is likely to affect the type of participation and governance institutions adopted (if any). Conversions of distressed firms with high levels of union membership and representation seem likely, all things being equal, to lead to a different pattern of participation and governance than in cases where employee ownership is introduced by an owner-manager of a firm without unions. These differing circumstances and outcomes have been reflected in differing findings in case study accounts, but it would be helpful if there were a more systematic exploration of this.

Second, it will be beneficial to disentangle the various forms of participation and governance potentially found in employee-owned firms. Whilst the literature clearly distinguishes work-group participation, for instance, from board-level representation, there is a tendency to view them as lying along a similar continuum with board-level representation been seen as a more advanced, though rarer, form of participation. From our perspective, however, the situation is more complicated than this. Participation in work-level decisions can be seen as fundamentally different from board-level representation (at least in employee ownership contexts) in that one provides voice to workers as employees whilst the other provides it to workers as owners. One is about participation, as usually defined, whilst the other is about corporate governance. Also, there is often an additional complicating factor in the form of union-based representation.

These various forms of voice may have different dynamics and express different sets of objectives for each of the groups of actors in the firm, and may differ according to the circumstances of ownership conversion. It is possible to identify conflicts between the various forms of voice, as perceived by the actors. For example, unions may prefer involvement in ownership-based governance institutions rather than in extensions of employee-based participation, despite their traditional reservations about employee ownership, for fear that extended employee participation may conflict with unions' role in employee representation. Contrary to expectations perhaps, managers may prefer employee involvement in governance institutions despite its peculiar monitoring implications (employee-owners monitor managers who monitor employees, who are also owners) because employee aspirations in task participation may be heightened by their sense of ownership rights, and hence may obstruct management's capacity to direct and co-ordinate work. Much may depend on the circumstances. This observation about managers might apply mainly to highly unionised companies where unions provide institutional backing for employee assertiveness in participation institutions. In non-unionised firms managers may find it easier to influence task participation so that it does not interfere with management 'rights' and activities.

Outline of the book

This book attempts to explore the origins, character, and outcomes of participation and governance in UK ESOPs. It is located in the Industrial Relations/Human Resource Management tradition of writing on employee ownership, though it draws on insights from writing in Labour Economics, Financial Economics, and Corporate Finance. The distinguishing feature of the approach here is that close attention is paid to the interests, objectives, and actions of the main social groups involved in conversions to employee ownership and the subsequent operation of employee-owned firms. We argue that the interplay of these, as they interact with the circumstances in which conversion takes place, has a powerful effect on configurations of participation and governance, and on the outcomes of these. A corollary of this approach is that formal ownership structures of firms provide only a partial guide to what happens in practice. The key thing is what individuals and groups do with institutions and practices of ownership, participation, and governance. Indeed, the selection of institutional forms will depend on the objectives and interests of those involved in the design of post-conversion firms. So, by way of differentiating between firms, a key criterion is not so much the percentage of equity owned by the workforce but the variations between firms in actors' objectives leading to these differences in equity ownership. But in turn the extent of equity ownership will help to institutionalise differences between firms, to guide future action, and hence help to differentiate between firms. There is thus a dialectic between structure and agency in the birth, life, and demise of employee-owned firms.

The data upon which these observations are based was collected over an extended period, commencing in 1990. A variety of information sources are drawn upon. During this period interviews were conducted with senior managers in over 60 firms with either an ESOP or a substantial element of equity-based employee ownership. From this, a database of 62 firms was constructed recording information on ownership and participation structures at the point of conversion, and on the circumstances of conversion. These interviews were supplemented with interviews with other actors in the firm, such as employee directors, trustees, union representatives, and with documentary information. Two other company-level databases were constructed. One comprised industrial relations/human resource management, participation, and accounts information of 93 bus companies, of which some were in employee ownership, some in private ownership (as a result of privatisation), and some in public ownership. The second comprised data on industrial relations/human resource management and participation for 25 firms outside the bus industry with employee ownership and a control group of 59 firms (of similar size and sector) without. Employee attitude surveys were conducted in six firms (mostly in the bus industry) and surveys of 'key respondents' to capture patterns of decision-making in governance institutions were undertaken in ten firms. The focus on the bus industry was deliberate as this industry was far and away the main site of employee ownership and ESOPs in the first half the 1990s. Overall, the data collected enables a comprehensive picture of UK ESOPs at the end of the twentieth century, as most of the known cases are included in our study. We hope that it complements survey-based and quantitative studies by providing greater information on the processes of employee-ownership conversion and operation. At the same time, the large proportion of ESOP firms in our study permits well-grounded generalisations.

Before we present the results from the empirical studies we examine the emergence of the ESOP. In Chapter 2 we consider various forms of ownership structure that can be viewed as antecedents of ESOPs. We suggest that the ownership, participation and governance structures of ESOPs can be viewed as a reaction to the perceived shortcomings of workers' co-operatives. By contrast, we view common ownership, 'conventional' share schemes, and management buy-outs as more benign influences on the development of ESOPs. In fact, to a certain extent ESOPs can be seen as a synthesis of these three corporate forms. In Chapter 3 we go on to examine the political influences on ESOP development. We suggest that this and other new forms of employee ownership benefited from the impetus given to share ownership by Conservative Governments in the 1980s and 1990s. The privatisation programme also created opportunities for workers to take over ownership of the firms that employed them. However, we also discern an anxiety about ESOPs emanating from a dislike of collectivist forms of organisation. As for the Labour Party and New Labour, we suggest that the notion of ESOPs was an important 'bit player' in the evolution of party policy that occurred during the latter half of the 1980s and early 1990s. However, aside from a few high-profile adherents such as Bryan Gould, party policy-makers did not display a deep commitment to the ESOP idea. This appears to have carried over into the New Labour Government. Whilst the government is deeply committed to extending the number of share ownership schemes and the number of share-owning employees, it is not yet clear how far the government wants to deepen ownership, in the sense of increasing the proportion of companies' equity that is held by employees. Overall, our suggestion is that ESOPs are liked by most but loved by none.

In Chapter 4 we present a more technical outline of the various forms of ownership structures that have been adopted by employee ownership firms since the 1980s. We outline the main characteristics of the two main kinds of ESOP – the 'case law' ESOP and the statutory ESOP. Direct share subscriptions and common ownership are also considered. Many firms in our study use a combination of these methods of securing employee ownership. To take Chesterfield Transport, for example, a case law ESOP was used in conjunction with direct subscriptions. Some of the equity acquired by the Employee Benefits Trust was to be retained in trust permanently to provide partial common ownership.

In Chapter 5 we start to present the empirical results. We examine first the contexts in which employee ownership conversions took place. By far the largest single group of firms were buy-outs during privatisation. Within this group, bus companies predominate. As mentioned previously, the bus industry was the single most important locus of employee ownership conversions in the final decade of the twentieth century. For this reason we discuss the case of the bus industry separately from the other privatised firms. Besides the privatisation group, we also discern a small group of what traditionally would have been called 'rescue' conversions. These were firms or parts of firms that were about to be closed by their owners, and employees mounted bids to purchase them. A third group we refer to as 'paternalist divestments' as the initiative for employee ownership came from paternalist owners who wished to protect their employees on their exit from ownership. Although the circumstances and motives for employee ownership differed between these three groups, we argue that corporate control is a unifying characteristic. In each group, key actors in the conversion sought to protect their firms from changes in corporate control that would have adverse consequences for incumbent managers and employees. Finally, there is a fourth group where ESOPs are created for what we call 'technical' reasons. Here the intention is not so much to develop employee ownership as to respond to regulatory problems emanating from pre-existing share schemes. Recently, this group has expanded considerably in size because the conjunction of statutory ESOPs with Save As You Earn share option schemes has created the potential for sizeable tax concessions to companies.

At the end of Chapter 5 we reconfigure our groups of employee ownership firms on the basis of who is involved in conversion. Thus we discern four groups. A 'representative' firm is one where employees and their representatives tend to be deeply involved in the transition to employee ownership. A 'risk-sharing' firm is one that is essentially a management buy-out, with an employee ownership component. 'Paternalist' conversions are initiated by owners or owner-managers. Finally, 'technical' firms are as defined above, and schemes in these firms tend to be initiated by finance and legal managers.

In Chapter 6, the focus shifts to participation in decisions and corporate governance. The main findings and approaches of the Industrial Relations/Human Resource Management literature on employee participation are considered, as are the main elements of the Corporate Governance literature. It is argued that in employee ownership firms, enhancement of *participation* by employees and *governance* by employee-owners might be observed. Furthermore, participation and governance might become intertwined, given employees' dual role. In the latter part of the chapter, we suggest influences on the composition and extent of participation and governance. We argue that the objectives of the main actors involved in conversion are likely to have a substantial impact on participation and governance, and attempt to show how variations in actors' objectives and philosophies might be associated with various institutional outcomes.

In Chapter 7, the findings relating to participation and governance in the four groups of firms (identified in Chapter 5) are reported. Clear differences are observed between them. In the 'representative' group there are substantial advances in employee-owner governance though these are secured in conjunction with already existing forms of employee representation. There is little evidence of developments in direct employee participation. In the 'risk-sharing' group there are few developments in either governance or participation. Firms in the 'paternalist' group display some innovations in shareholder representation, but these do not have such a direct impact on corporate governance as the new institutions in the representative group. Finally, there are no innovations in either participation or governance in 'technical' firms, though this is not to say that these firms are hostile to participation *per se*. In each case we link institutions of participation and governance to the objectives and philosophies of the actors involved in establishing employee ownership.

In Chapter 8 we examine the outcome of employee ownership, participation, and governance on employee attitudes. Here our results are consistent with those that have repeatedly emerged in the employee ownership literature. We find that the capacity for employees to participate in decision-making (mainly relating to their role as employees) has a critical influence on whether they feel like owners. In contrast to much of the literature, however, we find that the level of individual shareholdings also has an impact on employees' sense of ownership.

In the final chapter, the findings from the previous chapters are summarised and pulled together. We draw on our findings to reflect on important issues that have emerged in the employee ownership literature over the years. We consider whether there are characteristics of firms that make them more likely to become employee-owned, and also whether there are integral features of employee ownership that result in it being a short-lived phenomenon. We also attempt to draw out the implications of our findings for the literature on the performance of firms with employee ownership. Overall our conclusion is that studies of employee ownership need to pay close attention to the varying circumstances of ownership conversion, and to the objectives and philosophies of those involved in mounting the conversion. Variations in these are likely to be associated with differences in ownership, participation and governance.

2 The development of employee ownership

Introduction

ESOPs first appeared by name in the UK in the second half of the 1980s. The formation of an ESOP at the motorway service company Roadchef in 1986 is often proclaimed as the first ESOP in this country (e.g. Wright and Robbie 1992).[1] In this case an Employee Benefits Trust acquired 12.5 per cent of the company's equity, mainly from the estate of the recently deceased Finance Director (who had been committed to sharing ownership with the employees and who had been exploring the possibility of an ESOP just before his death). The formation of the ESOP at Roadchef was the first of a series of highly publicised ESOPs in the late 1980s and early 1990s. From this time ESOPs attracted a considerable level of interest in the business and quality end of the daily press.

How did ESOPs come about in the UK? Why did this form of employee ownership emerge at this time? We attempt to answer these questions in this chapter. Poole (1989) has identified three types of explanation for the development of economic democracy and industrial democracy over time. One, termed the 'evolutionary' perspective, posits a long-term and broadly linear development towards greater participation by employees, as a result of, *inter alia*, increased technical complexity of modern economies, higher levels of education, and a diffusion of democratic values. A second perspective, associated with Ramsay (1977), suggests that organisational democracy is a cyclical phenomenon. He suggested that employer interest in forms of *economic democracy* with weak control rights, such as profit sharing, tends to be most marked in periods of labour power and high employment when it becomes a useful tool to inhibit various forms of *industrial democracy*, such as union representation. Poole advocates a third approach, which combines elements of both the evolutionary and cyclical perspectives. Called the 'favourable conjunctures thesis', he suggests that organisational democracy advances in an uneven pattern and depends greatly on variations in circumstances. He emphasises managerial choices and values, in conjunction with the power and strategies of other groups in the firm, as critical influences on the development of economic democracy.

In this book we incline towards the 'favourable conjunctures' approach, for reasons to be outlined shortly. The evolutionary perspective is not a compelling one since, although there has been political and managerial support more or less continuously for over 20 years now, evidence from the past indicates that the use of financial participation can wane. The 'cycles of control' perspective too has its shortcomings, mainly in explaining recent developments in profit sharing and share ownership. Widespread use of share schemes recently has coincided with reductions in union density and power so it is difficult to view them as a tool to undermine organised labour.[2] Equally, the low incidence of ESOPs, as a potentially democratic form of ownership, might be seen as arising from weak pressures on employers in the 1980s and 1990s to find innovative ways of taming militant labour.

More recent explanations of economic and industrial democracy emphasise the role of product market competition, rather than labour market pressures, in bringing about certain types of schemes. Hyman and Mason (1995), for instance, argue that intensified competition has led to great interest in employer-sponsored forms of involvement (including profit sharing and share ownership), on the grounds that these may improve corporate performance. Meanwhile, interest in what they call 'participation' (i.e. employee *rights* to influence decisions) has faded away. They suggest that ESOPs have not 'caught on' in the UK because they are collectivist in nature and give employees control as well as return rights.

Our interpretation of both the emergence and limited development of ESOPs in the UK fits in with the 'favourable conjunctures' perspective. The favourable circumstances in the 1980s and 1990s were the presence of a raft of legislation (on 'conventional' share schemes) that could be adapted for ESOP purposes and a strong ideological current in favour of personal share ownership. At the same time ESOPs were a defensive reaction to major threats facing a number of types of firms. For some it was the threat of privatisation, for others it was the possibility of destructive restructuring and downsizing, and for some it was both. The ESOP form was selected in preference to other organisational forms, such as the workers' co-operative, because of their perceived shortcomings, especially in relation to labour involvement in management. At the same time, ESOPs appealed to organised labour because they appeared to give control rights seen to be muted or absent in other forms of economic democracy. In short, ESOPs seemed to give something to everybody. However, 'mass appeal' was not translated into widespread ESOP conversions, probably because of the control rights implications. As the Economics literature has suggested, owners are usually unwilling to dilute their control and residual rights by sharing them with employees, and are unlikely to do so voluntarily (Jensen and Meckling 1979).

In the next two chapters we explore the various elements of the 'favourable conjuncture' that encouraged the development, albeit limited, of

ESOPs in the UK. In this chapter, we first consider the features of ESOPs in relation to earlier forms of employee ownership and suggest that they are a reaction to the limitations of these. We then consider developments in employee share schemes over the last 20 years, and suggest that these provided both a fertile environment and specific legal mechanisms for ESOP development. ESOPs in the United States meanwhile provided a clear model for advocates of employee ownership in the UK. Finally, the emergence of leveraged management buy-outs in the 1980s suggested the potential for innovative forms of financing that could be used for employee acquisitions.

Workers' co-operatives

In the UK ESOPs developed as an alternative to workers' co-operatives. In several important cases where ownership conversion was underway, co-operative structures were initially considered but soon rejected. Co-operatives were perceived, by managers especially, to have several fundamental flaws, mainly relating to inadequate management organisation. The benefit of ESOPs was that they appeared capable of sidestepping these problems. Whereas co-operatives appeared to take the form of *labour-managed* firms, ESOPs were instead *labour-governed* entities. Thus, a clearly defined and specialised management function could operate within the employee-owned firm without undue day-to-day interference from employee-owners. Furthermore, as ESOPs permitted a form of ownership where top managers could have disproportionate ownership rights (rather than equal votes with workers), managers might have a substantial, possibly dominant, role in governance anyway. To elaborate on these differences between ESOPs and co-operatives, it will be useful to outline the core characteristics and development of co-operatives in the UK.

Workers' co-operatives emerged in the early years of industrial capitalism, in response to the dehumanising characteristics of the factory system. 'Born out of a long tradition of self-help, mutuality and industrial democracy, their origins can be traced back to labour movement struggles in the early nineteenth century for better working conditions' (Mason 1992: 193). By becoming owners of their work organisations, employees could be released from the role of appendage to the machine and could instead direct their own work activities. Furthermore, they could direct the overall policies of the firm. The divisions between employee and owners, and between workers and managers, would thereby be overcome. Co-operatives, however, offer even more than ownership. As Schuller puts it (describing Robert Owen's New Lanark 'experiment'), in the co-operative vision people are viewed as social beings, with housing, schooling etc. needs, rather than as a mere source of labour power (1985: 155). The co-operative form of organisation is viewed as a way of meeting these fundamental human needs.

The core principles of co-operative operation derive from those established by the Rochdale Pioneers in 1844. Currently they are set out in a statement of principles emanating from the International Co-operative Alliance (ICA). These require that co-ops are equitable organisations, with equal rights attaching to all members. They must be democratic organisations, run by people selected by the members of the co-operative, with members enjoying equal voting rights. Co-operatives should take an active approach to the education of their members, and should co-operate with other organisations organised on co-operative principles. Hobbs and Jefferis (1990) note that many co-ops in the UK supplement these requirements with the principles of common ownership, namely that the assets of the enterprise are collectively rather than individually owned. Membership is open only to those who are employed by the firm, and all employees have the right to become members (after a qualifying period in some cases). These principles are promoted by the Industrial Common Ownership Movement (ICOM), who have developed a set of model rules which supplement the core co-operative principles issued by the ICA. In the UK most new-start co-operatives take the common-ownership form (Mason 1992: 194).

Co-operatives enjoyed substantial growth from the 1970s, after a long period of decline. The handful of co-operatives in the inter-war period had been fairly stable but from the 1950s the co-operative sector virtually disappeared (see Jones 1975). The number of co-operatives then grew from around 30 in the mid-1970s to nearly 900 ten years later (Hobbs and Jefferis 1990). The main reasons for the rebirth of co-operatives appear to have been provision of some support from government coupled with a more general evolution of social values favouring democracy at work (cf. Poole 1986; 1989). The 1974–9 Labour Government passed the Industrial Common Ownership Act in 1976 to promote co-operatives in small-scale manufacturing enterprises, and established the Co-operative Development Agency in 1978. More famously, the government set up the 'Benn co-operatives' (in the *Scottish Daily News*, KME and Meriden motorcycles), so called because their development was spearheaded by the then Secretary of State for Industry Tony Benn. These were conversions of firms in deep financial trouble, and the co-operative model was viewed as a potential salvation for them. The growth of the co-operative sector appears to have received a further boost from the recession of the early 1980s coupled with the support of local Co-operative Development Agencies established by Labour local authorities (Hobbs and Jefferis 1990). As Poole remarks (1989), the growth of co-operatives is to some extent a counter-cyclical phenomenon as workers attempt to save failing firms by taking over management and ownership. In more theoretical terms, the opportunity costs for risk-averse workers are lower in downturns of the business cycle (though the risk may well in fact be higher) (Ben-Ner 1988). This theoretical prediction is supported by empirical studies, such as that by Perotin (1997) of French co-op formations.

Although the spectacular growth in co-operatives indicates a degree of success for this form of ownership and organisation, there are in fact many shortcomings (real or perceived) of the co-operative model. These provided the context and, in many cases, an explicit part of the rationale, for ESOP development. The root of the problem lies in the particular relationship between ownership, management, and control. Employees, as owners, not only have complete control of the direction of the business, they also typically expect close involvement in the management process, especially where self-management and personal development are important ideals in the firm. It is argued that this inhibits the emergence or appointment of a cadre of professional and expert managers (or conversely that where such a group does emerge the ideals of the co-operative have been lost (see Meister 1984)). These shortcomings of the labour-managed firm have been recurrently expressed within the Economics literature. It has been argued that a managerial hierarchy is necessary, where there are complex production processes, to co-ordinate and control the various labour inputs and the large volume of information to be processed (Williamson 1975).[3] Put another way, in 'team production' it is necessary to appoint a monitor to ensure that workers do not free-ride, as they may well be tempted to do because of the 1/n or 'free-rider' problem (Alchian and Demsetz 1972). Further criticisms of the co-operative form of management are that employees may prefer to channel funds which ought to be used for investments into wages (Vanek 1977; Jensen and Meckling 1979), and that there is a tendency to maximise revenue per worker rather than profits (Ward 1958; Meade 1972).[4] These criticisms reflect the much earlier observations of the Webbs that worker co-operatives would inevitably 'degenerate'. They argued that co-operatives would fail because of lack of relevant commercial knowledge on the part of the workers managing them, and because no one group would be able to co-ordinate and control the activities of the owner-managers (Webb and Webb 1914). In short, the co-operative firm will not pursue profit-maximising objectives and will be inefficiently organised internally (for a recent review of the arguments for and against labour-managed firms see Dow and Putterman 1999).

The experience of the Benn co-operatives in the late 1970s provided very powerful confirmation of the fears of those suspicious of co-operatives. The involvement of shop stewards and other workers in both strategic and day-to-day management, as well as in traditional forms of employee representation, meant that it was near impossible to develop a credible management function. Soon after the Benn experiment ended, Eccles provided a graphic account of these failures at the KME co-operative. Writing of shop stewards in the plant, he notes that 'they were ambivalent about their roles as workforce representatives and policy makers and, unprepared, they were in a poor state to take the initiative even if they had been united on what action was necessary' (1981: 397). The unions were given a key role in the management of the plant but 'they (union representatives) refused to accept that they had a dual role as representatives of the workforce and promoters of organisational competence' (ibid.: 378). A further problem was that it improved impossible to create institutions or procedures that could resolve sectional differences within the workforce (Oliver and Thomas 1990).[5] Given that they were 'rescue' co-operatives it is questionable whether these firms could have survived anyway, but the failures of internal management in these firms have lodged in the managerial psyche as damning evidence of the lack of viability of the workers' co-operative. They also provided clear danger signals to unions, and contributed to suspicion of the worker co-operative form of ownership and organisation amongst unions.

Elsewhere, it is a matter of debate how far these observations about management in co-operatives are well grounded or significant, but the perception that co-operatives suffer from these problems besets them with a plethora of serious difficulties. One, they typically find it difficult to raise capital from financial institutions because of doubts that debts can be repaid. Since they are precluded from raising finance by issuing equity to outsiders, they often depend instead on the financial resources of their members (both to finance conversion and for working capital), which may well be limited. Hence, co-operatives are often under capitalised and display low levels of capital productivity (Abell 1983).[6]

Two, there is a suspicion that the worker-owners of labour-managed firms will choose to maximise short-term revenue gains by taking 'excess' wages, thereby limiting the internal funds that are available for investment. In other words, worker-owners will behave as workers rather than owners, and will put their short-term interests as employees over those of the long-term health of the firm. In practice, these fears are rarely realised in the UK (and elsewhere), though the suspicion amongst managers that co-op members do not behave as 'responsible' entrepreneurs is seemingly a widespread one. In reality co-operative members tend to pay themselves lower wages than the norm, this being a trade-off for employment stability and job security. Robinson and Wilson found that average pay was significantly lower amongst co-operatives than otherwise similar privately owned small firms (1993). Carter (1990) argues that co-ops are dependent on 'sweated labour' because they are dependent for their survival on large contracts from larger firms. They secure these contracts on the basis of 'under-pricing', which passes through to lower wages. In the US, Craig and Pencavel's study of worker co-operatives in the plywood industry of the Pacific North-West[7] suggests that co-op members attach greater importance to job security than high wage levels since wage levels tended to be more responsive to the business cycle than employment, compared with 'conventional' firms (1992). The upshot of these observations is that the fears of economists and managers about the wage behaviour of co-op members are often unfounded. By the same token, though, this pattern of behaviour has contributed to suspicion of co-operatives amongst trade unions, who fear that co-ops undercut the 'going' wage rate.

Another focus of managerial suspicion of co-operatives is pay differentials. The underdevelopment of the managerial function, coupled with an emphasis on equality, means that managerial pay is lower than in 'conventional' firms. Within co-operatives themselves managerial pay is not much higher than that of other workers (or is even the same). The evidence tends to bear out these fears. Robinson and Wilson found that pay differentials were significantly lower in co-operatives than in small private firms, and that average managerial pay was significantly lower in co-ops than in the other firms (1993). Welford, in fact, found that over half of co-ops in his study paid the same rates of pay to all co-op members (1990). The criticism of this phenomenon is that managerial incentives are weak, and that this thereby reinforces the underdevelopment of management in co-operatives.

Widespread suspicion of the labour-managed aspects of co-operative organisation in the UK has meant that co-operatives tend to be concentrated in a restricted range of economic activities. They are typically very small – most (86 per cent) co-operatives have less than ten members – they tend to operate in declining product markets, and they are labour intensive (Hobbs and Jefferis 1990). They also tend to operate in localised product markets and are often unwilling to expand beyond local boundaries (Carter 1990; Robinson and Wilson 1993). The broader co-operative vision, which emphasises personal development and integration of work with the self, has led many to perceive workers' co-operatives as an 'alternative', 'lifestyle' form of organisation, outside the mainstream of economic activity. In its wide-ranging report, the Commission on Social Justice, for instance, noted that co-operatives 'are most effective in areas and sectors which are not attractive to conventional companies' (Commission on Social Justice 1994: 215).

Whether co-operatives are necessarily a peripheral or transient feature of modern society – 'islands of socialism in a sea of capitalism' – is open to question. There are large and successful co-operative movements in France, Italy, and Spain. Certain pre-conditions seem to be necessary to ensure co-operative survival and growth. The Mondragon network of co-operatives in northern Spain have benefited from the availability of loan finance via a locally-based bank, the Caja Laboral Popular (see Moye 1993; Whyte and Whyte 1988). The other feature of many co-operatives in these areas is an emphasis on representative democracy rather than collective management of day-to-day work tasks. Thornley (1983: 327) notes that co-operatives in Italy, which has the biggest co-operative sector in Europe, have shown less concern for individual involvement in decision-making than UK co-ops. An emphasis on involvement in governance rather than day-to-day management has also been observed in long-standing and successful UK co-operatives, and it may be that this shift in approach is necessary for survival either as a viable commercial entity or as a co-operative form of organisation. Cornforth (1995) suggests that as long as co-operative patterns of governance are retained, this does not detract from the co-operative vision. This echoes an earlier life-cycle perspective developed by Batstone (1983), who argued that representative democracy would gradually take the place of direct or 'primitive' democracy.[8]

To summarise, the key problem with co-operatives in the view of many observers is that labour manages the firm. Employees either manage themselves or else employees collectively manage the firm. For both academic and business commentators this means that these firms will be inefficient and ultimately doomed to failure. The fact that there are so few labour-managed firms is said to be proof that it is an inefficient form of operation (Jensen and Meckling 1979). The potential merit of ESOPs is that they do not have the ideological baggage of self-management and 'primitive' democracy associated with the co-operative form of organisation. It is usually accepted that the management of the firm will be conducted by a specialised group of 'professional' managers with clear decision-making rights. This was recognised as a clear advantage of ESOPs over co-operatives by managers involved in ownership conversions in the late 1980s and 1990s. Key figures in both central and local government also recognised these differences with co-operatives, and it is reasonable to conclude that many of the management-employee buy-outs in these years would not have occurred if the ESOP form had not been developed. It is almost certain that they would been sold as trade sales or management buy-outs if workers' co-operatives were the main employee ownership alternative. Furthermore, the large bank loans secured by leveraged ESOPs would almost certainly not have been available to workers' co-operatives (the Yorkshire Rider buy-out in 1988 was financed by bank loans of over £20 million). Meanwhile, for unions, the emphasis in most ESOPs on conventional patterns of management organisation provides a clear 'space' for traditional trade union activities of employee representation.

The upshot of these factors is that conversions to ESOPs have been successfully mounted in considerably larger firms than is the norm for the co-operative sector. Whereas co-operatives have often been perceived as a 'deviant' form of ownership and organisation, operating on the fringes of the economy, ESOPs have appeared as a potentially viable form of employee ownership for firms that are more in the mainstream of economic activity.

Paternalist common ownership

A second strand of employee ownership, which forms a historical context to ESOPs, is the conversion of firms to a form of collective ownership by paternalistic owners. There have not been many of these cases but the firms concerned have often been considerably larger than most workers' co-operatives. Their interest in our context resides in the use of trust structures to bring about a form of employee ownership, and in this respect they can be seen as precursors of ESOPs. The most well-known case here is the John Lewis Partnership. The key feature of this 'high-street' firm is that the owner, Spendon Lewis, placed the entire equity in trust in perpetuity for the benefit of the John Lewis workforce (see Flanders *et al.* 1968).[9] This was the final stage of a long-running experiment by Lewis about the impact of introducing partnership principles into the running of the business. Employees have no direct ownership rights themselves, and unlike ESOPs there are no mechanisms for distribution of equity to individual employees at any point. Instead a trust holds 'their' equity on their behalf. Collective ownership 'underwrites' two important features of employment at John Lewis. One, it provides for an annual profit share or dividend to be paid to all employees. This partnership sharing system predated the creation of the partnership trust in 1950 and reflected Lewis's belief that the rewards of economic activity should be distributed more equitably. The profit share has in the past been paid in the form of non-voting preference shares which in turn attract a dividend coupled with a cash bonus but in recent years a cash bonus has predominated. In good years this is substantial. In 1995, for example, £43 million was paid out in profit shares to the company's 33,500 employees. This was six weeks' pay for each employee, and was equivalent to 12 per cent of the wage bill (Buckley 1995).

Two, it underpins a system of governance which gives employees an important role in the direction of the firm, and provides for employee interests to be incorporated into key managerial decisions. There is a trust which has powers of last reserve and which formally removes the Chairman if the elected representatives of the partners vote for this. The main forum for employee representation is the Central Council, composed of 140 elected representatives. As Bradley *et al.* (1990) put it, the role of the Council in relation to management is akin to that of the legislature to the executive in the US political system. The Council can refer matters to the Board and has the power to demand an adequate response from the Chairman. It also selects five of the thirteen Board members. In exceptional circumstances the Council can set in motion procedures to remove the Chairman. The other six members of the Board are selected by the Chairman. The Chairman heads the management structure of the firm and functions in effect as a chief executive. As can be seen, the management structure is separate from the representative structure but its accountable to it at the apex of the organisation. Unlike workers' co-operatives, then, the John Lewis Partnership does not aspire to be a labour-managed firm. Employees have formal rights of representation in corporate governance, and also consultation rights at lower levels of the organisation, but they are not directly involved in management as such.

There are a few other cases of 'employee ownership' with similar structures to the John Lewis Partnership, such as the Scott Bader Commonwealth. This resin-making firm was transferred to common ownership by its Quaker owner Ernest Bader from the 1950s. The firm's co-ownership structure was viewed by Bader to 'represent essential steps towards a true

Christian Industrial and Social Order'. Like the John Lewis Partnership, the ownership and participation structure evolved over a long period of time. Initially (in 1951), shares were passed to employees but Bader retained a minority but controlling stake. In 1963 the shares were placed into a common ownership company – the Scott Bader Commonwealth. Although there was no individual shareholding, each employee had a vote. The workforce elects a governing council, which controls the distribution of profits, and two directors to the company board (see Hadley and Goldsmith 1995: 171).

These firms are the direct antecedents of ESOPs in several ways. One, they made use of trust structures (or similar) which were later to become the hallmark of ESOPs, though unlike their successors the facility of tax efficient profit share trusts were not available to them. In any case the objective was not to distribute equity to individual employees, who might subsequently choose to sell their shares to outsiders, but to maintain the equity on employees' behalf in perpetuity. Two, the collective ownership of equity is a distinguishing feature of John Lewis, Scott Bader and others. Shares are not held by individual employees, and hence cannot be traded by them. Three, like most ESOPs (but unlike most UK co-ops), there was a managerial group from the outset and an explicit attempt to formulate the division of rights and responsibilities between managers and employee-owner representatives and representative institutions. This is seen most clearly in the Constitution of the John Lewis Partnership referred to above. In Scott Bader, too, the structure of the company remained hierarchical from the outset (Hadley and Goldsmith 1995: 172). Despite the appeal to communitarian and religious values of teamwork and co-operation, employee involvement tends to centre on representation in governance systems rather than direct involvement in day-to-day management. As Hadley and Goldsmith put it:

> While the Code of Practice adopted in Scott Bader in 1972 clearly favoured co-operative rather than directive work relationships and individual managers could lead in a participative style if they wanted to, managerialist practice seemed more consistent with a belief that formal participation should be confined to the representational system and not become a required part of the decision-making processes in the workplace.
>
> (Hadley and Goldsmith 1995: 186)

Firms like John Lewis therefore provided a powerful model for those interested in promoting employee ownership in medium-sized and large firms. The problem of this model, however, is that conversions are heavily dependent on the goodwill and initiative of enlightened owners. The transfer of equity from these owners to the employee trusts was essentially a donation. Few owners are able to follow this example either because of the need to secure their own financial future should they choose to exit or the inheritance claims of their descendants. The alternative – that of selling their equity directly to the workforce – is rarely a practical option because of limited capital resources amongst the workforce. ESOP mechanisms, as we shall see, provide a way of resolving these difficulties by providing a low-risk method for transferring equity from paternalist owners to employees or employee benefit trusts.

Profit sharing and employee share ownership schemes

The third contextual influence affecting the development of ESOPs is the profit-sharing and employee share ownership schemes that became widespread in the UK in the 1980s. These became so popular at this time because of a raft of supportive legislation passed from the late 1970s onwards and because wider share ownership and 'popular capitalism' were strongly encouraged by successive Conservative Governments. The participation of the public and employees in public flotations of public corporations gave a strong, though often transient, boost to personal share ownership and certainly promulgated values associated with share ownership[10]. Leaving aside specific encouragement of ESOPs by government, the wider programme of financial participation assisted the development of ESOPs in two main ways. First, the centrality of wider share ownership in public policy provided a generally supportive environment for ESOPs to flourish by generating awareness of share ownership amongst workers and trade unions. Two, specific elements of the financial participation legislation were utilised to develop the ESOP form. At the same time, the vast majority of profit sharing and share ownership schemes tend to provide very limited management and governance rights to employees. Instead these schemes are primarily a form of additional remuneration. To some extent ESOPs can be viewed as a reaction to these features.

Most discussions identify two main forms of financial participation: profit sharing and employee share ownership (Commission of the European Communities 1996). However, there are sub-species of each, with variations based on the directness of the link between the reward and the performance of the firm. The two main forms are also often interconnected. Cash profit sharing usually provides the most direct and immediate link between reward and company performance. Deferred profit sharing, whereby the profit share is received some time after the period on which the performance bonus is based (typically several years), is clearly less immediate. It becomes less direct also if the profit share is paid in equity shares. Here, the reward derives from the market value of the shares and from the dividends accruing to the share. Both, of course, are contingently related to corporate performance. The main benefit of employee share option schemes, where the employee typically purchases the shares on favourable terms, also resides in growth in share value and dividend payments. A further distinction between cash profit sharing and share schemes is that the former provides a reward for behaviour and performance in the immediate past, whereas share schemes tend to reward future performance. Deferred schemes combine elements of both. In practice financial participation schemes may incorporate both direct and indirect elements, and also combine cash sharing, deferred sharing, and share ownership.

Profit sharing and employee share ownership schemes have a long history in the UK and other industrialised countries. Of the two, cash profit sharing has a longer pedigree, with profit sharing starting to be used in the second half of the nineteenth century (Church 1971; Hatton 1988). It has been observed that profit sharing became popular in periods of full employment and labour militancy (see Church 1971; Ramsay 1977, 1983), whilst schemes often fell into decay during downturns in the business cycle. Employee share ownership schemes are on the whole a more recent phenomenon, and emerged in larger and more sophisticated companies such as Imperial Chemical Industries (ICI) from the 1930s. There was a flurry of interest in financial participation in the immediate Second World War period, and the development of innovative forms of share scheme (see Copeman 1958), but on the whole interest seems to have waned during the 1950s and 1960s (see Baddon *et al.* 1989: 4–5). The resurgence of interest commenced tentatively in the early 1970s with the passage of legislation by Edward Heath's Conservative Government to promote executive and all-employee share option schemes, though this was soon repealed by the 1974–9 Labour Government. At the prompting of the Liberal Party, however, upon whom this Government was increasingly dependent for a working majority in the House of Commons, an all-employee deferred profit sharing scheme was introduced in 1978. After that, most of the legislation to promote employee share ownership schemes and profit sharing was passed by Conservative Governments led first by Margaret Thatcher (1979–1) and then by John Major (1991–7). The Blair 'New Labour' Government has passed further legislation to promote all-employee share ownership schemes and share option schemes.[11]

UK legislation over the last 20 years has provided statutory support for cash-based profit sharing, deferred share-based profit sharing, and various forms of share option scheme. Each scheme attracts tax concessions, which in most cases are mainly captured by the employee rather than the firm. Currently the main schemes are:

Approved profit sharing (1978 Finance Act). Up to 5 per cent of pre-tax profits can be used to buy ordinary shares in the company. These are placed in a profit sharing trust for at least two years, and if employees retain them in trust for a further year (three years before 1995), they attract no income tax liability as a benefit from employment. Instead employees are liable to capital gains tax on their growth in value. For most employees the capital gain is well within their tax allowance so no tax is due. Employees may be granted up to 3,000 shares or to the value of 10 per cent of their salary (whichever is the highest) subject to an overall limit of £8,000. Employees receive dividends on the shares, even when they are held in trust, and can acquire voting powers (though legally the trustees exercise voting rights on shares held in trust). Initially all full-time employees with five years' service were eligible to participate but this was widened to include part-time employees in the 1995 Finance Act (to comply with equal opportunity case law). In 1997–8 just under a million employees received share allocations, with an average value of £680 (Inland Revenue 1999c). This scheme is likely to be phased out as it is superseded by the All-Employee Share Plan.

Save As You Earn share option schemes ('Sharesave')(1980 Finance Act). In this scheme employees are able to take out options to buy shares in their employing company in three, five or seven years' time, at up to 80 per cent discount on current market values. To finance the option, employees save between £5 and £250 monthly using a Save As You Earn savings plan. There is no income tax liability on the interest accruing from the SAYE account, the value of any preferential terms on the option, or the growth in share value between taking-out and exercising the option. Instead there is a capital gains tax liability on the growth in value between exercising and selling the option.[12] In 1997–8 an average option of £2,500 was awarded to over one million employees (Inland Revenue 1999c). As SAYE is a voluntary option scheme, not all employees participate. At the beginning of the 1990s the average participation rate appeared to be about 20 per cent (Millward *et al.* 1992: 266). This appears to have been rising steadily, and the share ownership lobby group Proshare estimates that currently around 35 per cent of employees in firms with Sharesave participate in the scheme (Proshare 1998).

Company share option plan (CSOPs) (1995 Finance Act). This scheme, which may be used for selected employees, allows an option to be taken out to purchase shares in the company between three and ten years later. Unlike SAYE schemes no discount on prevailing market prices at the time of taking out the option is allowed. The structure of the tax breaks are similar to those for SAYE, with the maximum amount of options that can be taken out by any employee being £30,000. This scheme replaced the Executive Options scheme introduced in 1984. This earlier scheme had allowed both a discount on current market prices (if there was already an all-employee scheme in operation) and allowed options up to £100,000. In 1997–8 330,000 employees took out options worth on average £3,300. Since the reduction in the maximum level of options in 1995, this scheme has not been so popular as a method of top management remuneration. It is increasingly being used as a flexible all-employee scheme.

Enterprise Management Incentives Plan (EMI) (Finance Act 2000). This plan allows up to £100,000 of options to be made available to up to 15 selected employees in small and medium-sized enterprises (with gross assets of less than £15 million in 2000). The granting of the option is free of income tax whilst the gains are subject to business assets taper relief (which is more favourable than capital gains tax relief) from the date of the award of the option (rather than the date of exercise).

All-Employee Share Plan (AESP) (Finance Act 2000). This is a framework plan which provides for the passing of free shares to employees and which enables employees to buy shares from pre-tax income. Matching shares are also available. Free shares up to £3,000 per employee are available, awarded on the basis of performance measures. These shares are free of income tax and social security contributions if held for five years. Partnership Shares are also introduced, enabling employees to save up to £1,500 per annum out of pre-tax income. Although these are not options as such the employee may save in an accumulation account for a year to purchase shares at the end of the year. These too are free of income tax and social security contributions if held for five years. Those buying partnership shares are entitled to up to two matching shares for every share purchased. Dividend shares are also available from dividends reinvested from plan shares.

Share ownership schemes have become widespread in the UK. As of November 1998 there were 859 live approved profit sharing schemes, 1,201 Sharesave schemes, and 3,769 company share option Plans. Altogether about 1,750 firms had an all-employee share-based scheme (Treasury 1998). Looking at it from a workplace perspective, the 1998 Workplace Employee Relations Survey found that 30 per cent of all workplaces with over 25 employees had profit sharing and 15 per cent had share ownership schemes for non-managerial employees (Cully *et al.* 1998: 10).

These schemes are almost the polar opposite of workers' co-operatives in their distribution. With the exception of PRP (where there is a more even distribution) they are concentrated in large, multi-site, financially successful firms (see Gonzalez-Menendez *et al.* 2000). About two-thirds of Sharesave schemes and one-third of approved profit sharing schemes are found in listed firms (Treasury 1998). Approved profit sharing and Sharesave are most common in financial services where 22 per cent and 47 per cent of workplaces have them. Approved profit sharing is rare in manufacturing, where only 2 per cent of workplaces are covered by such a scheme (see also Pendleton 1997b).

In stark contrast to co-operatives, these 'conventional' share schemes are primarily a form of remuneration rather than a means of fostering partnership and developing employee ownership. Research into company objectives behind these schemes indicates that a range of motives lie behind the decision to introduce share schemes. Overall, there appears to be little difference between approved profit sharing and Sharesave options schemes, with the main reasons (in descending order of importance) being promotion of a sense of employee involvement, recruitment and retention of staff, increases in remuneration, improvements in productivity, and prevention of take-overs. Raising finance is the least important (Smith 1993). Promotion of a 'sense of involvement' may be viewed primarily in the terms used by financial economists. Share schemes appear to be aimed at aligning the interests of agents with those of principals by linking part of remuneration to the performance of the firm (and its stock price). By encouraging employees to identify with the firm and to feel more involved in it, it is hoped that employees will perform better, share information with other employees and managers, and be less likely to quit. The key point about employee involvement in this context is that it is not driven by the idealistic notion of self-expression and personal development often found in co-operatives. Instead, it is about encouraging employees to feel involved in a predetermined corporate entity. This point is captured well in a speech to the House of Commons by a recent Financial Secretary to the Treasury: employee share owners:

> have a real and identifiable interest in how their company does because they can benefit directly . . . there is an increase in commitment and motivation. They become more aware of their company's aims and objectives . . . can bridge the gap between employees, managers and shareholders by aligning more closely the interests of the workforce with the owners.
>
> (Roche 1999)

The relationship with participation and governance is very different in 'conventional' employee share schemes from that found in workers' co-operatives. In most cases, these schemes are introduced by managers with little input from workers or trade unions (Baddon *et al.* 1989; Smith 1993), even though they tend to be more commonly found in workplaces and firms with union representation and collective bargaining. This is especially true of Sharesave schemes, where there are significant differences in the level of union density and bargaining coverage compared with workplaces without schemes (see Gonzalez-Menendez *et al.* 2000). As ownership-based schemes, they do not provide the rights or the basis for employees to take responsibility for the management of firms with these schemes. That said, the evidence persistently indicates that firms and workplaces with share schemes have a range of mechanisms to facilitate employee involvement, such as team briefing, quality circles, work teams etc. (Poole 1988; Gonzalez-Menendez *et al.* 2000). These so-called 'high performance work practices' rarely provide rights to employees to influence or take what are defined as management decisions. Instead, they are designed to promote information sharing and to engender a sense of involvement (in much the same way as the share schemes themselves are).

Although share schemes do not confer rights to participate in management decisions, the fact that they confer ownership rights might facilitate involvement in governance.[13] In practice, this does not happen, for a host of reasons. In most cases, the proportion of equity passing to employees does not exceed 5 per cent so the capacity of employee votes to influence the outcome of issues put to the vote is low, even if employees voted *en bloc*. It is extremely rare indeed in the UK to find institutions that articulate the collective interests of employee shareholders, and companies certainly do not encourage the formation of these. Employee attendance at Annual General Meetings is also rarely encouraged, in part because of the disruption that could be caused to the normal operation of the business by mass absence, in part because of fears that employees might not appreciate that the AGM is primarily a formal, 'business' meeting rather than a forum for wide-ranging discussions of company affairs. A good case in point is the troubled retail company Marks and Spencer which, in 1999, announced that employee shareholders wanting to attend the AGM would have to do so at an 'over-flow' location connected by video link to the main meeting. Furthermore, they would have to take a day's annual leave to attend.

In practice, in the Anglo-American corporate governance 'system' voting is not the main form of corporate governance. Instead discipline is exerted on companies via the market for corporate control (see Jenkinson and Mayer 1992; Keasey *et al.* 1997). The threat of exit by shareholders is a powerful governance device since new owners may choose to replace the incumbent management. From this power comes a range of informal and often 'behind the scenes' forms of involvement in governance by major shareholders. Employee shareholders cannot hope to break into this form of governance because individually their holdings are much too small, whilst collectively they lack the institutions to articulate their ownership interests.[14] For many employees the transaction costs are often too high to mount a credible threat of unified exit. In any case, employee shareholders are likely to support the incumbent management in most cases on the grounds of 'better the devil you know'. Any ownership contender attempting to mount a take-over may be reasonably expected to introduce a number of measures harmful to employees (such as redundancies) to increase the returns to shareholders. It has been argued that managers of US firms introduce share schemes precisely to provide a degree of protection against the market for corporate control (Useem and Gager 1996). Investors therefore often display mixed feelings about employee share schemes. On the one hand, they provide a tool for aligning employee interests with those of the firm. On the other, they have a dilution effect, albeit usually a modest and inactive one, on control rights (and on earnings per share when there are new issues of shares). For these reasons, there are limits imposed by institutional investors on the level of new issues to support employee share schemes. It is possible to discern a tacit agreement that institutional investors will support managerially initiated employee share schemes as long as their primary function is remuneration rather than provision of a vehicle for involvement in corporate governance.

To summarise, most employee share schemes supported by legislation in the 1980s and 1990s provide limited involvement in ownership, and virtually no involvement in corporate governance. Whilst these firms tend to encourage employee involvement, with share schemes providing an additional form of involvement, this involvement functions entirely separately from employees' role as owners. In any case, control rights in this sphere are usually absent or are very weak. However, though most share schemes are not aimed at promoting employee ownership in the full sense of the word, the legislation governing these schemes has been capable of extension to provide an integral element of ESOPs structures, as we shall see shortly. Furthermore, the encouragement given to share ownership by government has provided a fertile environment for employee ownership campaigners to lobby for further legislative supports for employee ownership. At a deeper level the value attached to employee and individual share ownership from the 1980s has facilitated the development of equity-based ownership, as opposed to other forms of employee ownership.

ESOPs in America

When employee ownership campaigners looked for a new model of employee ownership from the mid-1980s they looked to the USA and in particular to the spectacular growth in ESOPs since facilitative legislation was passed in the mid-1970s. Study tours were organised by employee ownership research and lobby groups, such as Partnership Research. In some cases these included managers and trade union representatives of firms considering ownership conversion, and what they saw in the US led directly to the decision to use an ESOP back in the UK.

ESOPs were the brainchild of Louis Kelso who, as mentioned in Chapter 1, saw them as a way of facilitating a massive transfer of equity to employees and the public. They entered into public policy through the efforts of Senator Long, and were enshrined in 15 separate pieces of legislation between 1974 and 1987. Blasi argues that a consistent model underlay all of this legislation. Employee ownership would broaden ownership, encourage capital formation, improve labour-management relations, productivity, and profitability in firms, and create economic democracy. A further benefit, as employees built up their wealth, was that the overall level of state payments for welfare, unemployment benefit, and pensions could be reduced (Blasi 1988: 18–28). In fact, a major difference between employee share ownership in the US and the UK (and other European countries) is the use of schemes to provide a source of pension provision. By contrast, in the UK retirement income plans and employee share schemes have functioned almost entirely separately, mainly because a well-developed system of occupational pensions is in place in large firms.[15]

Tax incentives for ESOPs were mainly initiated by the 1974 Employee Retirement and Income Security Act, passed to regulate employee pensions. Under this legislation, where a company established an ESOP trust to purchase newly issued or pre-existing shares, the loan taken out by the trust to acquire them is guaranteed by the company. The company makes cash contributions to the ESOP according to the loan repayment schedule. In this scenario, repayment of the loan itself and the interest payments on it are tax deductible because they are ESOP contributions, as compared with a conventional loan where only the repayments are tax deductible (Conte and Svenjar 1990: 147). The ESOP thus appears to be a highly tax-advantageous mechanism. This, however, has been disputed by Conte and Svejnar (1990), and by Gordon and Pound (1990), on the grounds that there are alternative ways of securing the same level of deductions. Payment of the ESOP contributions in the form of wages would also attract company tax deductions. The following year, tax credits were introduced for ESOPs (those taking advantage of this were known as TRASOPs or PAYSOPs) but this legislation was repealed in 1986. Other important measures to stimulate the use of ESOPs were the granting of capital gains tax rollover relief (in 1984) to those owners selling stock to an ESOP where the ESOP came to hold 30 per cent of firm's equity.

Besides ESOPs, there are several other mechanisms for bringing about employee ownership of shares. 401(k) plans are defined contribution pension plans enabling employees to invest in the stocks of their employer and other companies. Employee contributions are tax deductible whilst the gains from the plan are exempt from capital gains tax. It is increasingly common for employers to provide 'matching' shares, the cost of which can be offset against corporation tax. This is a way of increasing participation in 401(k) plans, especially amongst lower-income earners, and thereby avoiding violations of the anti-discrimination rules governing 401(k) plans (National Center for Employee Ownership 1998). ESOPs can be used to provide the 'matching shares'. Meanwhile 423 plans are stock purchase plans which allow employees to buy shares at a discount and with favourable tax treatment.

It is difficult to estimate reliably the number of ESOPs in the US because of terminological imprecision and the use of ESOPs in combination with other employee share ownership plans. The National Center for Employee Ownership (1999) estimated that there were 11,500 plans in 1998 with a coverage of 8.5 million employees. Furthermore, there are currently about 2,000 401(k) plans which invest in stock of the employer. There are also thought to be about 3,000 stock option plans and about 4,000 stock purchase plans (National Center for Employee Ownership 1999). The level of incidence of ESOPs has, however, been disputed. On the basis of US Bureau of Labour establishment data, Mitchell suggests that ESOPs are not widely used (1995). These data suggest that at the beginning of the 1990s less than 3 per cent of the private sector workforce were covered by ESOPs (compared with more widespread estimates by employee ownership advocates of about 10 per cent). Mitchell argues that this situation shows 'how remarkable resistant business has been towards sharing the wealth, not how effectively the tax treatment of ESOPs has promoted such sharing' (1990: 21). This point notwithstanding, the perception (whether justified or not) that ESOPs are so widespread in the US gives a powerful message to those interested in employee ownership elsewhere.

Currently, most employees covered by ESOP arrangements are in publicly traded firms but most ESOP plans are found in privately owned firms (Blasi *et al.* 1999). The number of employees in ESOPs seems to be declining, mainly because of a shift in the use of ESOPs from large public firms to smaller private firms (National Center for Employee Ownership 1999). The level of employee ownership differs markedly between these two types of firm. Nearly two-thirds of publicly traded firms have 10 per cent or less of their stock held by ESOPs, whereas nearly half of private firms have 30 per cent or more of their stock in the ESOP. In fact, 20 per cent of privately owned firms with ESOPs are majority worker-owned, compared with 1 per cent of public companies (ibid.).

In terms of employee participation in management decisions and governance, public company ESOPs are very similar to 'conventional' share schemes in the UK. Blasi and Kruse (1991) found that employee stock ownership is not associated with direct employee participation within public firms. They also found very little participation by workers or their representatives in the governance of these firms. At the time the only publicly traded firms with employees on the corporate board were the well-publicised cases of Polaroid, Weirton Steel, NorthWestern Steel, TWA and Oregon Metallurgical (Blasi *et al.* 1999). A somewhat different picture emerges in the private company sector, where levels of employee ownership are somewhat higher. A study by Logue and Yates in 1999 found that worker directors were present in 17 per cent of cases. The lesson that these types of companies provided to British observers was that there was a mechanism for passing substantial levels of ownership to employees when owner-managers wished to exit, and which created forms of employee ownership which did not seem to suffer from the problems experienced by co-operatives and other labour-managed firms. Furthermore, the use of ESOPs to mount management-employee buy-outs of firms that were considerably larger than the typical UK co-operative was directly relevant to those considering how to introduce employee ownership into firms about to be privatised.

Management buy-outs (MBOs)

A final factor that was important in the emergence of ESOPs was the development of management buy-outs (MBOs). Whilst management buy-outs are, to use Wright *et al.*'s words, 'almost certainly as old as capitalism itself', few buy-outs occurred until the late 1970s (Wright *et al.* 1989: 405) mainly because of legal restraints, lack of financing availability and techniques, and lack of willingness of managements to mount them. The core features of the management buy-outs that emerged in the 1980s were: (1) incumbent managers (and increasingly outsiders) acquired a substantial proportion (50 per cent or higher in most cases) of the equity of the restructured firm; (2) the finance for these buy-outs came from debt. From an agency perspective, the merit of the MBO is that agency costs are lower than where there is a separation of ownership and control. At the same time, the reliance on debt finance exerts a strong disciplining effect on these owner-managers by generating prior claims on cash flow (Hart 1995b). This is often reinforced by rigorous performance contracts imposed by finance providers (banks and venture capitalists) and by performance-related remuneration for top managers (Thompson *et al.* 1990; Kaplan and Stromberg 2000). So, whilst MBOs create a form of insider ownership, they are a structure in which there tend to be very powerful incentive effects emanating from outside the firm.

It has been argued, most notably by Michael Jensen (1993), that leveraged management buy-outs were a market response to the managerial 'excesses' that occurred in managerially controlled firms in the USA. In this view the separation of ownership and control, that characterised publicly listed firms from the 1930s, had enabled managers to pursue their own 'managerialist' goals (Williamson 1964) that prioritised growth and size of firms rather than profitability and performance. By the 1970s it was clear that American corporations were not only badly organised to meet new competitive threats, but also that the growth of firms by merger and acquisition had created giant firms that were often worth less than the sum of their parts (see Donaldson 1994). The 'market response' was a rise in investor assertiveness (fuelled by a growing concentration of stock ownership in institutions), and a greater emphasis on the importance of 'shareholder value' (see Useem 1993). The corporate restructurings that followed from this included hostile take-overs, shut-downs and divestments. Management buy-outs and buy-ins were an integral part of this restructuring.

These developments in the US were also found in other economies. In the UK the annual number of buy-outs doubled from around 250 a year in the early 1980s to around 500 at the end of the decade. More significantly, the value of buy-outs multiplied by a factor of ten as the size of buy-outs increased (see Thompson *et al.* 1990: 73). There was also a shift in the character of MBOs. Whereas in the early 1980s many buy-outs were 'rescues' of failing firms, by the late 1980s many were voluntary divestments of past acquisitions by dissatisfied corporate parents (Thompson and Wright 1987).

There are several features of MBOs that are highly relevant to the development of ESOPs in the UK. One, they established the principle and role of leverage in buy-out transactions. In other words, they established that firms could be bought by loan finance secured against their future income streams. The relevance to employee ownership is clear: cash-constrained employees may be able to raise finance to buy their firms without raising capital on their own accounts. The type of businesses that seem most likely to be able to raise this kind of debt finance are those with a stable and secure cash-flow, and, as we will see later, many leveraged employee buy-outs had this characteristic. Two, management buy-outs were widely used for privatisation divestments. In fact, in the 1980s it was the most common form of privatisation transaction. During the decade there were over 100 privatisation MBOs compared with 24 primary flotations (Thompson *et al.* 1990: 74). Some 39 of the 73 units of the National Bus Company offered for sale from 1986 were acquired by MBOs and a further 11 were purchased by MBO companies (Wright *et al.* 1989: 410). Two NBC subsidiaries were acquired by management-employee buy-outs, one using an ESOP and the other direct employee subscriptions. When employees of local authority bus companies began to consider ways of acquiring ownership through privatisation in the late 1980s, the leveraged buy-out was a well-established mechanism for securing ownership of public sector companies.

Finally, there are powerful reasons for managers mounting buy-outs to include employees in their bid. Those mounting leveraged buy-outs assume a high degree of risk because of the need to meet debt servicing and repayment commitments. They usually operate to much more detailed and demanding funding contracts than is typical with other forms of finance. Managerial control and remuneration may well be explicitly and contractually linked to MBO performance. In these circumstances, there is a lot to be said for sharing risk with employees by involving them in ownership. It may reduce monitoring and bonding costs by aligning employee interests with those of the new principals. Wright *et al.* (1989) found that there is some form of employee share ownership in about 10 per cent of MBO deals, and in about 50 per cent of privatisation buy-outs. It might be predicted that employee share ownership is most likely in MBO firms with strong unions, where ownership involvement may be helpful in winning union support for the buy-out.

Summary

The development of ESOPs and related forms of employee ownership from the 1980s onwards can be seen as arising from the conjunction of several trajectories. One was the recent development of workers' co-operatives and a widespread perception in the business and trade union community that this form of organisation was either inappropriate, inefficient, or both. The second was the long-running but minority appeal of common ownership, and the perceived need by employee ownership campaigners to find a way to persuade departing owners to pass their businesses onto their work-forces. The third was the substantial encouragement given to employee share ownership and financial participation by governments since the late 1970s. To these must be added developments elsewhere, chiefly the huge growth of ESOPs in the USA from the mid-1970s.

The development of ESOPs and related forms of employee ownership in the UK in the late 1980s seems broadly supportive of Poole's notion of 'favourable conjunctures'. This approach 'encapsulates the notion of an uneven but advancing pattern which depends greatly on variation in circumstance and situation between and within particular nations' (1989: 6). From this perspective ESOPs resulted from the coming together of several developments in the sphere of employee ownership and financial participation. A further ingredient that we have not touched on here (see Chapters 3 and 5) is the role of privatisation. Many ESOPs, as we shall see, were a defensive reaction by managers and employees to the privatisation programme of the Conservative Governments. Other initiatives of these governments (i.e. share ownership legislation) were used to protect employees against hostile take-overs as a result of privatisation in a context where co-operative forms of ownership were seen as inappropriate. The structures associated with large common ownership firms such as John Lewis and Scott Bader provided a basis for developing relatively advanced forms of employee participation and industrial democracy which nevertheless protected the managerial role.

The view taken here, then, is that ESOPs were the outcome of several developments in the particular circumstances of the 1980s and early 1990s. To explore this further we will need to examine the role, interests, and objectives of those directly involved in creating employee-owned firms (in Chapter 5) and the orientation towards employee ownership of political parties and other opinion formers (in Chapter 3). However, they were not a simple or straightforward outcome of these developments. The experience of the 1980s, which saw both a retreat from the development of industrial democracy and trade union representation and at the same time the development of financial participation, suggests that the picture is complex and uneven. A further part of our argument is that ESOPs and other recent forms of employee ownership draw on opposing influences, and this introduces contradictory elements to their operation. For instance, the development of ESOPs was substantially dependent on the favourable statutory framework developed in the 1980s yet at the same time they were a reaction against its limitations of these. They drew on values and ideas associated with Conservative Governments (e.g. promotion of share ownership) to counter other initiatives, primarily privatisation, of these governments. They were also a fusion of collectivist ideas of industrial and economic democracy and the more individualistic and entrepreneurial values promoted by the Conservative Party in this period. ESOPs, then, were a complex response to the economic and social environment.

3 Employee ownership and politics

Introduction

In Chapter 2 we outlined the various forms of employee and management ownership that provided the backdrop to the development of ESOPs towards the end of the 1980s. We suggested that ESOPs possessed advantages over earlier forms of employee ownership, such as workers' co-operatives, and built upon recent legislation promoting employee share ownership. Following Poole (1989), ESOPs were seen to occur during a 'favourable conjuncture' of circumstances. We take this line of argument further in this chapter by examining the role of political factors in the emergence of ESOPs. Specifically this means that we focus on the aims and activities of the Conservative Governments during the 1980s and 1990s, and the development of Labour Party policies in opposition during the same period. We examine too the policy positions and initiatives of the Labour Government which took office in May 1997. Trade union orientations to employee share ownership in general and ESOPs in particular are also examined because union representatives have played a central and critical role in the formation of many ESOPs in the UK.

The focus on governments and political parties is a deliberate one. The development of all forms of employee share ownership seems to be closely bound up with the provision of a statutory framework. The much greater incidence of employee share ownership in the USA and UK as compared with many European countries correlates broadly with the extent of statutory frameworks. This has led many observers to suggest that government encouragement of financial participation via legislation and tax concessions is the single most important factor encouraging the take-up of financial participation (Uvalic 1991; Organization of Economic Cooperation and Development 1995; Vaughan-Whitehead 1995; Commission of the European Communities 1996). Whilst doubts have been expressed about the role of tax concessions by some American observers (e.g. Gordon and Pound 1990), the importance of legislation seems unquestionable. In the UK the clear legislative framework for 'conventional' share schemes has assisted the development of employee share schemes, and it seems unlikely that there would have been some five million employee shareholders over the last 20 years without statutory frameworks for employee share ownership.

That there is a statutory framework for ESOPs has helped this form of employee ownership to emerge in the UK, though it should be emphasised that a large proportion of ESOPs have not been governed by a single set of statutory regulations. Most have utilised an amalgam of trust and profit sharing legislation (see Chapter 4). By the same token, the somewhat imperfect development of specific ESOPs legislation (see Chapter 4) may account for the limited spread of this particular form of employee ownership. Besides providing a set of rules, legislative frameworks also underpin, as well as reflect, an ideological dimension to share ownership. The ideological climate in the 1980s, which emphasised the merits of entrepreneurial attitudes and ownership, was supportive of employee share ownership and some aspects of ESOPs. Share ownership legislation both reflected this ideology and helped to entrench it. The power of such an ideological climate is perhaps best observed in the United States, where the long-standing and deep-rooted tradition of support for individual and employee share ownership helps to explain the high incidence of ESOPs in that country (see Blasi *et al.* 1999). So, the combination of legislation and values may be viewed as elements of a 'favourable conjuncture', to use Poole's words (1989).

A feature of UK ESOPs which has been a source of strength and weakness has been that all political parties and both sides of industry have found them attractive. Thus, all have suggested that ESOPs are a good thing and have argued that their formation should be encouraged. As James Freeman, Managing Director of People's Provincial Bus Company (the first bus company ESOP) put it, 'we have been used as propaganda by politicians of every hue' (Economist 1988: 90). Some saw the ESOP as way of promoting 'deep' as well as widespread employee share ownership, some saw it as a way of developing substantial employee ownership without the dangers of labour involvement in management, and some saw it as a way of promoting industrial democracy alongside share ownership. The main difference is that Conservatives and management organisations such as the Confederation of British Industry and Institute of Directors (see Purkiss 1992) view ESOPs' primary function as spreading wealth, whereas Labour and the trade unions have emphasised their potential for extending industrial democracy. Members of both groups, however, subscribe to the view that greater participation of employees in ownership and profits will lead to attitudinal changes, which in turn will lead to improvements in company performance.[1]

The problem with all-party support for ESOPs has been that no one party has been especially committed to their development. With the exception of a handful of MPs, supported by a range of lobbying groups, no group has really pushed for legislation to promote ESOPs. In fact, to a large extent ESOPs have been viewed as an instrument to achieve other policy objectives. Thus, for the Conservative Governments of the 1980s and 1990s they generated worker support, which might not have been otherwise forthcoming, for a range of privatisation initiatives. They also helped to inhibit the danger that some privatisation initiatives might lead to private monopolies.[2] For the Labour Party, ESOPs can be seen as a 'bit' player in the political struggles of the 1980s and 1990s to shift the party away from its support for wide-scale and increased public ownership. ESOPs could be portrayed as a policy alternative supportive of social ownership and industrial democracy, though specific policy measures to promote this aspect of ESOPs have never been spelt out. Since being in office New Labour has focused its attentions on further development of 'conventional' share schemes and share option schemes for key managerial employees in small and medium-sized firms.

In this chapter we elaborate on these points by reviewing the views and orientations of the main political parties and trade unions towards ESOPs.

Conservative Governments in the 1980s and 1990s

Extension of share ownership was a central tenet of Conservative beliefs, and the activities of Conservative Governments in this area have been seen as one of their 'outstanding achievements' (Taylor 1988: 6). There were a number of legislative initiatives in the annual Finance Acts during the 1980s and 1990s to promote share ownership generally and to facilitate the development of ESOPs in particular. This support for ESOPs formed part of the wider programme to promote a 'share-owning democracy'. The privatisation programme of the Conservative Governments in the 1980s is also an important factor in explaining the development of ESOPs, albeit perhaps in a negative sense. Support for share ownership also has to be set in the context of Conservative views on industrial relations and trade unions. Financial participation was viewed as an ingredient of the programme to reform British industrial relations. Share ownership would promote a sense of common interest in place of the 'two sides of industry' (Employment Department Group 1994).

Clearly the Conservative Governments of 1979–7 provided support for ESOPs. This took two main forms: one was primarily legislative support, whereby the government established a statutory framework in which ESOPs could develop. These initiatives could be seen as facilitative in that they placed the onus on firm-level actors to develop employee ownership conversions within this framework. In this way they were typical of most other measures in the area of financial participation, where decision-making on implementation occurs at firm level but the context in which the decision is made is at least in part determined by government. This facilitative support primarily took the form of amendments and additions to legislation, primarily in the annual Finance Act and to revisions to the Companies Act. These legislative initiatives took a typical form: tax breaks were provided as an inducement to firms but a stringent set of regulations were introduced to govern access to these tax breaks. The main elements of these were the provisions for the statutory ESOP in 1989, the provision of capital gains tax rollover relief in 1991, and substantial relaxation of the 1989 regulations in 1994. An amendment to the Companies Act in 1989 allowed listed firms to provide loans and financial guarantees for the acquisition of its own shares when the shares were to be used for employee share ownership schemes. This encouragement should not be overstated. The regulations governing access to tax breaks for 'statutory' ESOPs were extremely restrictive to the extent that less than a handful of statutory ESOPs were established in the early 1990s (see Chapter 4). Tightly regulated access to tax benefits and relatively modest further concessions to those that were already allowable on a 'case law' basis can be compared with the regulations governing profit-related pay after 1991. In the latter case, the more 'liberal' taxation regime led to a massive increase in the number of firms using PRP, from around 1,000 to nearly 15,000 firms in the late 1990s (when the tax benefits were phased out) (see Inland Revenue 1999c).

The other form of encouragement was the provision of preferential terms for employee buy-outs during some parts of the privatisation programme. This may be viewed as much more active support as it involved the government in actively declaring a preference for ESOPs. In the privatisation of the Scottish Bus Group companies, for instance, bids from employee buy-out teams were given a 5 per cent price preference, all other things being equal. Similarly, Department of Transport guidance to local authorities concerning the privatisation of municipal bus companies noted that closed sales to management and employees would be acceptable in principle. In the preferred mode of competitive tendering, management or employee bids would benefit from a discount of up to 5 per cent (see Lynch 1990: 101). This reflected the government's 'firm view (as expressed by Michael Portillo) that the management and employees of companies should be given a reasonable opportunity to acquire the company' (see ibid.: 106). The employee buy-out of Tower Colliery in South Wales also received some encouragement and assistance at critical points from John Redwood, the Secretary of State at the Welsh Office. Speaking of Tower, he declared 'that's my kind of popular capitalism' (Milne 1996: 24).

The underpinning for government support for ESOPs came from its strong support for 'people's capitalism' and employee share ownership more generally. As outlined earlier, the government had given strong support for employee share ownership in the first half of the 1980s in the form of the savings-related share option scheme and the discretionary share option scheme. The rationale for employee share ownership was centred on the change of view and behaviour that was thought to follow from ownership of shares. As Conservative MP Ian Taylor has described it:

> for the individual employee, share participation can encourage a greater sense of involvement in the company. Each worker, instead of only being concerned with the salary slip at the end of each month, becomes part of the company, with a vested interest in its future well being...This is a shift in their role in the company and properly explained it could lead to an increased sense of responsibility. There is a real incentive to work as a team.
>
> (Taylor 1992: 14)

Michael Portillo, Secretary of State for Employment in the latter years of the Major Government, argued that:

> employee share ownership is a potent symbol. Employees who own shares in their company have both an investment and a responsibility for that company. Through share ownership they can gain a better understanding of how their companies work; of the economic climate with its opportunities and constraints; and of the need to increase efficiency in order to compete in world markets.
>
> (Portillo 1995)

He went on to observe that there are more worker shareholders then union members in the USA, and the apparent potential for share ownership to lead to a decline in attachment to unions was an implicit part of government support for employee share schemes.

As the 1980s progressed, this essentially instrumental conception of the role of employee share ownership was deepened by the philosophy of 'popular capitalism' and the 'enterprise culture'. In this philosophy, the vision was of a capital-owning democracy with high levels of share ownership and home ownership (Saunders and Harris 1990). This would reverse the long-running decline in the role of individual share ownership and would inculcate more entrepreneurial attitudes amongst the population at large (see Grout 1994 for an in-depth discussion of the attractions and limitations of 'popular capitalism'). This reached its apogee in the privatisation by share flotation of large public corporations such as British Gas, British Telecom, and the electricity generation and distribution companies. Employee share ownership schemes, but not ESOPs, were incorporated into all of these, the rationale being that 'employees will benefit from employee shareholding, closer identification with their businesses, greater job satisfaction, better motivation, and the prospect of the rewards that enterprise has brought those that work for other industries that have been privatised' (Department of Environment 1986: 2).[3]

Despite the ideological support for share ownership generally and policy support for ESOPs specifically, it has been argued that government support for ESOPs was lukewarm rather than strong. Drawing on interview data derived from employee ownership lobbyists, financiers and managers,

Kenner Thompson (1993) suggests that Conservative Governments were cautious towards ESOPs for several reasons. One, they were viewed as a collectivist version of share ownership and, given that several important battles had been won against the trade union movement, these governments were wary of providing new mechanisms for collective voice amongst employees. For this reason, her respondents argued, statutory ESOPs were initially beset with a very stringent set of conditions to qualify for tax breaks and a lack of meaningful tax incentives (see Cornford 1990 for further discussion of these). So, whilst support for ESOPs was provided it was of a nature that would not lead to substantial growth in employee-owned firms. Most firms would find the legislation too restrictive to be attractive. It was also the reason that statutory ESOPs were required to distribute their equity to individual employees within seven years. Whilst employee ownership would initially take a collective form, within a few years the pattern of employee share ownership would be similar to that in 'conventional' employee share schemes.

A surprising feature of the statutory form of ESOP created by the Thatcher Government in 1989 is that it embodies specific requirements supporting collective employee 'voice'. Most notably, the legislation required that most trustees (other than 'professional' trustees) be employees, and that these representatives be elected by a majority of the workforce (see Chapter 4). This certainly does not fit with the argument that the government was wary of creating new collectivist forms of worker organisation, unless requirements imposing these with regard to employee trustees is seen as a manipulative plot to stifle any enthusiasm for ESOPs amongst companies (and their owners). Probably the best way to see this aspect of the ESOP legislation is as a 'necessary evil'. The Conservative Governments of the 1980s and 1990s were certainly not sympathetic to industrial democracy[4] but felt that some protections against abuses by firms were necessary (i.e. to prevent firms using ESOPs to benefit only the higher-paid employees). This type of approach is perhaps exemplified by a speech by Norman Tebbit, former Chairman of the Conservative Party, at a conference on ESOPs organised by the Institute of Directors. He called for more ESOPs as a 'means of turning workers into capitalists'. He was scornful of those who saw ESOPs as a form of socialism. He argued that 'one has to distinguish the baby from the bathwater: the bathwater in ESOPs is egalitarianism. The baby is the motivational effect and the social cohesion that comes from the spread of capital ownership' (quoted in the Economist 1988: 91).

In fact, a second reason for the limited promotion by government, according to Kenner Thompson, is the fear that ESOPs would generate abuses that had been widely observed in the US. These included the use of ESOPs to benefit a small elite group of managers, to thwart take-overs in conjunction with 'poison-pills',[5] and as high-risk substitutes for other forms of pension provision. The recent use of ESOPs by PLCs to obtain a tax benefit using SAYE schemes (see Chapter 4) provides a good example of how facilitative regulations can provide loopholes which can be exploited by companies in ways that are not consistent with the objectives of government policy. This view is entirely consistent with the restrictive conditions imposed on the statutory ESOP. The extensive role for employees set down in the legislation can be seen as providing a mechanism to restrict managerial opportunism.

Overall, a reasonable assessment is that whilst Conservative Governments were clearly keen to encourage employee share ownership, their support for ESOPs was somewhat tentative. The association between ESOPs and industrial democracy, claimed by some advocates of ESOPs and promulgated at the time by the Labour Party, was not likely to endear them to the Thatcher Governments. Furthermore, whilst these governments were keen to promote worker share ownership, there was a wariness of worker *management* of firms. Workers' co-operatives were viewed with suspicion because of the perceived difficulties in developing effective management in co-ops. As a result, central government support for creating and maintaining workers' co-operatives was wound down by Conservative Governments. The Thatcher Governments therefore did not want to encourage a form of ownership which might lead to active worker involvement in management.[6] So legislation to support ESOPs was provided, but it took a form that was not likely to be attractive to managers in most firms. ESOPs appear to have been viewed as relevant in a limited range of circumstances.

The main area where ESOPs were seen as relevant was in management-employee buy-outs during privatisation, where more active support was given by Conservative Governments (at least for a time). Referring to the bus industry, Michael Portillo (Secretary of State for Transport at the time) suggested that management-employee buy-outs were 'the best solution for the company in very many cases' (quoted in Lynch 1990). Support for employee ownership during privatisation was, however, very much conditioned by the specific objectives and context of particular privatisation initiatives. In the bus industry, promotion of competition was a central element of government policy, and there was the danger that open sales would lead to further market dominance by a small number of large companies. Furthermore, practical encouragement for ESOPs during privatisation was a feature of the late 1980s and early 1990s when the philosophy of 'popular capitalism' was strongest and when the healthy state of Treasury finances meant that revenue maximisation need not be a primary objective of privatisation. By contrast, later in the 1990s when government finances appeared less secure and when a paramount concern was to effect privatisation quickly (before a possible change of government), much less encouragement was given for employee ownership conversions. None of the management-employee bids for British Rail operating companies was successful, though one management buy-out (Chiltern Railways) was approved. As has been widely remarked in the privatisation literature (e.g. Heald and Steel 1986), government objectives for privatisation have shifted over time, and fluctuating support for ESOPs has been a result of this. In fact, support for ESOPs seems to have faded somewhat in the course of the 1990s. There were no references to ESOPs in the Conservative manifesto for the 1997 election (Conservative Party 1997). In fact, there was little reference to share ownership at all, other than a pledge to bring forward a facility for companies to provide matching shares to employee share purchases.[7]

To summarise, though the Thatcher and Major Governments sponsored a set of measures in the late 1980s and first half of the 1990s that were favourable to ESOPs, government support was limited and conditional. The main perceived value of ESOPs was as an extension of the programme of individual employee share ownership, to which Conservative Governments were deeply committed, rather than as a new form of employee ownership and management. ESOPs were seen primarily as a means for spreading wealth rather than an as a route towards industrial democracy (Taylor 1988: 7). Fears that ESOPs might embody something more than conventional share schemes meant that support tended to be restricted to specific sets of circumstances, and that support tended to be hedged with restrictions.

As we shall see, the apparent potential for ESOPs to provide models of organisation that went substantially beyond conventional employee share schemes provided a powerful advantage to critics of the Conservative Governments.

The Labour Party

Recently, both the Labour Party and the Trades Union Congress have tended to view ESOPs as a significant advance on 'conventional' all-employee share schemes. In the Labour Party's case, its orientation to ESOPs has been conditioned by its support for extensions of industrial democracy, its traditional relationship with the trade union movement, its suspicion of 'popular capitalism' during the 1980s, and, most important of all, its evolving policy on public ownership. The merit of ESOPs for party reformers was that they provided an alternative to state ownership that nevertheless embodied other key aspects of Labour philosophy. Despite the apparent ideological appeal of ESOPs to Labour policy-makers, their orientation to ESOPs was primarily an instrumental one.

In the 1970s the Labour Party was wary of company share schemes on the grounds that they were an ineffective means of bringing about capital redistribution, provided little scope for increasing worker involvement and influence in corporate decision-making, and potentially undermined trade union representation (Baddon *et al.* 1989). These views closely mirrored those of the union movement, as expressed in the Trades Union Congress' document *Industrial Democracy* (Trades Union Congress 1974). Instead

Labour's support for economic and industrial democracy focused on the separate areas of worker representation on the boards of large companies, common ownership through public ownership, and on encouraging co-operatives amongst small and medium-sized firms (see Schuller 1985). Although the 1974–9 Labour Governments did not implement the proposals of the Bullock Commission on Industrial Democracy, there were extensions of public ownership (via the activities of the National Enterprise Board) and support for workers' co-operatives (see Chapter 2). Of course, Labour did introduce the current share-based approved profit sharing scheme in 1978 but this was an outcome of co-operation with the Liberal Party (to prop up the minority Callaghan Government).

In the 1980s Labour Party policy warmed towards all-employee share schemes and vocal support was given to ESOPs in particular. This reflected the substantial change in Labour's economic and industrial philosophies and policies during the decade. The concept of ESOPs provided a weapon in the fight that took place after the 1983 election to shift Labour party policy away from an emphasis on public ownership and nationalisation, and away from a hostility towards market forces. ESOPs were a useful talisman for the revisionists in the centre left and right in their struggle to reshape party policy. To see how and why this was so, it is necessary to briefly trace the recent history of Labour industrial policy.

In the early years of the 1980s party policy incorporated many of the elements of the Alternative Economic Strategy, as associated with writers such as Stuart Holland (1975), and reflected the ascendancy of the left.[8] *Labour's Programme 1982* (Labour Party 1982) and the 1983 manifesto *The New Hope for Britain* (Labour Party 1983) focused on the policy arena which traditionally provided the main battleground between left and right of the party – public ownership. In these, the party promised to renationalise those companies already privatised by the Conservatives and to extend public ownership to new companies and sectors. Industrial policy would be directed through large increases in public investment and planning agreements between government and companies. Away from the commanding heights of the economy, workers' co-operatives were seen as a useful means to promote worker ownership and industrial democracy. Indeed the party proposed to create a statutory right for workers to convert their enterprises into co-operatives through acquisition of the assets of the employer.

The debacle of the 1983 election defeat for Labour began a shift away from the *dirigisme* of *Labour's Programme*, and in particular a rethinking of the role of public enterprise and ownership. The left was weakened and divided after the election, and members of the party's centre and right began to reassert themselves in policy debates (Smith 1992a). A further factor was the gathering momentum of privatisation. The high levels of public involvement in the share flotations of major public corporations generated debates within the party as to whether, how, and to what extent there should be a return to the status quo of public ownership, let alone the major expansion envisaged in the Alternative Economic Strategy (Thompson 1996). Furthermore, participation by employees in the preferential share option schemes incorporated in many of the public flotations also meant that Labour's traditional hostility to share schemes was less sustainable. It was clear too that a sizeable number of workers were participating in the SAYE schemes introduced in 1980.

Several key party thinkers, such as Bryan Gould and Roy Hattersley, sought to reformulate Labour's socialist objectives in the context of the ideological and policy shifts that had occurred during the first five years or so of Conservative rule. Whilst both Gould (1989) and Hattersley (1987) emphasised the role of public ownership, the role of public enterprises was viewed primarily in an instrumental way rather than as an end in itself (Thompson 1996). Both drew attention to new forms of social ownership, as alternatives to nationalisation along Morrisonian lines. ESOPs occupied a prominent role in these new visions. They were so important because they had the potential to achieve Labour's traditional goals of common ownership, to extend industrial democracy, and to improve relationships at work, whilst using mechanisms (i.e. share ownership schemes) that had attracted a considerable amount of support during the Thatcher years. In the Labour context, therefore, ESOPs were a 'benign' policy instrument because they could apparently achieve traditional goals in new contexts, thereby sidestepping the political problems associated with either nationalisation or with explicit revisions of core canons of party ideology. As such they provided useful ammunition in the battles to reshape party policy. Discussing share ownership, Bryan Gould commented:

> [it is] far better to develop a concept and practice of share ownership that serves the socialist interest in diffusing power, rather than the capitalist preoccupation with preserving and concentrating the privileges of capital. The ESOP offers us the chance of doing exactly that.
> (1989: 144)

Labour leader Neil Kinnock was also becoming sympathetic to flexible forms of social ownership, and he too advocated the development of worker-owned enterprises at this time (see Jones 1996: 118). This approach was incorporated into the policy document *Social Ownership* (Labour Party 1986), published shortly before the 1987 general election. Here it was suggested that there should be some renationalisation, coupled with encouragement of financial participation such as ESOPs, with the proviso that the collective elements of these schemes, including voting rights and equal access, be emphasised. On the whole, though, the 1987 election manifesto *Britain Will Win* (Labour Party 1987) viewed common ownership as occurring through public ownership. Most of the text in this area emphasised the importance of regaining some control of privatised corporations through share acquisitions by the government. There were no specific references to ESOPs in the manifesto, though there was a commitment to 'encourage the establishment and success of co-operatives of all forms' (1987: 6).

The policies presented by Labour in the 1987 election have been seen by many commentators (e.g. Smith 1992a) as a 'half-way house' or, as Jones describes them, 'tentative and piecemeal' (Jones 1996: 120). The party's defeat in this election led to pressure for further revision of party policy. This resulted in the Policy Review of 1989 (Labour Party 1989) which once again emphasised the role of ESOPs and workers' co-operatives (Smith 1992b). The Review stated that 'our ideal is an economy in which enterprises are owned and managed by their employees' (1989: 13). It especially commended the 'democratic ESOP' (i.e. ESOPs that transfer real powers of control to the workforce), and promised to provide appropriate tax incentives to facilitate conversions. It did so in the context of an acceptance of the reality of the market economy, and a rejection of nationalisation as a policy goal. Indeed, Gamble commented that it was the 'most explicit rejection of the policy of expanding public ownership' ever made by the Labour Party (Gamble 1992: 65).

By the mid-1990s the battles over Labour's economic and industrial policies were largely won, and ESOPs and indeed employee share ownership more generally were uncontentious, if not central, elements of party policy. In the 1993 election manifesto *It's Time to Get Britain Working Again* (Labour Party 1992) it was noted that:

> employees should have the opportunity to own collectively a significant stake in the company for which they work, through a democratic Employee Share Ownership Plan (ESOP) or a co-operative. We will strengthen support for such schemes and consult about the possibility of creating a new tax incentive to encourage companies to establish or extend an ESOP or set up a co-operative.
>
> (ibid.: 14)

Labour politicians were critical of discretionary share schemes (and their contribution to a 'fat cat' company culture) and argued that 'popular capitalism', in the sense of deep and widespread support for share ownership, was a myth. They suggested that share schemes should be used to provide more of a role for worker involvement in decision-making, and for this reason tended to view ESOPs as an ideal form of share scheme.

However, over the course of the debates during the previous ten years Labour had adopted a similar rationale to the Conservative Party concerning the benefits of share schemes to firms. The acceptance of the efficiency benefits of share schemes is well illustrated by this comment before the 1997 election by Alistair Darling, currently a member of the Labour Cabinet. He noted that:

> the importance of securing participation by the workforce, by providing proper motivation to get improved performance, and therefore success, is a major part of the philosophy of stakeholding. . . . Employee share ownership, for example, can play a major role in providing motivation and incentives to individuals to work.
>
> (1997: 18–19)

The findings from US research on ESOPs that efficiency gains were dependent on employee participation in decisions were used to link arguments about efficiency to those of employee rights and democracy.

Although ESOPs were an uncontentious element of party policy by the mid-1990s, they were not a central plank of Labour's platform. Two sets of events briefly suggested they might become more important. One was the apparent acceptance by Labour leader Tony Blair of the philosophy of 'stakeholder capitalism' in a speech in Singapore in February 1996. 'Stakeholder capitalism' encapsulates a set of ideas about corporate governance that had generated considerable interest since the early 1990s (see Kelly *et al.* 1997), and especially since the publication of Will Hutton's *The State We're In* (1995). Its advocates (Kay 1997; Parkinson 1997) proposed that company directors should be required to pursue the interests of stakeholders (major suppliers, employees etc.) as well as investors. Revisions to company law would be necessary to effect this. The advantage of ESOPs is that they can bring about the formal accountability of directors to workers without contentious changes to company law and without the complexities of differentiating stakeholders from other bodies in some kind of a relationship with the firm (see Pendleton 1997a). In other words, employee ownership can bring about employee stakeholding using current models of corporate governance. However, 'stakeholder capitalism' slid from the political agenda as the 1997 election approached, and the initial enthusiasm for it on the part of the Labour leadership did not lead to any elevation of collective employee share schemes in the policy agenda.

The other important event was the initiative by Tony Blair to jettison Clause 4 of the Labour Party Constitution, which had traditionally provided the justification for nationalisation and public ownership. This proposal had the potential to provide support for ESOPs in so far as they could have been highlighted as an alternative means to secure Labour's objectives (in much the same way as had occurred in policy debates in the late 1980s). Some Labour advocates of ESOPs (Stuart Bell MP for example) were quick to pursue this line of argument. However, it became clear during this episode that the fundamental ideological battles about public ownership had been largely won in the earlier debates. The proposed revision of Clause 4 was primarily a formal adjustment to the reality of party policy, driven by the perceived need to demonstrate to the electorate that Labour had decisively rejected its traditional policies. Blair and his colleagues did not need to draw substantially on a raft of alternative policies to secure acceptance of the changes they proposed. Unlike Gaitskell's attempt to revise the party Constitution at the beginning of the 1960s, the groundwork for Blair's new set of aims and values had been laid over a ten-year period.

The role of ESOPs as an uncontentious but not central part of Labour's programme was maintained in the 1997 election. The 1997 manifesto – *New Labour Because Britain Deserves Better* – reiterated the party's support for ESOPs and co-operatives though no specific policies were mentioned. It was noted that 'we are keen to encourage a variety of forms of partnership and enterprise, spreading ownership, and encouraging more employees to become owners through Employee Share Ownership Plans and co-operatives' (Labour Party 1997). Since gaining office, however, New Labour has concentrated on 'conventional' share schemes in general rather than ESOPs in particular. The government's objective, as set out in the 1998 November Budget Report, is to 'promote long-term shareholding by employees to build a stronger sense of partnership in industry and increase productivity'. The Chancellor has written that he wants 'to reward long term commitment by employees . . . to encourage the new enterprise culture of team work in which everyone contributes and everyone benefits from success . . . to double the number of companies in which all employees have the opportunity to hold shares' (Treasury 1998). To this end, a new All-Employee Share Plan has been incorporated in the Finance Act 2000 (see Chapters 2 and 4 for further details of this).

It is interesting to observe that the Labour Government's rationale for employee share ownership is expressed in virtually identical terms to that of its Conservative predecessors, though the language of 'partnership' has replaced that of 'popular capitalism' in discussions of the broader context. The orientation of the legislation may be seen as a corporate one, in that the advantages of share schemes are expressed primarily in terms of the benefits of aligning employee interests with those of the firm and of increasing employee commitment. This orientation may be seen as a pragmatic one given that the sponsors of employee share schemes are virtually always managers rather than workers or unions (the exception being employee buy-outs). Perhaps the main difference with the Conservatives is that New Labour has emphasised the importance of worker participation, noting that productivity benefits are more likely when share schemes 'are combined with modern management practices which promote active employee participation' (Inland Revenue 1999a: 2). Unlike the statutory ESOPs legislation, however, the current legislation does not attempt to define or stipulate what participation mechanisms should be conjoined with share ownership schemes. In this sense, the new legislation is in the same tradition as all of the earlier legislation on 'conventional' share schemes. It is also in keeping with the traditional reluctance on the part of UK governments to introduce employee participation through legislation.[9]

That the government has concentrated on 'conventional' share schemes is perhaps not surprising given that there are very many more Approved

Profit Sharing and Sharesave schemes than ESOPs. Furthermore, the use of statutory ESOPs by firms with Sharesave plans to gain substantial tax concessions has not endeared ESOPs to the government. The upshot of this is that no major innovations have been introduced to stimulate the growth of ESOPs. That said, the All-Employee Share Plan has been designed to appeal to small firms as well as public limited companies, and can in principle operate in conjunction with an ESOP trust. Shares held in a statutory ESOP trust can be passed to a trust set up under the new legislation without loss of tax benefits granted earlier to the ESOP. Furthermore, the provision for rollover relief to owners selling shares to a statutory ESOP has been incorporated in the new legislation.

Trade unions

Trade union views on employee share ownership schemes traditionally mirrored those associated with the Labour Party. Indeed, union views on this topic were an important influence on Labour Party thinking. Yet as in the case of Labour, the prevailing views of the union movement have subtly shifted over the last 15 years or so, and, as for Labour, ESOPs provided a model of share ownership which met many of the unions' traditional criticisms of employee share schemes. Up until the 1950s the TUC displayed limited interest in financial participation. A report prepared for the 1957 Congress was sceptical of the benefits of financial participation and fearful of the impact on union functions. This view tended to predominate through the 1960s and 1970s (see Callaghan n.d.). During the 1980s some unions came to view share schemes generally, and ESOPs in particular, more favourably. By the end of the century, the TUC's position was that it 'welcomed the Government's commitment to extend and promote employee share ownership' (TUC 1999a).

Trade union suspicion of employee share ownership schemes centred on several issues (see Baddon *et al.* 1989; Pendleton 1992). One, share schemes usually fall outside the remit of collective bargaining. Share schemes are often not negotiable, either because participation in them by employees is optional or because the criteria for their operation are established externally by legislation and the Inland Revenue. Two, share schemes have been widely seen as a means of circumventing unions and collective bargaining. If workers became owners, they may come to see less need of union representation and may develop attitudes similar to those of other owners of capital. This view has been held for many years in the trade union movement but the apparent conjunction of 'popular capitalism' and measures to weaken unions during the Thatcher years reinforced this suspicion in the perceptions of many union observers. Comments in official publications and speeches about the number of worker shareholders overtaking the number of trade union members, as mentioned earlier, has not helped in this respect. Three, a recurrent fear about financial participation schemes and workers' co-operatives is that the separation between employees and employer is blurred as employees also become owners. This might compromise the union role as the union could become drawn into representing owners as well as employees. If, for instance, unions are party to a strategy of retrenchment, as representatives of *owners*, it becomes difficult for them to provide protection against redundancy for their members as *employees* (Pendleton *et al.* 1995b: 581).

Besides these criticisms, which centre on the relationship between share ownership and union representation, unions have had a further set of criticisms of financial participation in relation to inequalities of power and capital. These fears were well expressed in the TUC's document *Industrial Democracy* in the 1970s (Trades Union Congress 1974). It was argued there that financial participation schemes tend to provide little real control over managerial decisions. Common ownership principles are rarely incorporated and the amount of equity passing to workers insufficient to bring about any real shift in control. Two, it was argued (primarily in relation to option schemes) that financial participation ties up workers' savings and exposes them to risks which they are not on the whole well placed to shoulder. Three, it was also argued that financial participation did little to counteract inequalities of wealth. High-income earners were able to benefit disproportionately from schemes, and hence they could reproduce rather than ameliorate existing patterns of inequality. Furthermore, public sector workers did not usually have access to these schemes, so sectoral inequalities were reinforced.

The generally negative view held by the trade union movement began to change in the 1980s under the twin pressures of widespread employee participation in privatisation share subscriptions and the wider diffusion of employee share schemes. As Baddon *et al.* (1989: 48) note, the initial trade union response to privatisation – that their members not take up preferential share offers – failed dismally. A further twist is that both share-based profit sharing and employee share option schemes are more likely to be found in firms with union recognition and collective bargaining arrangements (see Pendleton 1997b; Gonzalez-Menendez *et al.* 2000; see also Baddon *et al* 1989). Some unions, such as the Banking, Insurance and Finance Union (BIFU), began to incorporate profit sharing into their bargaining agendas (Incomes Data Services 1986).[10] Others, such as the British Airline Pilots Association (BALPA) and the Engineers and Managers Association (EMA) put forward proposals to establish financial participation schemes (see Baddon *et al.* 1989: 47)

These moves by individual trade unions have entered onto the agenda of the broader trade union movement. The 1987 Trades Union Congress passed a motion, initiated by the main Post Office and British Telecom unions, which called on the union movement to recognise employee share ownership schemes as a form of 'social ownership' (Trades Union Congress 1987: 534–43). This 'social ownership', which echoed the title of a Labour

Party document published the previous year, incorporated employee ownership as a way of forcing privatised corporations to operate in the public and employees' interest. A motion critical of employee share schemes was rejected at the Congress in the following year, whilst a motion in 1989 called upon unions to develop and support initiatives which transferred ownership of new companies in the public service arena to their workforces (Callaghan n.d.: 7). As a TUC document has put it, 'the general policy stance might be described as "engaged scepticism"' (TUC 1999b). This contrasts with the situation only a few years before, where the orientation of unions was described as 'bored hostility' (Incomes Data Services 1986).

The emergence of ESOPs in the late 1980s provided a model for the type of employee share ownership that unions could not only accept but actively support. The twin reservations, expressed for instance in TUC submissions to the NEDC in 1986 (Callaghan n.d. : 6) and to the CBI Task Force on Wider Share Ownership (TUC 1990), about exposure of employees to risk and lack of influence in key decisions, could be met by the capacity of ESOPs to distribute large portions of equity free of charge, the collective nature of ownership (at least in the early stages), and the potential for employee involvement in key decisions. They seemed to offer a form of privatisation that was more acceptable than the large-scale public flotations or private sale of publicly owned companies to other industrial interests. The TUC has continued to look benignly on ESOPs for these reasons, whilst being sceptical of 'conventional' employee share schemes where employee participation in decisions is absent.[11] As the TUC has suggested in response to the new share scheme legislation, 'simply owning shares in the company will not, on its own, increase worker motivation and commitment. By using share ownership as part of a wider package to increase employee involvement, however, the company and the employees can benefit' (TUC 1999a: 6). The main criticism of ESOPs advanced by the TUC is the transient character of employee ownership in many cases: it has suggested therefore that legislation be amended to permit statutory employee trusts to own shares permanently.

The support of the TUC for ESOPs has been mirrored by that of a small number of individual unions. The Electrical and Power Engineers' Association (EPEA) and the Electricity Supply Trade Union Council argued (unsuccessfully) that ESOPs should be created during the privatisation of the electricity supply industry in England and Wales. The Engineers and Managers Association (of which the EPEA became a part) took an active role in the purchase of a power station by management and employees in the privatisation of the Northern Ireland electricity generation industry. Similarly the General Municipal Boilerworkers' Union were closely involved in the formation of the Roadchef ESOP. Perhaps the clearest expression of union support for ESOPs was provided by Gavin Laird, then General Secretary of the AEU who, in his submission to the Social Justice Commission, baldly stated that 'my members want ownership' (Commission on Social Justice 1994: 214).[12] Union support for ESOPs has been also expressed in practical terms through Unity Trust Bank, the trade union-backed bank, which has been a key provider of ESOP, though not buy-out finance,[13] especially in the early years of UK ESOPs.

However, in many cases the support for ESOPs from individual unions can only be described as grudging. The policy of the Transport and General Workers' Union passed in 1987 noted that 'some circumstances favour the tactical validity of recourse to such devices as ESOPs as a last resort in defence of negotiated wages and conditions against the threat of take-over, break-up and asset stripping'. A union spokesman pointed out that 'we balance ESOPs as a tactic, a last-resort device to safeguard wages and conditions, against our aim of achieving public integration in the passenger industries' (see Lynch 1990). ESOPs were viewed as an instrumental, defensive device rather than as a form of organisation offering opportunities for workers and industrial democracy. The problem with ESOPs for unions such as the TWGU was, in addition to the problems outlined earlier, that they could expedite privatisation (by encouraging local authorities to sell their bus companies, for instance). This mirrors the support given to ESOPs by the Conservative Government at the end of the 1980s. It contrasts with the development of support for ESOPs in the Labour Party as a response to the privatisation programme.

This fear that ESOPs might actually encourage privatisation meant, according to local and regional officials and representatives interviewed by the author, that union headquarters organisations often gave little assistance to local representatives when ESOPs opportunities arose. The NALGO representative on the employee buy-out committee of a major bus company noted that he had little support from NALGO because the union opposed privatisation, and that he had had 'a difficult time with local and national officials'. In discussing this particular case, the 'NALGO National Committee eventually said it was against privatisation but that it would leave it to individuals to decide what to do'. As a result, detailed advice on various aspects of mounting the buy-out, such as the implications for pensions, had to be obtained from sources outside the union movement. This contrast between the views of national union officers and those of local representatives involved in employee buy-outs has also been observed in the US literature on ESOPs (McElrath and Rowan 1992). It seems to reflect a contradiction between employee pragmatism when jobs are at stake and union policies that are based on maintaining a separation between capital and labour.

Summary

In this chapter we have attempted to outline the evolution of policy towards ESOPs amongst the two main political parties and the trade union movement. In the case of the Conservative Governments of the 1980s and

1990s we have suggested that ESOPs were a by-product of the concern to promote employee share ownership and 'popular capitalism'. Practical assistance for ESOP development was provided by a statutory framework and by preferential bidding procedures during privatisation. Support for ESOPs, however, was tempered by unease about the possible association between ESOPs and industrial democracy, and also about the potential for abuse by firms. The legislation supporting ESOPs was therefore quite restrictive.

The Labour Party too has supported ESOPs but, we have argued, mainly for ulterior purposes. This is not to discount the passionate support given to ESOPs by key policy-makers such as Bryan Gould. The wider acceptance of ESOPs in the higher echelons of the party has to be viewed, however, in the evolution of party policy on public ownership from the mid-1980s onwards. The apparent potential of ESOPs to promote industrial and economic democracy was an ideal counterpoint to more traditional views on public ownership and nationalisation. In reading policy documents from the 1980s and early 1990s it is difficult to gain any strong sense of positive commitment to, or indeed understanding of, ESOPs in Labour policy. With traditional Labour policies on public ownership now decisively jettisoned, discussion of ESOPs amongst Labour policy-makers has faded somewhat. Since gaining office, however, the New Labour Government has devoted considerable attention to promoting employee share ownership, along lines similar to that of its Conservative predecessors. The main innovations in the current approach are an emphasis on creating flexible frameworks for employee share schemes and a 'transatlantic' interest in the use of share option schemes in start-up, 'knowledge economy', and high technology companies.

We have restricted the discussion in the chapter to the two main political parties in the UK as, on the whole, these have had the most direct impact on the development of employee share schemes. The intention is not to downplay the views of other parties, especially as the Liberal Party played a pivotal role in the establishment of the Approved Profit Sharing scheme in 1978 (see Chapter 4). In the 1992 election the Liberal Party promised to establish rights for every employee in 'substantial' companies to acquire a share in ownership and/or profits, and also to establish rights to participate in decisions (Liberal Party 1992). By the 1997 election, this French-style commitment to compulsory share schemes had been downgraded to a promise to promote profit sharing and employee share ownership (Liberal Democrat Party 1997). Meanwhile the nationalist parties have had little to say on ESOPs and employee share ownership as it is not obviously a devolution issue (within the context of current discussions and policies concerning divisions of powers between Westminster and national assemblies).

We have examined too the evolution of policies towards employee share ownership on the part of the TUC and the union movement more generally. The orientation of trade unions to share ownership can be seen as moving from 'bored hostility' to 'engaged scepticism'. This policy shift reflects the growth in share schemes in the economy over the last 20 years or so. The TUC and constituent unions remain cautious about share schemes for a variety of reasons summarised earlier, but within the range of share schemes ESOPs have been the preferred option. This is because ESOPs apparently have a much greater potential for industrial democracy than other forms of employee share ownership. Later chapters will attempt to show whether this belief is justified.

4 The structures of employee ownership

Introduction

In this chapter we examine the ownership structures that have been adopted by firms converting to full or partial employee ownership in the last 15 years or so. Our focus is primarily ESOPs but, since many firms using ESOPs also tend to use other mechanisms for achieving employee share ownership, our remit is inevitably wider than this. We examine direct share ownership, where employees subscribe directly to company shares, and also the use of ESOPs in combination with the earlier forms of employee ownership identified in Chapter 2 (collective ownership and co-operative ownership). As will become apparent, ESOPs are regulated by a complex amalgam of legislation on share schemes, taxation, financial services, trusts, and company practices, as well as legislation specifically aimed at ESOPs. Stock Exchange listing rules, accounting regulations and the codes of practice of institutional investors add to this mix. Our intention, though, is not to provide a comprehensive picture of the legal and taxation position of ESOPs. Instead our aim is to highlight the main features of ESOP structures, as a guide to understanding ESOPs in practice in subsequent chapters.

The perspective that guides the account here is that, within the constraints imposed by regulation, those involved in bringing about ownership conversion choose institutions and structures that reflect their interests and seem likely to meet their objectives. Despite the extent and complexity of ESOP regulation, ESOPs can provide a moderately flexible vehicle for achieving corporate or employee objectives. They may be used to resource existing employee share schemes aimed at enhancing employee remuneration or may be established to bring about a 'partnership' of employees (i.e. to develop meaningful ownership of the firm).[1] They may be used as a vehicle for highly leveraged employee buy-outs or as a means of facilitating divestment by owners. Given that there is some flexibility in the use of ESOPs to meet particular circumstances, the structural characteristics of ESOPs tend to vary (within the constraints set by the laws, regulations and codes governing ESOPs).

The defining feature of an ESOP is the presence of a trust(s) to acquire, hold and distribute equity. The main ESOP trust usually has borrowing powers to enable it to purchase shares for eventual distribution to employees. These shares may be newly issued by the main company, purchased on the open market or purchased directly from owners. In privately owned companies, this trust can also act as a 'market-maker' by providing a market for employees wishing to sell their shares. In the UK there are two main forms of ESOP in terms of legal and taxation characteristics: the 'case law' ESOP and the 'statutory' ESOP. Until the late 1990s case law ESOPs were the more common of the two as they were perceived to be more flexible than statutory ESOPs. The tax position of the latter was clearer but this was seen to be outweighed by the greater weight of regulation on statutory ESOPs, especially in relation to the composition of the trust mechanisms. In this chapter we outline the main characteristics of each type of ESOP, and then go on to discuss other forms of employee ownership that can be used in conjunction with them: direct share subscriptions, collective ownership, and co-operative forms of ownership.

Case law ESOPs

The first ESOPs in the UK took what came to be known as the case law form. Their main features are an amalgam of institutions and procedures, deriving from various trust, company, and taxation legislation (Reid 1992). They were developed in the mid-1980s by employee ownership lobbyists and experts, who attempted to integrate the characteristics of ESOPs in the USA with the particular legal and taxation context in the UK. This type of ESOP acquired the name 'case law because corporation tax relief on contributions from the company to the Employee Benefits Trust was established by case law and general taxation principles rather than specifically by statute. There is no specific legal identity for case law ESOPs as such.

The main component of a case law ESOP is an Employee Benefits Trust (EBT), and indeed it is possible to operate an ESOP with just an EBT. There are no legal restrictions on the way that shares are distributed to employees. In fact, there is no legal requirement as such that shares be distributed at all. Where shares are transferred from the EBT to employees, they may be distributed using an Approved Profit Sharing scheme, an approved Sharesave scheme, a (discretionary) Company Share Ownership Plan, or an unapproved share purchase or share option scheme.[2] Most case law ESOPs use an Approved Profit Sharing scheme for this purpose as it makes shares available to all employees reasonably quickly and, of course, provides tax benefits to its recipients. These ESOPs therefore also need to make use of a Profit Sharing Trust (PST) designed in accordance with the 1978 approved profit sharing scheme described in Chapter 2. For this reason ESOP structures are sometimes referred to as 'twin trusts' (Hurlston 1998).[3]

The basic 'twin-trust' ESOP structure is shown in Figure 4.1. As shown, a new company ('Newco') is created to effect a buy-out (Step 1). An EBT is established by the new company in Step 2. The EBT takes out a loan from a bank or other financial institution (Step 3) to purchase shares in the new company (Step 4). Employees may also subscribe directly to shares (Step 5), though this is not integral to the process. The receipts to the new company, along with any other loans and financial assistance, are used to pay for the acquisition of the company (Step 6). From time to time, contributions from pre-tax profits are passed to an Approved Profit Sharing Trust (Step 7). These contributions are then used to acquire shares held in the EBT (Step 8). The receipts from this activity are used by the EBT to repay the original loan from the bank (Step 9). Meanwhile, the Profit Sharing Trust allocates shares to individual employees in accordance with approved profit sharing legislation (Step 10). Equity can be passed from the EBT to the PST as quickly or slowly as profits permit but it is common to plan for the overall period of transfer to coincide with that of the repayment of the ESOP loan. In effect, the ESOP functions as a device to enable employees to obtain equity in their firm in the current period using profits expected to be generated in the future. As Hurlston points out, there is nothing new about the institutions that together form the ESOP structures – what is novel is the use of trusts to borrow funds to finance equity acquisition (1998). There are some variants on the basic position outlined above. Shares may be gifted to the EBT by the company, whilst shares that are purchased by the EBT may be acquired on the open market or newly issued.

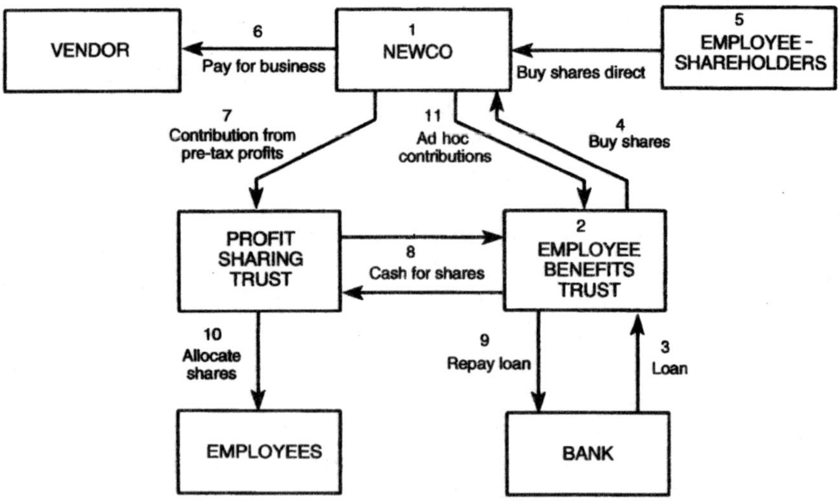

Figure 4.1 The use of a 'case law' ESOP in buy-outs.
Reproduced with the kind permission of Capital Strategies.

The EBT can also function as a market for shares in privately-owned companies. Where there is not a readily available market for shares, the value of employee shares may be adversely affected by the lack of liquidity. The EBT can resolve this problem by undertaking to purchase shares from employees (possibly as a fall-back if employees cannot sell them to their colleagues) or establishing a 'dealing day' when employees can buy or sell shares. Since an open-ended undertaking to buy shares could lead to unpredictable financing requirements for the EBT (it may have to raise further loans to buy back shares) it is common for a buy-back facility to be made available only to departing employees. In fact, in many cases employees leaving the firm are required to sell their shares back so that ownership is kept within the firm.

Case law ESOPs offer tax concessions to both the company and the employee. A corporation tax deduction can be secured for gifts made by the company to the EBT to repay a loan taken out to acquire shares. This deduction is not, however, explicitly stipulated in legislation and hence needs to be agreed with the Inland Revenue on a case-by-case basis. As in the US, the tax deduction may be allowable to cover both the interest payments and repayment of the principal. However, as corporation tax deductions can only be claimed for expenditure of a revenue nature it is not possible to claim a deduction for the establishment of the trust itself. There is a statutory tax deduction for contributions to PSTs in Approved Profit Sharing schemes.[4] The 1978 scheme also allows a deduction for the 'reasonable' expenses of the PST. The employee benefits from the tax concessions associated with the approved profit sharing scheme. If shares are retained in the PST for the two-year holding period plus one year, employees are not subject to income tax on the shares. Instead they are liable to capital gains tax on any eventual sale of the shares but the capital gains tax exemption limit is such that most employees would not pay any tax.[5]

A good example of a case law ESOP is the Yorkshire Rider buy-out from the West Yorkshire Passenger Transport Authority in October 1988. The purchase was a highly leveraged one with share capital accounting for only £0.5 million compared with a purchase price of £23 million. Forty-nine per cent of the equity was acquired by two EBTs with the benefit of a loan from Unity Trust. The remaining 51 per cent was bought directly by directors and senior managers. financed by a loan from Unity Trust Bank. An Approved Profit Sharing Trust was created to distribute equity to the workforce. An immediate distribution was made to employees of 125 shares each plus 25 shares for each year of service in excess of two years. These shares were passed to the PST and held in accordance with the statutory requirements on behalf of their beneficial owners. From then on, 125 shares were passed to the PST for each eligible employee each year, financed out of profits. Employees were not able to sell their shares to each other. In fact they could not be sold at all whilst they were still employed by the company. On leaving the company, however, they were required to sell their shares back to the trust at the current value (share valuations were provided twice a year). Dividends were not paid on the shares as profits were used primarily to pay back the head loan and finance the distribution of shares to employees.

The Yorkshire Rider case law ESOP was formed during a leveraged management-employee buy-out. Case law ESOPs have also been used where private owners have wanted to pass on all or part of the company to the workforce. In these cases the owner sells or donates their equity to a EBT, typically for distribution eventually using a PST. Whereas the EBT acquisition of shares in a leveraged buy-out tends to be a one-off transaction, in divestment cases it is not uncommon for several tranches of equity to be passed to the EBT over time. The motorway services company Roadchef, for instance, gradually built up its employee ownership component using a case law ESOP. Initially, in December 1986 12.25 per cent of equity was passed to an EBT, composed of 7 per cent acquired from family owners and 5.25 per cent new issue. This was followed by a second tranche of 15 per cent in 1988, also acquired from family owners. Another 5 per cent was acquired from similar sources over the next three years, so that by the early 1990s around a third of the ownership of the company was in the hands of the ESOP.

A third use of case law ESOPs can be found in publicly listed companies. Here the reasons for establishing an ESOP tend to be quite different. These companies usually have an array of employee share schemes, though these typically form a smaller proportion of equity than that found in private company ESOPs. These share schemes, be they share option or profit-sharing schemes, are resourced by the issue of new shares. This of course leads to dilution as the equity base is added to and detracts from earnings per share (EPS). To counter this problem, institutional investors (who are by far the largest owners of shares in the UK) impose, via the Association of British Insurers, strict limits on the issue of new shares for employee share schemes. These rules limit the extent of dilution to 10 per cent over any ten-year period (5 per cent for executive schemes). Stock Exchange listing rules also require that employee share schemes involving the issue of new shares be approved by shareholders. ESOPs are attractive to those firms who are in danger of breaching ABI limits since they enable equity to be acquired on the open market rather than through new issues. Furthermore, shareholder approval is not always necessary for share schemes where previously issued shares are used (and where directors are not beneficiaries of the scheme). ESOPs started to be used by listed firms after 1989, when the Companies Act gave greater freedom to firms to provide financial assistance and loan guarantees for the purchase of their own shares for the purpose of resourcing an employee share scheme. Since the EBT is established to resource present and future share scheme commitments in these cases, there tends not to be the 'once and for all' acquisition of shares as found in leveraged ESOPs. Instead, the EBT purchases shares on the open market when prices are favourable, when the company makes finance available, and when shares are needed for distribution. The levels of equity held in the EBT tends to be much lower than in either leveraged buy-outs or in cases where owners choose to divest to their workforces.

Reliable information on the number of case law ESOPs is hard to come by as they are not specifically recorded in Inland Revenue statistics, and tend instead to be subsumed in the statistics for Approved Profit Sharing schemes. Furthermore, as ESOPs tend not to be precisely defined, there is a certain amount of latitude in decisions about whether a particular firm has an ESOP. Much of our knowledge of ESOP numbers derives from the activities of ESOP lobbying organisations (such as the Employee Share Ownership Centre, formerly the ESOP Centre) keen to publicise conversions to employee ownership. Since some ESOPs may desire anonymity or their creation may have been handled by professional advisers not specialising in employee ownership work (and hence information has not been 'fed' into the network of those interested in employee ownership), these estimates probably slightly understate the number of ESOPs. With these provisos in mind, it has been estimated that the total number of case law ESOPs in the mid-1990s was between 50 and 100 (IRS Management Review 1998: 34).

There was a flurry of ownership conversions using the case law form in the late 1980s and early 1990s, but since the mid-1990s the number of these ESOPs has declined, for three reasons. One, quite a large number of case law ESOPs sold out from the mid-1990s onwards. Two, the decline in privatisation activity from the mid-1990s reduced the pool of firms likely to consider employee buy-outs. Three, the availability of a different form of ESOP from 1989, and especially from 1994 (when the 1989 legislation was relaxed), provided an alternative route to employee ownership.

In our database there are 32 firms with 'twin-trust' case law ESOP structures. These comprise 52 per cent of the firms in the study. Although we cannot be sure of the precise numbers of the total ESOP population, it is clear (given the informed estimates presented above) that we have a substantial proportion of the ESOP population in the database. The proportion of equity passed initially to case law ESOPs in our firms ranged from just 2.41 per cent to 100 per cent. The average transfer of equity was 36 per cent (median=25 per cent). Average total employee ownership, however, is higher in these firms since some used other mechanisms in addition to the case law ESOP. Mean total employee ownership is 43 per cent (median=30 per cent). In addition to the firms with case law ESOPs, there are a further 13 firms with an EBT, established either to hold equity in perpetuity or to act as a 'market-maker' for shares that were initially bought directly by employees. Overall, 73 per cent of firms in the database set up an EBT.

The function of the Employee Benefits Trust

At this point it is worth outlining the functions of the EBT in more depth as this institution is the centrepiece of case law ESOPs. It is also an interesting institution in so far as there is considerable scope for variation in its purpose. These variations derive from differences in the interests and objectives of those involved in establishing EBT, and the role of the EBT raises sometimes difficult issues about governance and participation.

The root of the ambiguity in the role of EBTs is that their fiduciary duty is to act in the interests of the beneficiaries (i.e. employees) but their operations are to a large extent governed by the company. The company usually provides financial assistance and acts as financial guarantor to the trust, and would typically seek to be a party to any measures to change the functions of the trust (Reid 1992). In some instances the company will have responsibilities and powers in the removal of trustees. Accounting regulations (UITF Abstract 13: *Accounting for ESOPs Trusts*) treat ESOP trusts as part of the main company, and require that the assets and liabilities of ESOP trusts be entered onto the main balance sheet and that income and expenditure be included in the main Profit and Loss account. Nevertheless, the discretionary nature of these trusts means that trustees must make decisions subject to the terms of the trust deed and in accordance with its legal duties. The typical duties include the requirement to act independently, to be impartial between beneficiaries, to act in the beneficiaries' best interests (as perceived by trustees), to preserve and enhance the assets held by them, and to exercise a duty of care if the trust is a major shareholder in the company (see Watts 1998):

The lack of a specific legal identity for case law ESOPs means that several specific powers and duties have to be incorporated in the deed of the EBT, especially where it is used to facilitate substantial employee ownership. For instance, the trust deed normally has to explicitly specify that the EBT deals solely in the equity of the company (see Reid 1992: 36). This is because the trustees' fiduciary duty to enhance the value of the assets held on beneficiaries' behalf would normally preclude investment in just one company as this would be viewed as unduly risky. Furthermore, the trust deed will normally need to give the trustees explicit powers to buy and sell shares, and to specify the method of share distribution, be it via an approved profit sharing trust, an approved option scheme, an unapproved scheme, direct sale, or gift to employees. If shares are to be retained in trust on a more or less permanent basis, the trustees need to be provided with the power to do this in the trust deed (Carnell 1992: 122).

The role of EBT trustees is wider than that of PST trustees as the latter have a narrow, and limited 'technical' function i.e. to distribute shares to their beneficial owners in accordance with the 1978 profit sharing legislation. By contrast, EBTs are the legal owners of the shares held by them, even though shares are held for employees' benefit. Whereas PST trustees are required to vote in accordance with employee shareholders' instructions (once shares are appropriated to employees), EBT trustees cast their votes in accordance with their perception of employees' best interests (which they may see as best indicated by an employee ballot) (Carnell 1992: 122).

Even though the trustees of the EBT have independent powers and responsibilities, accounting standards in the UK (UITF13 *Accounting for ESOP Trusts*) now treat employee benefits trusts (in both case law and statutory ESOPs) as part of the main company. This reflects the reality that EBTs generally are part of the company (see Carnell 1998). Accordingly the balance sheet of the main company incorporates the assets and liabilities of the trust, whilst its Profit and Loss account reflects the trust's income and expenditure. In accounting terms the company is held to own the shares held in trust on employees' behalf. This accounting regulation derives from the concern, expressed in UITF Share Options for Directors, that employee share schemes, executive schemes in particular, should be classed as remuneration since most firms use schemes for this purpose. As such, share schemes should be viewed as a cost to the company in the same way as core salary, rather than as a cost to shareholders. An exemption can be secured from this accounting regulation if there is 50 per cent or higher employee ownership. In these cases employee ownership is perceived as underpinning a 'partnership' of employees rather than simply providing additional remuneration. In legal terms, however, this muddies the water somewhat as eligibility for corporation tax deductions may depend on the proportion of equity transferred to the trust and the intentions of those effecting the transfer.

That EBTs have both the duty and power to act independently, and at the same time form part of the company, means that the composition and function of trusts can be a difficult and contested issue (Carnell 1992: 123). In case law ESOPs there is considerable legal freedom in the choice of trustees (unlike the statutory ESOP): trustees may be employees, outsiders, a company providing trustee services, or a subsidiary of the company. A corporate trustee tends to be the preferred model as it confers limited liability. In addition, corporate status means that the decisions of trust directors do not necessarily have to be unanimous. Where a company subsidiary is used, employees may be appointed as directors of the subsidiary. Given the ambiguity of status of the EBT, several scenarios are possible. On the one hand, it can be argued that trustees should be selected by the workforce as they are the beneficiaries of the EBT. On the other, it can be argued that trustees should be selected by the company as the EBT is simply a corporate mechanism to store ('warehouse') shares prior to distribution. Which definition of the EBT's role is paramount depends on the overall objectives and character of the ESOP, and the aims of those involved in creating it.

A further set of issues concerns the extent to which EBTs are involved in corporate governance and the *management* of the firm. On the whole, EBTs would find it difficult to take an active role in management as this would exceed the powers normally provided in the trust deed. They could, however, legitimately seek an active role in *governance*, especially if they hold a substantial proportion of the equity. The grounds for doing so would be the fiduciary duty to protect the beneficiaries' investment. If, however, the EBT is perceived as primarily a 'passive' warehouse for shares, the implication is that it should not be actively involved in corporate governance.

The composition and role of the EBT is therefore intimately bound up with issues of employee participation, governance, and industrial democracy. In practice the selection of trustees and the activities of the trusts seem likely to be powerfully influenced by the level of involvement and objectives of the various constituencies in the firm. Where employees or their representatives are deeply involved in the development of employee ownership, it may be anticipated that the trusts are more likely to have some employee representation.

The statutory ESOP

After the initial flurry of ESOP creation in the late 1980s, ESOP campaigners drew attention to a number of problems in establishing ESOPs via the case law route. These concerns were taken up by Members of Parliament from all of the major political parties, and a lobbying campaign was set in motion to provide a clearer legal identity for ESOPs. The main problems were outlined by Conservative MP Ian Taylor (1988). He argued that the administrative complexity and expense of establishing an ESOP was off-putting to potential converts. At least two trusts had to be established, one to raise loans and the other to distribute shares in a tax-effective way. A second problem was that the taxation status of contributions by the company to the EBT was unclear, as there was no statutory basis for them. Since general taxation law requires that deductions from corporation tax are based on revenue but not capital expenditure, the company contributions had to be demonstrably not for capital purposes. Tax deductions could therefore not be claimed for the expense of establishing the trust. Furthermore, the acquisition of shares might be perceived as a capital item and hence regular payments by the company might be viewed as instalments of a fixed capital sum (see Arrowsmith and Anderson 1992: 75–6). A third problem at the time was that PLCs were prevented from giving guarantees in respect of an EBT's external borrowings or providing direct financial assistance (see Reid 1992: 44). Four, private owners selling their companies to case law ESOPs were liable to capital gains tax on the proceeds where there was an increase in the value of the firm. By contrast, those owners selling their firms to PLCs could claim capital gains tax rollover relief if they reinvested the proceeds in certain kinds of assets.

The result of the lobbying campaign was the so-called 'statutory' ESOP, introduced in the 1989 Budget. This legislation provided for the creation of Statutory Employee Share Ownership Trusts (ESOTs) or Qualifying Employee Share Trusts (QUESTs) to acquire, hold, and distribute equity. Two clear taxation advantages over case law ESOPs were provided (Reid 1992: 38), mainly relating to the uncertainties in corporation tax treatment referred to above. One, voluntary contributions by the company to the QUEST were made tax deductible by statute rather than case law. Two, the expenditure incurred in establishing the trust was allowable for tax deductions. So, this legislation provided a clear legal status for ESOPs and provided a set of statutory as opposed to case law principles for the taxation treatment of them.

However, several important conditions had to be met to obtain this preferential treatment, chiefly relating to the function and composition of the QUEST itself. The powers of the trustees were more circumscribed than those of trustees in many case law ESOPs'.[6] Initially shares could only be passed directly to beneficiaries or to an approved profit sharing scheme, and could not be used in conjunction with a share option scheme. Nor could they be sold on the open market. They also had to be transferred on equal terms, as in the approved profit sharing legislation. Where they operated in conjunction with a PST (so as to give tax concessions to employees receiving shares), transfers to the PST had to be on the basis of full market value. Initially, the law required that equity held by the QUEST be fully distributed to individual employees within seven years.

In addition to these regulations governing the purpose of the QUEST, there were stringent conditions governing its composition. The legislation initially stipulated that there be at least three trustees, all of whom had to be UK residents, and of whom at least one should be a professional person, such as a solicitor. Directors, or anyone with a material interest in the company (defined as a 5 per cent or more equity stake), were precluded from trust membership. Furthermore, a majority of the trustees had to be employees of the firm, and selected by a majority of the whole workforce (i.e. not just a majority of those voting in a ballot) or by their elected representatives. These conditions can be contrasted with EBTs in case law ESOPs where those establishing the trust are given considerable latitude in the composition and selection of trustees.

More or less from the outset, ESOP campaigners and specialists campaigned for a more liberal set of regulations. They achieved some success in this as a number of important revisions were made during the course of the 1990s. From 1991, owners selling equity to a statutory ESOP could claim capital gains tax rollover relief as long as the QUEST acquired at least 10 per cent of the company and the departing owner reinvested in 'chargeable assets' within six months.[7] In 1994 the Finance Act extended the time for share distribution to 20 years and removed the requirement that a majority of trustees be drawn from the workforce. Furthermore, only half of the non-professional trustees had to be selected by the workforce or their representatives, and where an election was held trustees were elected by simple majority of those voting (rather than of the whole workforce).[8] From then QUESTs could be comprised of either individual trustees or a single UK corporate trustee (whose directors had to fulfill the same requirements as those set for individual trustees). Other reforms included compulsory eligibility of part-time workers on the same terms as full-time workers (1995), exemption from the Financial Services Act regulation on collective investment schemes (1995),[9] and from 1996 the capacity to operate ESOPs in conjunction with SAYE schemes. The Finance Act 1996 also removed the requirement that beneficiaries had to have a minimum of one year's qualifying service, thereby making QUESTs a feasible instrument for mounting employee buy-outs.[10]

On the whole, the approach of governments in the 1990s was to dilute the obstacles to ESOP formation rather than to provide positive inducements to their formation. Even so, observers have identified continuing obstacles to QUEST formation. These include the liability of vendors to claw-back of rollover relief if the QUEST violates statutory regulations and the requirement that companies forming QUESTs be UK-based (Pett 1998). Against this, it is thought that other recent changes in tax regulations may encourage the formation of statutory ESOPs even though they are not focused on them specifically. The phasing out of retirement relief and the abolition of reinvestment relief is thought likely to increase the attraction of QUESTs to business owners wanting to exit, by increasing the relative value of rollover relief (see Mason 1998).

Up to mid-1996 it is thought that around 30 statutory ESOPs had been created in the UK, all of them in private companies. Most of these were created after the relaxation of the statutory framework in 1994 (see Pett 1998), and it is thought that less than five were created before then (IRS Management Review 1998: 38). Since 1996, when SAYE schemes were allowed to be used in conjunction with QUESTs, there has been substantial growth, and as of March 2000 there were 399 QUESTs, mainly in publicly listed firms.[11] The new attraction of the statutory ESOP resides in the capacity to obtain a tax deduction for the growth in value of a SAYE option (and the initial discount) provided shares are issued to employees through the QUEST rather then directly (Carnell 1998). The potential for this tax relief arises from the interaction of QUESTs, SAYE schemes and recent accounting regulations. In 1997 SAYE schemes were exempted in UITF 17 (*Employee Share Schemes*) from the requirement that the cost of share schemes be accounted for at full market cost and that any discounts and option gains be entered onto the Profit and Loss account. By issuing new shares for SAYE schemes via a QUEST there is no cost (of option gains and discounts) to the Profit and Loss account but the internal transfers of funds (minus employee subscriptions) to the QUEST to meet the full market cost of issuing shares to the QUEST itself can be set against corporation tax. In effect the company secures a tax relief for operating a SAYE scheme (see Carnell 1998 for a very clear explanation of this complicated process).

In our database there are eight firms with statutory ESOPs, two of whom operate them in conjunction with non-statutory EBTs. This represents about a quarter of the total QUEST population in the mid-1990s (before the substantial growth in QUESTs in PLCs after 1996). The proportion of equity passed to statutory ESOPs at conversion ranged from 13 per cent to 100 per cent. The average proportion of equity initially held in the QUEST was 49 per cent (median=38 per cent). The average total level of employee ownership, including other forms besides the QUEST, was 68 per cent (median=90 per cent). Overall, then, the average level of employee ownership tends to be higher in statutory than case law ESOPs.

Direct ownership

Case law and statutory ESOPs are not the only ways firms have increased employee ownership in recent years. Some firms have become substantially employee-owned via employees subscribing directly to share capital and by employees raising some or all of the finance necessary to acquire the firm. These kinds of conversions to employee ownership are sometimes referred to as 'worker capitalism' (e.g. Wright *et al.* 2000) because the mechanism and characteristics of shareholding by employees are similar to any other purchase of shares by investors. In practice it is not always possible to make a clear distinction between ESOP arrangements and direct acquisition of shares by employees because 'case law' can distribute shares using direct purchase mechanisms. Some firms have used a combination of ESOPs and direct share purchases. Others have converted to employee ownership via direct purchases but have then created an EBT to buy back shares from employees leaving the firm. In this section we outline the main characteristics of direct share purchases, and then consider the arguments in favour of this approach rather than the ESOP method.

The clearest form of direct purchase is where employees subscribe directly to shares without any use of an ESOP or EBT. A good case in point here is the National Freight Consortium buy-out in 1981. In 1982 about 40 per cent of the workforce and their families subscribed to 82.5 per cent of the new company's equity (see Bradley and Nejad 1989: 59–61). NFC was initially acquired by its management via a high-leveraged buy-out. A condition of the loan package was that employees, pensioners, and their families would be invited to subscribe to a substantial part of the equity of the new company shortly after the formal transfer out of public ownership had taken place. Opportunities for employee purchases of shares were also provided in the large privatisation flotations in the 1980s, usually on preferential terms. Typically up to 5 per cent of equity was available to employees.[12] This approach has also been found in privatisation transactions in Asia, Latin America, and Africa (see Wright *et al.* 2000).

There have been a few instances in the bus industry where substantial employee ownership was brought about by direct share purchases. The first company to became employee-owned using this method was the Luton and District subsidiary of the National Bus Company in 1987. After this, other cases included Derby City Transport (privatised from local authority ownership in 1989) and Clydeside 2000 (privatised from the Scottish Bus Group in 1991).[13] In the case of Clydeside 2000 the workforce raised about £750,000 to provide it with an equity stake of 70 per cent, with Luton and District and the senior management each acquiring 15 per cent. Seventy per cent of the workforce of 835 invested in multiples of £200. The employee subscriptions ranged from the minimum of £200 to £2,000, with one individual contributing £12,000. These direct subscriptions by employees raised just over 50 per cent of the total cash sale price of the company. In the highly publicised employee buy-out of Tower Colliery in South Wales in 1994, employees each contributed £8,000 to finance the purchase from the National Coal Board.

In some cases direct share subscriptions have been used in conjunction with an EBT (and sometimes also with an Approved Profit Sharing Trust). Here shares might initially be placed in an EBT as part of the purchase of the company but then more or less immediately offered for sale to employees. A good example here is Quadron, the management-employee buy-out in 1993 of Woodspring District Council's (Weston-super-Mare) contract services department. At the buy-out, 90,000 shares were purchased by an EBT using a loan provided by Unity Corporate Advisors (the successor to Unity Trust) and 81,000 of these were immediately offered for sale to the workforce supplemented by a free transfer of the remaining 9,000.

In other cases EBTs have been created to buy back shares from departing employees in buy-outs that were brought about primarily by direct share acquisition. In Tayside Buses (an employee buy-out from Tayside Regional Council in June 1991) all 592 employees subscribed £500 to meet the purchase prices of just under £3.3 million. Since ownership was limited to current employees, and as each share had a book value of £500, a mechanism was necessary to relieve departing employees of their equity stakes. As purchases by other employees could not be guaranteed (and indeed was viewed as undesirable given the emphasis on equality of ownership in the company), it made sense to create an EBT. Shares purchased by the EBT were then made available for purchase by new employees.

Finally, some firms creating ESOPs also used a degree of direct share ownership to supplement ESOP-facilitated share acquisitions. In the first ESOP in the bus industry, People's Provincial Buses employees subscribed £750 to help fund the purchase of the company. Out of a workforce of 212, 189 participated in the scheme, a participation rate of just under 90 per cent. £700 of each contribution were used to acquire preference shares, and the remaining £50 bought ordinary voting shares. These ordinary shares comprised 20 per cent of the ordinary share capital of the company. The remaining 20 per cent was acquired by an EBT, funded by a loan from

Unity Trust. In this case the employee subscriptions raised £143,250 of the £730,000 sale price of the company (i.e. 20 per cent).[14] Initially, transfers from the EBT to employee accounts were financed out of profits using an approved profit share scheme, in line with 'classic' ESOP principles, but from 1994 EBT shares were sold to the workforce. At this time employees had acquired 51 per cent of the ordinary share capital with the remainder still held in the EBT.

A similar approach was adopted in Chesterfield Transport, where 85 per cent of the workforce subscribed £800 to purchase £750 of non-voting preference shares and £50 of ordinary voting shares. This subscription contributed around 10 per cent of the sale price of the firm and enabled the workforce to acquire directly 15 per cent of the equity. Eighty-five per cent was initially acquired by an EBT. Like Peoples' Provincial, further distributions of shares to employees were made by a combination of free transfers financed out of profits and share sales (with new employees given preferential access for share purchases).

That direct ownership and ESOP structures tend to be intertwined in practice, at least in the case of management-employee buy-outs during privatisation, is well illustrated by the case of London United Busways (a buy-out from London Transport in November 1994). Initially this privatisation was a management buy-out facilitated by venture capital. As part of the buy-out, however, it was decided to offer a significant share of the voting capital to employees. Seventeen per cent of the ordinary share capital (plus non-voting preference shares) was made available for direct purchases by employees in February 1995. The receipts from this purchase were used to contribute to repayment of around £5 million of loan stock sold earlier to financial institutions (to effect the original buy-out of the company). Meanwhile, an EBT had been created and 4 per cent of voting share capital had been placed in it. This 4 per cent was transferred to employees free of charge in portions governed by length of service. After this distribution, the primary function of the EBT was to acquire, warehouse, and resell shares initially bought by employees under the offer outlined above.

Although ESOPs and direct share subscriptions have often been used together, the two methods do have different characteristics and implications. Within the employee-owned sector of the bus industry there was an intense debate, sometimes acrimonious, about the respective merits of the two routes to employee ownership. Advocates of direct employee ownership argued that direct share purchases provide a more immediate and direct sense of ownership than is found in most ESOPs. Whereas it can take three years (five years before 1995) for employees to receive shares allocated to them using ESOP mechanisms, in the case of direct ownership employees receive their share certificates from the outset. The shares are held by them rather than on their behalf. It is argued therefore that share ownership of this type is more 'meaningful' to the employee. It is also sometimes argued that the direct subscription method is more 'individualistic'. Since there is no collective shareholding by trusts, there are normally no ownership-based employee institutions with a collective voice in corporate governance.

A further argument is that as employees have to finance their share acquisitions themselves, they bear a much higher degree of risk. It has been argued that this engenders a more 'responsible' form of ownership, with employees much more aware of the importance of corporate success and the relevance of their own work behaviour to this. Typically, employees use either redundancy payments or bank loans to finance their acquisitions. Since the latter clearly leads to costs to the employee (i.e. interest payments to banks), it is usually necessary to channel a large part of the employee subscription into preference shares providing regular interest payments rather than equity shares to cover the costs borne by the employee. In other words a substantial part of the employee investment does not directly contribute to ownership as such. Critics have argued that the degree of risk shouldered by employees is unreasonable since at least some firms taking this route have highly uncertain prospects. The benefit of leveraged ESOPs, where shares are transferred free of charge to employees using approved profit sharing schemes, is that employees do not bear any investment risk (though there is risk to their employment if the firm fails).

A further corollary of the direct ownership route to employee ownership is that there are pressures militating against equality of ownership. In the extreme case, where direct purchase is the sole or main mechanism for acquiring ownership and where substantial sums are sought from employees, those members of the workforce unable or unwilling to raise the finance are excluded from ownership. The average participation rate in our firms was 67 per cent (median=70 per cent), with the lowest being 13 per cent. Just under one-third of firms had participation rates in excess of 90 per cent, and these tended to be firms that emphasised the democratic aspects of employee ownership.

Within the group of employees willing and able to participate, the exigencies of raising capital mean that inequalities of ownership are highly likely. In one of the firms in our study the largest subscription was 50 times greater than the smallest. Over two-thirds of our firms with some form of direct share purchases had unequal levels of subscription. However, some firms making substantial use of direct employee contributions have placed great emphasis on equality of participation. Several of the bus companies, such as Tayside, Preston, Kelvin Central, People's Provincial, Chesterfield, and Southampton Citybus, offered shares in equal blocks. However, in most of these cases the buy-out involved a substantial degree of leverage and the employee contribution formed a relatively small part of the finance necessary to acquire the company. It should also be borne in mind that share allocations in ESOPs are rarely equal. It is common for top managers to have a larger share than other employees, whilst distribution within the employee group is not necessarily equal (though distribution must be on 'equal terms' if an Approved Profit Sharing scheme is used). In practice, all but the first distribution of shares tend to be done equally, with the first distribution combining an equal portion and a portion linked to length of service. Forty-four per cent of firms for whom information was available linked some or all of the first distribution to employment tenure. There was just one case where APS share distributions were linked to salary levels.

One way of controlling the effects of unequal ownership is to place limits on the proportion of equity that can be held by any one individual. Several of the employee-owned bus companies which used direct share subscriptions, such as Greater Manchester South, Southampton Citybus, Preston, and Merseyside Transport, limited the proportion of equity that could be held by any individual to 1 per cent. Some also placed limitations on voting rights whatever the level of ownership.

A further advantage claimed for direct share subscriptions over ESOPs is that the administrative costs and effort of establishing trusts are avoided. Some of our respondents from firms with ESOPs structures indicated that the establishment and administration of the trusts and the constantly changing share register were the most important downside of moving to employee ownership. Against this, mounting a buy-out can be even more precarious than where an ESOP is used, as there are more actors involved in financing the purchase. Companies involved in direct ownership buy-outs typically have to expend a great deal of effort and time extolling the virtues of the buy-out to the workforce and arranging access to sources of loan finance for them. It is often not known until the eleventh hour whether employee participation will be at the level perceived to be necessary.

In several cases studied during the research, companies using direct subscriptions to fund much of the employee share acquisition had either weak asset bases, a history of poor trading performance, or no trading record at all. The highly leveraged buy-outs that have characterised some privatisation ESOPs were not feasible because outside investors would not have been willing to bear the risk. Unlike many ESOPs, therefore, the employee contribution may form a substantial part of the finance necessary to acquire the company. Critics of the direct subscription route to employee ownership amongst our respondents argued that where managers retain a substantial share, some of the costs of securing managerial control are in effect transferred to the workforce

In our data-set of 62 firms there were 23 firms (37 per cent) that made some use of direct employee share purchases during the conversion to employee ownership (i.e. not including those that subsequently distributed shares using share option schemes). Thirteen of these firms (56 per cent) had employee benefits trusts operating either as another medium for employee ownership or to buy-back shares from leavers (or both). In these firms the proportion of equity acquired directly by employees ranged from

3 per cent to 100 per cent. The mean level of direct share acquisitions was 52 per cent of equity (median=42 per cent). Average total employee ownership (i.e. including equity held in trust in some cases) was 64 per cent (median=70 per cent).

Collective ownership

In most ESOPs the usual course of events is for shares to be distributed from the EBT to individual employees over time. This contrasts with the practice in some long-established employee ownership firms, of which the most well known is the John Lewis Partnership, of holding all of their equity in trust in perpetuity without allocation to individuals (see Chapter 2). However, use of ESOP mechanisms is not inconsistent with this collective approach to ownership. Employee benefits trusts (though not QUESTs) can retain some or all of the equity in trust, if the Articles permit it. In fact, there is some use of long-term collective ownership alongside individual allocations to employees in our firms. Thirteen firms (21 per cent) intended to hold equity in trust in the long term. Of these, six were EBT-only firms (i.e. there were no mechanisms or intentions to distribute equity to individuals), six had a 'conventional' ESOP twin-trust structure with regular distributions to individuals, and one was a statutory ESOP. Whilst the latter was legally required to distribute equity to employees within 20 years, the intention was to hold the equity collectively in trust for as long as possible within the confines of the legal requirements.

There are two main types of reason for holding equity collectively in trust. The first is that distributions to individuals can lead to unstable employee ownership. Unless there are requirements in the trust deed and Articles to the contrary, employees may sell their shares to outsiders, thereby diluting employee ownership. To preclude this, most firms (75 per cent in our sample) require that employees sell their shares back to the trust or other employees when they exit the firm. A larger source of danger to employee ownership is the possibility that employees may vote to sell the company (e.g. where there is a take-over bid). Whilst employees do not own the shares not yet vested to them, the trustees of an EBT may feel bound to cast their votes in the same way as employees, on the grounds that the clearest expression of beneficiaries' interests will be made by the beneficiaries themselves. Where, however, it is stipulated in the trust deed that equity will be retained in trust, the trustees are in a better position to act independently of employees. In some firms the independence of trustees is reinforced by a stipulation that the beneficiaries include future as well as current employees. We noted earlier (in Chapter 2) that John Lewis is virtually immune from the danger of conversion out of employee ownership by virtue of the wording of the trust deed. The second reason for retaining equity in trust is that it can underwrite the involvement of trustees in company and management decisions. If trustees have a 'blocking' share, so that their consent is required for either normal or special resolutions, then management and other owners will generally need to heed their views.

There appear to be two forms of collective ownership amongst the firms in our sample. In the first, the purpose of the retained equity is to maintain employee control of key decisions. Typically, the benefits trust containing the retained equity has a substantial number of employee representatives or indeed is controlled by them. This approach is found exclusively in the bus industry management-employee buy-outs in our sample. Firms maintaining equity in trust included Mainline (26 per cent) and West Midlands Transport (25.5 per cent). Since the Articles required a 75 per cent vote in favour of major strategic decisions, such as acquisitions and divestments, this gave the trustees effective blocking control. Chesterfield Transport provided the basis for trust involvement in all major decisions by retaining 51 per cent of equity permanently in trust. In Merseyside Transport just 1 per cent was to be retained in trust but the Articles attached a 'golden share' formula to this to achieve a similar effect.

The other form of collective ownership is found in firms where employee ownership has arisen out of employer divestment and paternalism. Here the intention was not so much to underwrite the involvement of trustees in decision-making but to protect the firm from take-overs and to provide a source of employee benefits. Most of these firms had a majority of the equity held permanently in trust. Most did not have any provisions for distributing equity to individual employees. As in the case of John Lewis Partnership, the annual dividend on shares held in trust provided a source of profit-sharing payments to employees.

An important issue arising where the objective is to retain shares in trust is that of payment to acquire the shares. The financing mechanism in the 'classic ESOP' typically involves a loan to the EBT to purchase equity, with the loan being repaid by the EBT as transfers are made to the profit-sharing trust. If shares are to be retained in trust some other means of paying for the acquisition or retention of shares may be necessary. In the case of Chesterfield Transport it was anticipated that the portion of equity to be retained in trust, which had initially been acquired using a loan, could be financed by the growth in share value. The total loan repayment could be met by the profit transfer payments into the trust to acquire some of the shares at current values for the purposes of distribution. This type of financing is feasible in high-leverage buy-outs, where substantial increases in share value can be anticipated. In divestment cases, some other means of acquiring shares for the EBT is likely to be necessary since future increases in share value cannot be relied upon (because high levels of leverage are not used to acquire the firm) and, in any case, profit-finance distribution of shares to employees is not usually the objective. Gifts of shares, or substantially discounted shares, may well be the main means of effecting the transfer from owners to trusts. In five out of eight cases in our sample this was the method used.

Co-operative ownership

A key feature of workers' co-operatives is that ownership rights are distributed equally amongst the workforce. The ownership shares are usually held equally, and it is usual for each employee to be allocated one vote. In common-ownership co-operatives ownership shares are not held individually but each employee has a voting right by virtue of their employment. ESOPs do not necessarily embody these characteristics. In fact most do not. Ownership tends to be distributed unequally in ESOPs, both between employees and other owners (such as top managers) and within the employee group itself. In most cases, a 'conventional' corporate governance model is used, whereby voting rights are linked to size of shareholdings. Thus voting rights tend to be unequal in ESOPs.

However, there is nothing to prevent a policy of one person, one vote in principle. Shares could be distributed equally to employees so that equal voting powers could be achieved, especially as this is one option amongst the 'equal terms' provisions of approved profit sharing. Alternatively, a special class of voting shares, one of which is allocated to each employee, could be created to supplement the bulk of the share capital. Another possibility is that the Articles of Association could provide for equal voting rights on certain specified key issues, such as acquisitions and divestments, whilst leaving other issues to be voted according to the number of shares actually held. These possibilities indicate that ESOPs are not necessarily an alternative to workers' co-operatives. Instead, ESOPs may incorporate co-operative philosophies and practices. As Mason has put it, 'the ESOP legal framework is very "co-op friendly" (1992: 200). ESOPs, embodying co-operative principles, are sometimes referred to as 'Democratic ESOPs'. They may also be known as 'Employee Common Ownership Plans' (ECOPs) where the equity is held in trust rather than distributed to employees but voting rights are equal (Mason *ibid.*).

In our sample there are seven firms (11 per cent) that had incorporated co-operative principles. Most were buy-outs, and in six cases employees had subscribed directly to shares to part-fund the acquisition of the company. These subscriptions were equal, and in all but one case this provided the basis for equal ownership and voting rights. In two cases, one person one vote was based on the provision of a special class of voting shares (either because share subscriptions, though equal, were not universal or because the purpose of the ESOP institutions were to raise capital externally). Three of them made use of an ESOP 'twin-trust' structure, and a further three created an EBT to buy back shares where necessary (to maintain insider ownership).

Summary

In this chapter we have provided a fairly technical exposition of the main features of case law ESOPs, QUESTs, and other forms of employee share ownership. As has been emphasised, these various forms are not mutually exclusive. Many firms adopting ESOPs in the 1980s and 1990s used a combination of case law ESOP structures and direct share subscriptions. Some firms have utilised both case law ESOPs and QUESTs. The choice of share ownership mechanisms in each case appears to be a function of financing constraints, tax benefits, the potential for flexibility, and the salience (to those involved in introducing employee ownership) of employee involvement in trust decisions. The decision to use a particular configuration of share ownership institutions can be seen as the outcome of a calculation of the costs and benefits of each of these. For many owners, the perceived costs of employee involvement and lack of flexibility outweigh the tax benefits of the statutory ESOP. By the same token, the discovery of substantial tax benefits for SAYE schemes using QUESTs tipped the balance in favour of QUESTs for many PLCs at the end of the 1990s. Much will depend on which groups of actors in the firm are involved in ownership conversion, and how their objectives interact. ESOP and employee ownership structures need to be seen as instruments for achieving actors' objectives rather than as ends in themselves (Pendleton *et al.* 1995a). These observations will be pursued further in Chapter 5, when we consider the circumstances and objectives of employee ownership in our sample of firms.

5 Contexts and reasons for employee ownership

Introduction

In this chapter we examine why firms introduce employee ownership. We consider the circumstances in which employee ownership emerges, the characteristics of employee ownership firms, and the objectives of the key actors involved in the ownership conversions. We suggest that the interaction of contexts, company characteristics, and actors' objectives has a powerful effect on the level and type of employee ownership. Drawing on our data-set of 62 firms with employee ownership, we find three main sets of circumstances in which employee ownership occurred. These were privatisation of public sector organisations, divestment of private sector companies or operating units, and compliance with regulatory guidelines in publicly listed companies. The privatisation group, which is by far the largest, is separated into two sub-groups. One comprises bus companies, and the second is composed of other privatised firms. We also distinguish two sub-sets within the divestment group. The first is composed of employee or management-employee buy-outs of operating units or subsidiaries earmarked for divestment or closure, and the second is composed of firms that have been passed on to their employees by owners wishing to exit (in part or in whole).

In this chapter, then, the basis of the categorisation of employee-owned firms is the circumstances in which the conversion occurs. In outlining each set of firms we consider the characteristics of firms in each group, and the involvement and objectives of key groups of actors. In so doing, we hope to illuminate why employee ownership was chosen by these firms, and also to explain the particular configurations of ownership adopted. Towards the end of the chapter we reformulate the categories of employee ownership firms on the basis of the main actors involved in the conversion process. We thereby distinguish four sets of firms. These are 'representative' firms, where employee representatives tend to be deeply involved in conversion; 'risk-sharing' firms, where managers are the primary movers for conversion and where employee ownership tends to be at low levels'; 'paternalist' companies, where divesting owners have a powerful influence on the decision to become employee-owned; and 'technical' firms, where managers introduce ESOP mechanisms to comply with regulatory frameworks. This fourfold categorisation is a refinement of one made some five years ago on the basis of a smaller survey population (see Pendleton *et al.* 1995a).

The circumstances of employee ownership conversions

Ben-Ner and Jones (1995) suggest that a fundamental problem with many studies of ESOPs is that they do not address the specific circumstances in which ownership conversion takes place, and do not consider the motives and objectives of those involved in it. This is unfortunate, they argue, since the circumstances in which employee ownership comes about are likely to have a significant bearing on events post-conversion, such as the economic performance of the firm. A failing firm that converts to employee ownership to save jobs is likely to be very different from a successful one that introduces an ESOP to bind firm-specific human capital to the company. The pattern of involvement of various actors – owners, managers, workers, and unions – is likely to differ, and this is likely to have an important influence on the distribution of both ownership and control rights.

Studies of ESOP characteristics in the United States tend to find that no theoretically derived reasons for employee ownership (provision of incentives, flexibility etc.) are particularly strongly associated with ESOP creation (Kruse 1996). Partly, as Kruse points out, this may be because the measures and proxies are inadequate. Partly, the difficulty of discerning distinct predictors or characteristics of ESOP firms may be that there are distinct sub-groups of ESOPs whose characteristics cancel each other out. As Gordon and Pound argue:

> it is likely that some ESOPs will be undertaken primarily to boost long term performance and that some will be used primarily to defend against take-overs. Traditional approaches to evaluating these policies, which typically depend on examining average effects, will fail to capture either the potential gains from good ESOPs or the potential costs of bad ones.
>
> (1990: 526)

As we have seen in Chapter 2, US ESOPs take a variety of forms. Most pass just a small proportion of equity to employees (Blasi and Kruse 1991). In essence, they are 'conventional' employee share schemes introduced by management. There are some ESOPs, however, where large proportions of equity are acquired by employees, and these may more properly be seen as employee-owned. There are a number of distinct groupings within this category. Some are 'rescue' conversions of failing firms (such as the Rath Packing Company, discussed by Hammer and Stern 1986), some are employee buy-outs of firms scheduled for closure (see Hammer *et al.* 1982), some are the outcome of concession bargaining with unions, as in the case of the US steel and airline industry (Gordon 1998; Best 1999), and some are divestments by retiring owners. The latter appear to be growing in importance, but the conversions of large airlines have attracted most attention.

In many cases a significant motive behind ownership conversion is maintaining 'insider' control by protecting firms against take-overs. As far as privately owned firms are concerned, there is a danger that firms sold to others will be rationalised or closed down, with possible job losses. In the case of publicly listed firms, the operation of the market for corporate control may mean that under-performing firms undergo a change in ownership and control, with the result that earlier 'implicit contracts (i.e. job security) may be terminated (Schleifer and Summers 1988). Employee ownership, then, may be perceived primarily as a defensive strategy concerned with preventing changes in control that might have highly adverse effects on the workforce and its managers.

Although some large-scale surveys question whether corporate control is the most important reason for the creation of most ESOPs (Chang 1990; Blasi and Kruse 1991; Kruse 1996), econometric evidence from a more restricted sample of buy-outs suggests that control considerations are very important. Chaplinsky *et al.* (1998) found that 60 per cent of employee buy-outs had experienced take-over pressure in the year immediately preceding the ownership conversion. Beatty (1994) found that the presence of other anti-take-over devices, such as 'poison pills' and supra-majority voting provisions, are the strongest predictors of ESOP creation. Useem and Gager's (1996) survey of over 700 publicly listed firms found that firms facing a hostile take-over environment are likely to seek to seek greater employee shareholding. They argue that managers attempt to change their owners when faced with threatening shareholders. As Gordon and Pound (1990) point out, a benefit of ESOPs in this context is that ESOP trustees can be appointed by management without shareholder assent, and are likely to be sympathetic to management or employee interests. Besides blocking take-over bids, employee ownership may discourage buy-ins by outside investors because the diffusion of control rights may be perceived as increasing monitoring costs (cf. Jensen and Meckling 1979).

Whilst most ESOPs with substantial employee ownership may be created to maintain the control of incumbent 'insiders', there may well be variations in involvement and objectives according to the specific circumstances (Pendleton *et al.* 1995a). Thus, in owner divestments the objectives of the departing owner may be paramount. By contrast, in employee buy-outs of failing firms, employee interests and objectives may be the most important influence. It seems likely that these factors will affect the design and implementation of employee ownership institutions, such as the level, distribution, and type of employee ownership. This echoes the findings of earlier literature on workers' co-operatives that the orientations of founder owners have a critical influence on the design and functioning of co-operative structures (Cornforth *et al.* 1988).

It seems plausible that the factors that are often identified as potential 'determinants' of employee ownership, such as a concern to develop optimal labour contracts and secure wage concessions, may either be important for just some sub-groups of EOPS or else may be subsidiary factors in these conversions. Thus achieving wage flexibility, by exchanging wage claims for equity claims, may be important in those cases where there is competition from lower-wage new entrants and where unions are otherwise resistant to wage cuts (i.e. as in airlines). By contrast, securing downward wage flexibility in owner divestment ESOPs may be relatively unimportant. Another common explanation for the use of financial participation – that high or growing product market competition encourages firms to transfer risk to employees – may also only apply to some groups of ESOPs. In others, the capacity to share ownership and profits with employees may be based on product market security.

The suggestion overall, then, is that US ESOPs with substantial employee ownership tend to arise for defensive corporate control-associated reasons, and that other factors thought to encourage financial participation come into the equation according to the specific circumstances of conversion. The specific circumstances will also affect the degree of involvement, of various groups of actors. In turn, the balance of power, involvement and objectives of those involved will affect key features of the ESOP, such as the level and distribution of ownership.

Circumstances of ownership conversions in UK ESOPs

We suggest that the formation of UK ESOPs have many similar features to those of the US, though the specific circumstances tend to differ. We argue that in most cases ESOPs are formed for defensive reasons. They are created to prevent those take-overs that might lead to restructuring and job loss, or to prevent wholesale closure. Achieving employee co-operation, information-sharing, horizontal monitoring, and greater work effort tend to be important perceived benefits of employee ownership but, we argue, they are not the primary reasons or catalyst for ownership conversion. The motives of those involved differ between firms: in some cases, owners or managers embrace paternalistic sentiments concerning the justice of greater employee access to company profits. In other cases, managerial support for employee ownership is the outcome of a 'hard-headed' calculation that employee involvement is necessary to secure the purchase of the firm and to repay buy-out debts.

In our study we collected data on the circumstances in which conversion took place and the reasons for it. We expected that the balance of reasons would probably differ between contexts. From what we knew of ESOPs prior to data collection, we anticipated that most cases of employee ownership would be created either during privatisation or where private owners were seeking to divest in whole or in part. Table 5.1 provides details of the

Table 5.1 The circumstances of employee ownership

Circumstances	*Number of firms*	*Proportion (%)*
Bus company privatisation	26	42
Other privatisation	13	21
Total privatisation	39	63
Divestment – 'forced'	6	10
Divestment – 'paternalist	10	16
Total divestment	16	26
'Technical'	5	8
Other	2	3
Total	62	100

circumstances in which conversion took place, and the number of firms in each category.

Most cases (nearly two-thirds) of employee ownership came about as a result of privatisation. Two-thirds of the privatisation cases were in bus companies. The next largest group after the privatisation cases was divestments from privately owned companies. This group accounted for just over a quarter of cases. Most of the firms in this category became employee-owned as a result of owners deciding that they wanted to exit by transferring ownership to employees. The minority sub-group in this category are firms where employees mounted buy-outs in response to threats of closure. The third group – which we term a 'technical' group – is composed of PLCs who established employee benefits trusts to resource existing and planned 'conventional' share schemes. Finally, there are two firms that are difficult to categorise. One was a 'start-up' firm that established a statutory ESOP to hold 25 per cent of the firm's equity for distribution to employees once the business commenced active trading. The other was a workers' collective which established an ESOP when there was a large issue of shares to raise capital: the ESOP was created to maintain control of the collective by the current employees. Since these two firms are exceptional cases we exclude them from the ensuing discussion.

Table 5.2 indicates that there are substantial variations in employee ownership in our sample of 62 firms. Whilst average employee ownership is 56 per cent, there is considerable variation around this figure.[1] The lowest level of employee ownership is 2 per cent and the highest 100 per cent. The 'forced divestment' group has the highest average level of employee ownership, followed by the bus companies. These tended to have the highest level of employee and representative involvement in the conversion process. The next highest average employee ownership is found in the 'paternalist divestment' group. This reflects the concern of many owners in the sample to secure the future of the firm by passing large proportions of equity to employees. However, in all four groups there is substantial variation in

Table 5.2 Levels of employee ownership (percentage of total equity acquired by employees)

Circumstances of conversion	*Average ownership (SD)*	*Median ownership*	*Minimum ownership*	*Maximum ownership*
Bus privatisation	66 (33)	69	10	100
Other privatisation	34 (29)	25	2	100
'Forced' divestment	85 (36)	100	13	100
'Paternalist' divestment	58 (41)	60	7	100
'Technical'	5 (2)	4	3	8
All firms	56 (38)	49	2	100

ownership, with some firms having just a small proportion of employee-owned stock and others being entirely employee-owned. Twenty firms (i.e. just under a third) are entirely employee-owned. Meanwhile, all of the 'technical' ESOPs in PLCs have less than 10 per cent employee ownership.

Since we argue that employee ownership has to be understood as a defensive move to protect the firm and its employees from potentially damaging changes in corporate control, it is important to look at total levels of 'insider' ownership by executive directors and managers, as well as broadly based employee ownership.

As is clear from Table 5.3, most firms in our study had majority insider control. In fact, the average level of insider ownership is very high in each group, other than the technical group. Virtually all firms were fully owned by insiders. Bus privatisation and the two divestment groups were majority-owned by employees in most cases, with managerial ownership 'topping-up' insider ownership even further. The main difference between managerial and employee ownership is found in the other privatisation group, where only two firms are majority employee-owned but most are insider-owned. The average level of insider ownership is 70 per cent, double that of broad-based employee ownership.

As the circumstances of employee ownership conversion differed between groups of firms in the study, we thought it possible that the reasons for becoming employee-owned may well differ. To explore this further, we asked

Table 5.3 Levels of 'insider' ownership (percentage of equity owned by insiders)

Circumstances of conversion	*Average ownership (SD)*	*Median ownership*	*Proportion with majority insider control*	*Proportion with majority employee control*
Bus privatisation	85 (23)	100	92	62
Other privatisation	70 (34)	75	85	15
'Forced' divestment	100 (0)	–	100	83
'Paternalist' divestment	95 (14)	100	100	60
'Technical'	35 (20)	40	20	0
All firms	81 (28)	100	87	49

the main respondent in each firm (usually the managing director) to assess the importance in their firm of a variety of reasons for developing employee ownership.[2] A seven-point scale was used, where 1=little or no importance and 7=of very great importance. The items listed on the questionnaire were taken from surveys of firms with financial participation by Poole (1989) and Baddon *et al.* (1989), supplemented by additional items that were potentially relevant in an employee ownership context. We are unable to provide results for the 'technical' group due to a large number of missing values.

Table 5.4 indicates that there are differences between the groups but none of these are statistically significant.[3] We believe that each reason has to be interpreted in the light of the specific circumstances of the ownership conversion, and for this reason we explain the findings from this table in more detail when we discuss in depth each ownership group. Here we note that encouragement of employee commitment and co-operation, and creation of business awareness, are the most important reasons for bus companies, followed by encouragement of employee shareholding. Encouragement of employee co-operation and creation of business awareness seem to be less important for other privatised firms. However, raising share capital is comparatively more important for this group. Encouragement of employee shareholding is of lesser importance to 'forced' divestment companies, whereas provision of rewards to employees and promotion of industrial democracy are very important. Paternalist companies attach most importance to encouragement of employee commitment, provision of employee rewards, and prevention of take-overs.

A final consideration before embarking on a more detailed outline of the circumstances of employee ownership is the level of union involvement in the ownership conversion. We knew that unions were deeply involved in

Table 5.4 The reasons for employee ownership (means)

Reason for conversion	*Bus privatisation*	*Other privatisation*	*'Forced' divestment*	*'Paternalist' divestment*
Encourage employee commitment	4.44	4.56	4.67	4.00
Encourage employee co-operation	4.50	3.67	4.33	3.67
Encourage employee shareholding	3.83	3.89	2.67	3.33
Create business awareness amongst employees	4.06	3.00	3.33	3.00
Reward employees	3.56	2.78	4.00	3.89
Prevent take-overs	3.39	2.33	3.00	3.89
Attract/retain staff	3.33	2.44	3.00	2.78
Raise share capital	2.61	3.44	2.33	1.67
Constrain wage claims	1.50	1.33	1.67	1.00
Promote industrial democracy	3.00	2.11	4.00	2.33

Table 5.5 Involvement of unions in ownership conversions (means)

Union involvement	*Bus privatisation*	*Other privatisation*	*'Forced' divestment*	*Paternalist divestment*
Overall union involvement	4.64[a]	1.71	3.00	2.25
Importance of union agreement	4.73[a, b]	1.71	2.50	2.25
Union involvement at the outset	4.59[a]	1.57	3.25	2.13

Notes

[a] Difference with 'other privatisation' group and 'paternalist divestment'group significant at 0.001.

[b] Difference with 'forced divestment' group significant at 0.05.

some firms but not in others, and wanted to discover whether patterns of union involvement differed between the groups of firms. Table 5.5 presents the results of three questions where respondents were asked to assess the involvement of union representatives on a scale where 1 is 'little or no involvement' and 5 is 'very great involvement'.[4]

Union representatives are clearly much more involved in the conversion to employee ownership in the bus privatisations than in the other privatisation group and the paternalist group. They are also more involved than in the forced divestment group though the difference is not significant. However, the importance of securing union agreement to employee ownership is more important in the bus group than in any of the other three groups. At a later stage in the chapter this type of result will be drawn upon to reformulate the categories of employee ownership firms. At this stage, however, we merely note that the involvement of union representatives is likely to affect the pattern and characteristics of ownership conversions.

Although the findings presented above help to provide a picture of employee ownership firms as a whole, our emphasis on the relevance of the varying circumstances in which employee ownership occurs means that these types of findings are more meaningful when considered in relation to specific groups of employee ownership firms. We therefore proceed to a more detailed discussion of the circumstances, characteristics, and objectives of ownership conversions.

Privatisation: bus companies

By far the largest group of employee ownership firms in our study had their origins in privatisation initiatives (39 out of 62 i.e. 63 per cent). Whilst all firms in this group converted to employee ownership from some form of public ownership, we distinguish between bus companies and other companies undergoing privatisation because employee ownership conversions were so widespread in the bus industry at the time. As Table 5.2

showed, the average level of employee ownership is higher in the bus industry than in the other privatised group. Furthermore, the proportion of firms with majority employee ownership is higher: 62 per cent compared with 15 per cent.

The bus industry has been the main location of employee ownership conversions using ESOPs and other forms of share ownership in the last 15 years. Table 5.6 provides summary details of employee ownership conversions during privatisation. It includes all firms known to have become employee-owned, not just those in our database (but excludes the small

Table 5.6 Employee ownership in the bus industry (firms converting to employee ownership)

Name of firm	*Date of privatisation*	*Origin*	*Employee ownership (% of equity)*	*Insider ownership (% of equity)*	*Number of employees at buy-out*[a]
Luton and District	1987	NBC	100	100	641
People's Provincial	1987	NBC	100	100	281
Yorkshire Rider	1988	PTE	49	100	3,457
Busways	1989	PTE	49	100	1,897
Derby City Transport	1989	LA	59	75	349
Grampian Transport	1989	LA	33	84	569
Chesterfield Transport	1990	LA	100	100	359
Lowland Scottish	1990	SBG	30	70	264
Eastern Scottish	1990	SBG	30	N/a	1,094
Cleveland Transit	1991	LA	49	100	411
Clydeside 2000	1991	SBG	70	85	828
Kelvin Central	1991	SBG	92	100	1,556
Tayside Buses	1991	LA	100	100	617
West Midlands Transport	1991	PTE	90	100	5,912
Western Scottish	1991	SBG	68	100	1,934
Lincoln City	1991	LA	60	60	80
Merseyside Transport	1992	PTE	100	100	2,646
Brighton Borough	1993	LA	100	100	264
Hartlepool Buses	1993	LA	100	100	160
Mainline Partnership	1993	PTE	100	100	2,806
Preston Buses	1993	LA	100	100	274
Southampton Citybus	1993	LA	100	100	446
Strathclyde Buses	1993	PTE	80	100	2,543
Centrewest	1994	LT	19	75	1,486
Greater Manchester North	1994	PTE	25	25	2,440
Greater Manchester South	1994	PTE	51	51	2,000
London General	1994	LT	14	28.9	2,112
London United	1994	LT	9.5	54.5	1,544
Metroline	1994	LT	25	55	1,189

Notes

[a] Number of employees at the end of the financial year immediately preceding the buy-out except for Western Scottish and Clydeside 2000 where it is the number of employees at the buy-out.

number of firms that were acquired by employee-owned firms on privatisation). Since 26 of these 29 firms are included in our study we can be confident that our data provides a comprehensive and well-founded picture of employee ownership in the industry.

The first employee-owned firms came about during the privatisation of the subsidiaries of the state-owned National Bus Company (NBC) in the latter half of the 1990s. These were followed by several voluntary privatisations of local authority and Passenger Transport Executive (PTE) firms. The next wave of conversions was amongst subsidiaries of the Scottish Bus Group (SBG) in the period 1990–2. Five of the eleven subsidiaries of the SBG were privatised to management-employee buy-outs. These tended to have high levels of employee ownership. After these firms, there was then another wave of voluntary local authority and PTE privatisations, in which typically the employees had a controlling ownership stake. The main exception was the privatisation of Greater Manchester Buses, where employees and managers in Greater Manchester North (the company was split into two at privatisation) had a minority share. Finally four of the ten London Buses companies were partially bought by their employees when that company was privatised in 1994. Employees had a minority stake in all of these. Indeed, these companies had a higher equity involvement of institutional investors than virtually all of the preceding buy-outs.

To understand why employee ownership was so widespread in the bus industry we need to examine contextual features of the bus industry. A key consideration is that the bus industry had undergone fundamental restructuring in the mid-1980s. Prior to the 1985 Transport Act, the vast majority of scheduled bus services in the UK were provided by public sector operators (the National Bus Company, Scottish Bus Group, Passenger Transport Executives, London Transport and local authorities), who were protected against new entrants by a strict regulatory regime. The 1985 Transport Act changed all this by removing barriers to entry (other than basic safety requirements and route-reporting requirements) and by setting in motion the privatisation of the National Bus Company. Deregulation led to an influx of private sector operators into provision of local tendered and commercial bus services, though the extent of this differed widely between areas (see Evans 1990; Stokes *et al.* 1990).[5]

An important characteristic of new entrants was that their labour management and industrial relations characteristics were the polar opposite of those of public sector operators. Whereas union density was very high in public sector firms, union membership was non-existent in most private sector firms and unions were rarely recognised. Furthermore, working practices and pay determination tended to be regulated by collective bargaining in the public sector but not in the private sector (James *et al.* 1985). Employment costs tended to be considerably lower in the private sector operators. Indeed, a fundamental objective of the 1985 Transport Act was to reduce wage costs in the public sector firms (Heseltine and

Silcock 1990). The policy was successful in that bus employees' earnings, virtually alone amongst privatised industries, have declined substantially, from being about 5 per cent above average manual earnings in the mid-1980s to about 15 per cent below in the mid-1990s (see Pendleton 1999: 783). A further feature of privatisation policies was that privatisation of NBC subsidiaries had led to rationalisation and redundancies in many cases. The key problems facing public sector companies towards the end of the 1980s, then, was that they were facing severe pressures to cut wages and to reduce employment so that they could compete with the new low-cost entrants.

We can demonstrate the difficulties facing public sector firms by comparing firms about to become employee-owned with a wider set of bus companies already privatised or still in public ownership (though as the numbers are small, these findings must be treated with caution). The first important point to notice is that the performance of firms that subsequently chose employee ownership was substantially worse than that of other firms.[6]

It is clear from Tables 5.7 and 5.8 that the firms becoming employee-owned in 1991 and 1993 were in trouble. Both groups of firms were turning in losses in the years immediately preceding conversion, and in some respects were performing significantly less well than the control group of other similar-sized public sector and privatised bus companies. The local authority owners of most of these firms could not have continued to bear these losses, given the tight constraints on local authority finances imposed by central government. The choice for both firms and local authorities was either cutbacks in services and employment or sale to another firm. The local authorities concerned would have found either option unpalatable. Sale to another company would take services outside public control and would probably have led to asset sales and employment reductions. Some local authorities therefore encouraged the managers and union representatives of their bus companies to consider employee ownership as a 'third way'. Equally, some managers and union representatives foresaw that

Table 5.7 Performance of bus companies becoming employee-owned in 1991 compared with other bus companies

Performance measure	*Employee ownership conversions in 1991*	*Non-employee ownership firms*
Average profit margins 1989 (%)	−4.18	2.87
Average profit margins 1990 (%)	−5.63	2.05*
Average return on capital 1989 (%)	−0.80	8.58
Average return on capital 1990 (%)	−7.68	6.53
N	*5*	*70*

Note
* Z statistic significant at 0.05.

Table 5.8 Performance of bus companies becoming employee-owned in 1993 compared with other bus companies

Performance measure	*Employee-ownership conversions in 1993*	*Non-employee ownership firms*
Average profit margin 1990 (%)	−1.88	2.51**
Average profit margin 1991 (%)	−0.318	4.22**
Average profit margin 1992 (%)	−0.49	4.29*
Average return on capital 1990 (%)	−1.15	7.70
Average return on capital 1991 (%)	−0.18	16.75**
Average return on capital 1992 (%)	1.61	20.70**
N	*6*	*69*

Notes
* Z-statistic significant at 0.05.
** Z-statistic significant at 0.01.

local authorities would have to divest even if government intentions to privatise the rest of the industry did not materialise. They therefore initiated discussions with their owners about privatisation by management-employee buy-outs. It was apparent from an early stage that the ideological viewpoints of some councils was such that privatisation via management buy-outs would not be acceptable. Management-employee buy-outs appeared to be a form of privatisation that would be acceptable to anti-privatisation local authorities. As well as providing protection to workforce interests, the presence of workers as owners appeared to offer the possibility that this group would protect service levels because of desire to maintain employment levels.[7]

These firms faced additional challenges. One, though these firms dominated their local markets, they were facing more intense competition than other companies. Whilst the mean market share for employee ownership firms was nearly 80 per cent and significantly higher[8] than that of other bus companies, they faced competition on about half of their routes compared with about one-third elsewhere. However, as public sector operators they were faced with the problem that they were unable to compete by expanding services outside their territorial area (Barry 1989). Privatisation would give firms greater freedom of action to compete effectively. At the same time the capacity to ward off competition would help to preserve the local networks of services built up over many years and viewed as an important public service by local authorities.[9]

A further problem for these firms resided in their wage costs, which tended to be higher than in other firms in the public and privatised sector, let alone the emergent private sector.

As Tables 5.9 and 5.10 show, firms becoming employee-owned had higher wage costs per employee and as a proportion of costs, though these differences are not significant in the case of 1991 conversions. Clearly, action to reduce the wage bill was necessary to tackle the poor performance of these

Table 5.9 Wage costs of bus companies becoming employee-owned in 1991 compared with other bus companies

Wage measures	*Employee ownership conversions in 1991*	*Non-employee ownership firms*
Average wages in 1989	Higher than average	Lower than average
Average wages in 1990	Higher than average	Lower than average
Wages as proportion of costs in 1989 (average %))	61	59
Wages as proportion of costs in 1990 (average %)	59	57
N	*5*	*68*

Table 5.10 Wage costs of bus companies becoming employee-owned in 1993 compared with other bus companies

Wage measures	*Employee ownership conversions in 1993*	*Non-employee ownership firms*
Average wages in 1990	Higher than average*	Lower than average
Average wages in 1991	Higher than average**	Lower than average
Average wages in 1992	Higher than average	Lower
Wages as proportion of costs in 1990 (average %))	66**	57
Wages as proportion of costs in 1991 (average %))	66*	57
Wages as proportion of costs in 1992 (average %))	66**	60
N	*6*	*68*

Notes
* Z-statistic significant between the two groups at 0.05.
** Z-statistic significant between the two groups at 0.01.

firms if these firms were to remain in public ownership. On the other hand, if these firms were privatised by trade sales, it was likely (given earlier experience) that acquirers would take action to reduce wages and conditions of employment. Equally, management buy-outs would need to address the wage issue, and the possibility of unions being able to obstruct reforms in this area posed a major risk for those mounting buy-outs. Including employees in ownership could make buy-outs more feasible because employee consent to post-buy-out concessions in pay and employment would be easier to secure. The capacity of employee ownership to reduce the cost-base of buy-out firms could be attractive to potential financiers, thereby potentially reducing the costs of leverage (cf. Chaplinksy *et al.* 1998).

For worker, and unions, employee ownership appeared to provide a way of protecting pay and conditions, or of providing alternative forms of remuneration, or at least maintaining union capacity to influence the determination of employment conditions. We have seen earlier in Table 5.5

that unions were more involved in the bus industry firms than any employee ownership group. Union involvement in conversion was very high in virtually every case, and union agreement to the form of ownership conversion was seen to be significantly more important than in any other group. In fact in a third of cases, union representatives were responsible for starting the conversion process. The attractions of employee ownership were described by one union respondent as 'employees controlling their own future in terms of job security, wages, investments, conditions, how the company is run. . . . No outside owner dictating terms and requiring dividends. All the rewards are for the employee shareholders both present and future.' The deep involvement of unions in the conversions to employee ownership led to a specific configuration set of ownership institutions, which will be described in Chapter 7. The more unions were involved in ownership conversion, the higher the level of employee ownership ($p=0.438$, significant at 0.042). In addition, the more unions were involved, the more important was the prevention of take-overs as a reason for converting to employee ownership ($p=0.505$, significant at 0.033).[10]

Although unions sought employee ownership to prevent take-overs by firms who would probably have reformed pay and conditions of employment, employee ownership went hand in hand with concession bargaining in most cases. Employee ownership made wage and employment concessions palatable whilst, at the same time, these concessions were necessary for employee ownership to have any chance of success. The necessity for concessions is reflected in the relative importance attached to securing employee co-operation and creating business awareness as reasons for converting to employee ownership (see Table 5.4). In some cases pay-cuts were agreed. At Kelvin Central, 85 per cent of the workforce supported pay cuts shortly after the buy-out. Similarly, in Greater Manchester South, 93 per cent voted for pay reductions just before the buy-out was finalised. In other cases, improvements in working practices were achieved, such as greater flexibility in work scheduling. As one respondent put it, 'Productivity has improved significantly, mainly due to tightening up of driver schedules. Employee ownership created a climate in which such improvements could be achieved with a lower level of hostility.' In one case, employee concessions directly financed share acquisition. At Strathclyde Buses, half of each employee's 'subscription' was financed by an efficiency deal introducing shorter holidays and a longer working week. These were to be returned in a phased way as buy-out loans were repaid. These types of concessions are reflected in our data on bus company employment and wages. Each of the employee ownership year groups on which we have relevant financial information (those converting in 1991 and 1993) registered employment falls between the year in which the buy-out took place and the following year, and more negative changes compared with the control group.[11] Average wages for the 1991 group also fell by 6 per cent, compared with an 11 per cent growth for the control group[12] (though in subsequent years wage growth was higher). The important point about these concessions was that they were introduced by agreement, and that employee ownership ensured employees and their representatives could maintain some control of them.

Employee ownership came about in the bus industry, then, because the interests of the various key actors – managers, workers and local authorities – coincided, albeit from differing starting points and for different reasons. For all parties the primary motive was a defensive one rather than an ideological conversion to employee ownership. Union representatives too on the whole did not view employee ownership as a good thing in itself. ESOPs were the preferred method of ownership conversion because they posed little direct financial risk to employees, whilst for managers they seemed to permit the continuation of 'conventional' management structures. For union representatives, ESOPs were also preferable to workers' co-operatives because they did not appear to challenge the traditional role of union representation in the way that co-ops were perceived to (see Pendleton *et al.* 1995b). As we shall see in Chapter 7, the coincidence of managerial and union interests in this particular context led to the development of distinct forms of employee participation and corporate governance. Once employee ownership had taken root in a few major companies, imitation effects became a powerful determinant of future conversions.

Other privatised firms

The other privatised firms are more diverse than the bus industry. Out of 13 firms, three were in the coal industry, three were offshoots from local authorities, three were divestments of ancillary and specialised functions from a variety of public sector organisations, three originated in nationalised industries other than coal, and one was a trust port. The proportion of equity held by employees is 30 per cent or under in eight of them, and these firms can be viewed primarily as management buy-outs. Three others are joint management-employee buy-outs whilst one is an employee-led buy-out. There is considerable size variation in this group of firms. In 1995, the smallest firm had 55 employees whilst the largest had 28,000. All but the largest firm, however, had under 1,500 employees, with the median number being 981.

The reasons for privatisation varied enormously. In the nationalised industry cases there was little choice, as central government had decided that privatisation would take place. Similarly, the health authority off-shoot was 'thrown-out' (the Managing Director's words). In the local authorities and civil service, the decision to seek privatisation was taken by the managers and employees concerned. Private ownership was believed to give greater flexibility in the compulsory competitive tendering and market testing processes, and hence enhance the likelihood of winning contracts. Since it would become possible to secure additional contracts to the one held or sought with the authority owning them before privatisation, it would be possible to spread overhead costs and hence compete more effectively with major firms.

A clear contrast between this group of firms and the bus companies is that union involvement in conversion was much less widespread and extensive, even though unions were present in all but one firm (average union density was 40 per cent). Union representatives had little involvement or no involvement at all in just over two-thirds of cases, and securing union agreement to the buy-out was not seen as important. Only in one case was employee ownership initiated by union representatives. In one firm local union representatives refused to have anything to do with the conversion because it was seen to expedite privatisation. Where unions were involved, however, the reasoning was very similar to that in the bus industry. As one UNISON official described the conversion of a local authority direct works department, 'it was against a background of opposition to a management buy-out and the threat to job security of over 500 jobs that all the trade unions agreed to pursue the concept of an employee buy-out' (Evans 1994: 1).

Since employee ownership was initiated and developed by managers without significant input by union representatives, employee interests did not enter into the calculus of decision-making to the same extent as in the bus industry. The balance of reasons on managers' part for moving to employee ownership in these firms tended to be different to those in the bus companies. Whilst encouragement of employee commitment was very important, as in bus firms, encouragement of employee co-operation was less important. Our interpretation is that these managers needed to align employee interests for the buy-out to succeed, but securing employee consent to major changes to working practices and employment conditions was less important. This was either because union-based regulation of working practices had been limited in extent and depth or else because joint regulation had been substantially weakened earlier. Creation of business awareness amongst employees was significantly less important probably because employees and their representatives were unlikely to have such an extensive role in the direction of the firm post-buy-out as in the bus companies.

A notable feature of this group of firms is that ESOP structures were less widespread than in either the bus companies or other groups of conversions. Eight of the thirteen firms did not use an employee benefits trust to acquire equity at conversion. Instead direct employee subscription to shares was the method used. In part, this reflected a belief amongst managers that ESOPs were a cumbersome device with high administrative costs. Also, it was claimed that ESOPs had limited motivational properties because share ownership is indirect. The most important factor though was that the high-leverage ESOP mechanism was not available to these firms because financiers would not have funded buy-outs of this type. Most of these companies had no prior trading records. Some of them had no assets at the point of conversion. Ten of the thirteen firms were dependent on one or a small number of major contracts that had not been secured prior to the buy-out itself. As one Company Secretary put it:

> they (the management) persuaded (the parent public corporation) that in competition with other companies they could have a bash at buying it: a company with no accounts, no systems, in fact no management on site apart from site management . . . a company in name only. It was not an easy fund-raising activity. . . . Basically, with no accounts available, the whole thing was an absolute mess. Its future was based on contracts which we had to have to agree the deal but without actually having a costing structure to gauge whether the contracts were either going to be a profit or a loss.

Raising debt capital from banks to support a leveraged buy-out was a much more difficult option in these circumstances than in the bus industry, where firms were well established and where the nature of commercial activity was essentially cash-flow positive. Employee ownership (by share subscriptions) provided both a source of buy-out finance and a way of aligning employee interests with those of managers who, as majority owners, were taking on much of the risk. It is for these reasons that raising share capital was a more important reason for moving to employee ownership than in any of the other groups (see Table 5.4).

The configuration of employee and insider ownership in these firms reflected the circumstances of these conversions. In eight of the thirteen firms the share of the equity owned by top managers was greater than that owned by employees. In eight cases also institutional investors held some of the equity (the average was 30 per cent). Most of these firms may therefore be viewed as essentially management buy-outs with an employee ownership component. The size of the employee share was influenced by two sets of considerations. One was that employee interests should be aligned with those of managers and investors, given the level of risk facing managers and investors. The other was that employee ownership should not be so great as to dilute the control and return rights (and hence incentives) of managers. In one case, the Managing Director reluctantly acquired 88 per cent of the company because the main bank financing the buy-out was not prepared to support it if the employee share was more substantial.

'Forced divestment' companies

This is a small group, composed of six firms that converted to partial or full employee ownership in the face of closure by parent companies. As such, they might be viewed as 'rescue' buy-outs, as they were aimed at saving employees from unemployment. These firms are found in the coal mining industry, stevedoring, manufacturing, and advertising. With one exception, the buy-outs were mounted by employees. In the remaining case, the conversion could be seen as an 'orthodox' management buy-out, were it not for the use of an ESOP. The level of employee ownership was 100 per cent in the five employee buy-outs, and just 12.5 per cent in the management-led buy-out. As might be expected, given the dominance of employee-led buy-outs, the size of firms in this category tended to be smaller than the others. The average size of the employee buy-out firms was 121 employees in 1995, with the smallest having 34 and the largest 239. The management buy-out had 280 employees in 1992.[13]

The five entirely employee-owned firms were highly unionised yet, whilst those organising the conversion had experience as union representatives, local union organisations were not as deeply involved as in the bus industry (see Table 5.5). Nor was securing the agreement of union representatives so necessary. Ironically, perhaps, union agreement seems to have been most important in the minority buy-out. Here, the dynamics were not dissimilar to those seen in the bus firms. Significant employee concessions were necessary to improve low levels of labour productivity. As part of the ownership deal, trade union representatives agreed to a package of concessions that reformed shift patterns, sick pay, attendance bonuses etc. As the Managing Director described it:

> 'prior to the buy-out we went over to the Post House Hotel and agreed a ten-point plan . . . there was a ten-point plan and if they did not accept that or agree to it I wasn't going to buy the company. . . . If we hadn't bought it [the company] they realised it would have been closed. Eight million pounds sales and three million loss – it was part of the group that had become a financial dumping ground.

Four of the firms used ESOP structures to hold some of the equity at conversion and a further one used an employee benefits trust as a 'market-maker'. This group is notable for the use of statutory ESOPs: three of the firms had a QUEST. In the circumstances of an employee buy-out, it was possible to take advantage of the tax benefits of QUESTs without suffering what are widely seen as the disadvantages, such as employee majorities on the trust. A further distinctive feature of this group is that two of the firms were organised on co-operative principles whereby employees had equal shares and voting rights. It is noticeable that promotion of industrial democracy was a more important reason (though not significantly so) for conversion to employee ownership in this group than any of the other groups (see Table 5.4).

Most of these firms were not dependent on large loans to effect the buy-out, mainly because there were relatively little physical assets or 'goodwill' to purchase. In four cases, employees subscribed to shares using redundancy payments from the termination of their employment with the original company. Thus, the employees of Barry Stevedores subscribed £5,000 of their redundancy money from Associated British Ports which, after the demise of the National Dock Labour Scheme, decided to exit from stevedoring (see Turnbull 1993; Turnbull and Weston 1993). Half of this sum purchased shares directly, whilst the other half was loaned to an EBT. As profits were made, they were passed onto the trust, which issued shares to employees and repaid the loan to employees at the same time. At the well-publicised employee buy-out at Tower Colliery in South Wales, miners put up £8,000 each to buy the pit financed out of their redundancy money from British Coal.[14] In a rather different case, the buy-out of St Luke's advertising agency was financed by the payment of commission to the original parent company.

As these firms were not dependent on external finance to anything like the extent of the privatisation firms, they had greater freedom to implement preferred ownership and management structures. As mentioned already, the level of employee ownership was 100 per cent in five cases. As they were employee-buy-outs of threatened firms, a key priority was saving jobs. As a result, changes to labour management after conversion tended to focus on reforms of payment systems rather than employment-reducing measures to improve productivity. Thus, Tower abolished the British Coal bonus system whilst Barry Stevedores introduced a tonnage-based bonus system. In terms of management, there was greater freedom to organise management structures than in most of the companies discussed earlier. Two of the three stevedoring ESOPs elected their executive directors, whilst St Lukes has a highly participative and democratic style of working (see Chapter 7).

'Paternalist divestment'

This group is composed of ten firms that became partially or fully employee-owned as a result of owners' decisions to spread ownership amongst their employees. Unlike all of the firms discussed so far, these are not buy-outs in the normal sense of the word, though in some cases owners used the ownership transfer to completely exit from ownership and management of the firm. Instead, they reflect a 'paternalist' concern to provide employees with a greater share of the fruits of their labour and the financial well-being of the firm (Pendleton *et al.* 1995a). Often this transaction was effected on the retirement of the owner. There is considerable variation in employee ownership within this group: it ranges from 7 per cent to 100 per cent, with an average of 57 per cent. In every case there is majority insider ownership. In fact, there is wholly insider ownership in eight of the ten firms. In every case an EBT is present, and in two cases there is a statutory QUEST. In seven cases some or all of the equity is retained in trust rather than distributed to individual employees. The size distribution of this group is very similar to the other privatised group. The median number of employees was 891 in 1995, with the smallest firm having 88 employees and the largest 39,600. All but the largest firm had under 1,500 employees.

The most important reasons for moving to employee ownership, according to our respondents, were to reward employees, to encourage employee commitment and co-operation, and to prevent take-overs. Unlike the bus industry and 'forced divestment' firms, it was not imperative to undertake major restructuring of pay and conditions after conversion. The reason for these differences is that these firms were successful firms with a history of good trading performance. Instead, the reasons for conversion to employee ownership focused on protecting the firm and its employees, as well as binding employees closer to the firm. This may be seen as a typical expression of paternalism: the firm looks after employees who have been committed to the firm. But those responsible for bringing about employee ownership in these firms did not seek to promote industrial democracy. This was one of the least important reasons for ownership conversion, and on average it was less important than in the bus industry and forced divestment firms (see Table 5.4).

In contrast to the other groups of firms so far, the initiators of employee ownership tended to be owners or owner-managers rather than managers (who subsequently became owners). Were there any differences in union involvement? For a start, union membership was much lower in these firms than in bus companies, other privatised companies or 'forced divestment' firms. Three of the firms had no union membership at all (or at least none that was known of by management respondents) and the highest density level was 55 per cent. The average was 19 per cent, which was very similar to that in the control group of non-employee-owned firms. Given these features of industrial relations it is perhaps not surprising that the level of union involvement in ownership conversion was significantly lower than in the bus company group. Unions were less involved at the outset, were less involved overall, and securing union agreement to the conversion was less important.

These conversions came about because of owners' desire to divest. Since owner divestment is a common event, it is worth enquiring why these particular firms took the employee ownership route. Clearly owner philosophies are of very considerable importance here but there may be characteristics of these firms which also contribute to the decision. Bearing in mind the propositions found in the Economics literature that financial participation is useful where monitoring of individual effort is costly (see Alchian and Demsetz 1972; Weitzman and Kruse 1990), we examined whether the incidence of team production and non-manual work differed between these firms and the control group. No significant differences were observed. We also examined the product market context of the two groups of firms. Here the findings indicated that the 'paternalist divestment' firms faced significantly higher intensity of competition (Z-statistic significant at 0.013) and a higher number of active competitors in their main product market (Z-statistic significant at 0.032).

We infer from this that an influence on the decision to develop employee ownership was a concern to protect their firms from competitive threats. The supposed commitment-inducing properties of employee ownership would assist the firm to maintain competitive advantage whilst maintenance of insider ownership would prevent the firm being acquired by a predator. If owners had exited via trade sales, there was the perceived threat that the firm would have been purchased by an active competitor who would subsequently rationalise or break up the business. To preserve the firm it made sense to divest to the employees. In the well-publicised case of the Baxi Partnership, Philip Baxendale sold the company to an EBT for precisely these reasons. He decided soon after he inherited the company that he did not want his children to take over the business – 'it is not in the interests of the children nor of the businesses'.

> He was equally adamant that Baxi should not be sold to a competitor or floated because he knew this would soon lead to loss of jobs or closure of the factory in Bamber Bridge (near Preston), a former cotton town where Baxi is an important employer.
>
> (Gourlay 1995)

Similarly, family owners of Tullis Russell wanted to divest but, as the then Chairman commented, 'a trade sale would mean total insecurity for the company and its workforce. Flotation on the Stock Exchange is permanent insecurity' (Buxton 1995). As in the other cases in this group of firms, employee ownership provided an exit route for owners that maintained the firm intact and protected employees.

Our interpretation of the circumstances of the divestment group is therefore that a combination of employer philanthropy and maintenance of insider control were key reasons behind the transition to employee ownership. In contrast to many in the privatisation group, firms of this type tended to be successful performers and were often market leaders for their products. Employee ownership was not part of a strategy to 'rescue' the firm but was instead a measure to ensure the continued well-being of the firm and its employees.

'Technical' ESOPs

This small group of firms comprises just five firms, of which all are listed. The ownership background is therefore rather different from all of the other firms. One firm was in primary metals production, one in estate agency, one in shoe production and retailing, and two in chemicals. By listed company standards these are not large firms. The smallest had 220 employees in 1995, whilst the largest had just over 4,100.

The unifying characteristics of these firms are that they are all PLCs and all had share schemes prior to the creation of an ESOP trust. These firms created these trusts primarily for technical, corporate finance reasons rather than to advance the cause of employee ownership *per se*. ESOPs were created not as an instrument to further advance employee ownership but to protect existing share option scheme commitments. Most of these firms were facing the prospect of falling foul of Stock Exchange and Association of British Insurers (ABI) limits on the amount of new equity that can be issued to resource employee share schemes (see Chapter 4). ESOP trusts were created therefore as a means of acquiring the company's shares on the open market as an alternative to the issue of new equity and consequent share dilution.

The level of employee ownership was much lower than in any of the other employee ownership groups. The highest proportion of ownership was just 8 per cent (though this is high by 'conventional' share scheme standards). Insider ownership was somewhat higher, reflecting partial family ownership and, in one case, an earlier management buy-out. One of these firms was majority-owned by insiders such as top managers and family owners.

The circumstances of ESOP creation in these firms were therefore quite different from those in either the privatisation or divestment groups. Whereas managers in the two other main groups of firms were attempting to provide a substantial degree of protection from the market for corporate control, in these cases the firms were already exposed to outside ownership interests. ESOPs were essentially an attempt to placate these owners, fearful of share dilution arising out of 'conventional' employee share schemes. In fact, in one of these cases managerial plans to expand the level of employee share ownership to 10 per cent had to be scaled back to 3 per cent because of objections from institutional investors (who owned 53 per cent of the equity). In one of the other cases the EBT was designed to create a secondary market and thereby to maintain share price levels, as well as to meet the ABI limits on share schemes. A major institutional shareholder was known to want to offload its shares (25 per cent of the equity) but the market in the company's shares was 'turgid' (the Company Secretary's words) because of the high level of family ownership (dispersed through a large, extended family), and restrictions on voting rights. The ESOP provided a way of maintaining the capital value of the family's shareholding (and indeed that of the institutional owners) by providing a source of demand for shares in the stock market. Although these ESOPs can have a role in divestment, it is much more limited than in the case of the private company divestment group. When asked whether the ESOP would provide an exit route for insider owners, the Finance Director of one of these firms commented emphatically that 'it's not capable of buying sufficient shares and the other shareholders didn't like the idea'.

However, the context in which the ESOPs were created affected which groups of managers were involved in the implementation process. In contrast to both the privatisation and divestment groups, where employee ownership was typically driven (on the management side) by managing directors and chief executives, in these cases finance managers, company secretaries and legal specialists tended to be the architects of ESOP arrangements. In none of these cases were union representatives directly involved in the creation of ESOP mechanisms. In fact, the existence of an ESOP is not necessarily communicated to employees, as it is primarily a technical mechanism. As the Company Secretary of one of these companies commented (talking about an approach from another researcher:

> 'and then the interviewer was saying to me, do you mind if I talk to some of your shop floor employees about the benefit they are getting from the ESOP and I said with respect they wouldn't even know we have an ESOP, and he said why wouldn't they know? I explained that the ESOP buys on instructions from a handful of people here and holds the shares, so as far as the employee is concerned he doesn't know the significance of it.

Discussion: a reformulation of employee ownership types

This review indicates that there are different sets of circumstances to employee ownership conversion, and that differing sets of reasons tend to be important in these differing sets of circumstances. There are also variations in the key actors involved in employee ownership conversion, with unions tending to be deeply involved in bus privatisation and 'forced divestments'. There are also variations in the levels and form of employee and insider ownership between the groups. These findings reinforce the merits of examining ESOPs in relation to the circumstances of their conversion rather than grouping them all together. However, a unifying feature is that most ESOPs are formed for defensive reasons. Most are aimed at preventing changes in ownership and control that would have adverse affects on pay and employment.

However, it is clear that the grouping of firms primarily on the basis of the circumstances of conversion is not entirely satisfactory since some of these groups exhibit substantial intra-group differences. For instance, the 'forced divestment' group is composed mainly of 100 per cent employee buy-outs but also contains one management buy-out with just 12.5 per cent employee ownership. It seems appropriate to group this exceptional case with other management buy-outs. Meanwhile, like the bus companies, the other buy-outs in this category have extensive employee involvement in the conversion process. Similarly, there are a minority of firms in the 'other privatisation' category who also have extensive union involvement. It is appropriate, then, to reclassify these firms in with the bus privatisation companies.

Thus we distinguish four groups. The first is composed of employee and management-employee buy-outs where employee representatives had a substantial role in designing and implementing the conversion to employee ownership. This group therefore comprises the bus companies, most of the 'rescue' conversions, and some of the other privatisation group. In these cases, the proportion of stock held by employees is high (70 per cent). As in an earlier paper, firms in this category are referred to as 'representative' ESOPs (the reasons for this nomenclature will become clear in Chapter 7). The second group is composed of management buy-outs, which have some employee ownership component. Here the primary group is the managers mounting the buy-out. This group is composed of most of the non-bus company privatisation group and the remnant of the 'forced divestment' group. In these cases, the level of employee ownership is significantly lower than in the employee buy-outs (18 per cent). Given the objectives of these managers, we call these 'risk-sharing' ESOPs.[15] The third category is the 'paternalist divestment' group, and the distinguishing feature of this is that *owners* are the driving force behind employee ownership. Average employee ownership in this group is high (58 per cent). Finally, we retain the 'technical' group as originally conceived, as the primary objective (of managers introducing ESOP structures) is to deal with corporate financing difficulties arising from share ownership schemes rather than bringing about employee ownership in itself.

So 'representative' ESOPs have a substantial involvement of employee representatives in conversion, 'risk-sharing' ESOPs are introduced by managers, and 'paternalist' ESOPs are created by owners. Do any of the theoretical reasons for employee ownership identified in the literature apply to all of these groups, or just to some of them (as suggested at the beginning of the chapter)? Or are they not relevant at all? The first point to note is that the 'lock-in' arguments associated with Margaret Blair (1995) and Charles Leadbetter (1997) have little explanatory power in the UK context. Both authors have suggested that employee ownership should be viewed as a way of binding firm-specific human capital to the employer. Returns from employee ownership provide a pay-off for investments in firm-specific human capital by employees and help to ensure that this capital is not dissipated by labour turnover. However, there is very little evidence from our sample to support this perspective. In fact, what it noticeable about many of our firms – the bus companies especially – is that workforce skills tend to take a generic rather than a firm-specific form. The vast majority of jobs in any given bus company are very similar in skill and task requirements to any other bus company. Some of the manufacturing firms in the 'paternalist' group have jobs that require skills or knowledge with a certain degree of firm-specificity but these tend to be the exception. And there is very little evidence of so-called 'knowledge-based' firms in our sample. The St Lukes advertising agency is the only firm that could be readily placed in this category.

Another set of arguments sees employee ownership as a way of reducing monitoring costs in contexts where monitoring of individual performance is difficult to undertake satisfactorily (Alchian and Demsetz 1972). Once again, there is little evidence that is consistent with this interpretation in our sample. Many of the occupations found in our firms – be it bus-driving, coal-mining, provision of local authority services etc. – are relatively straightforward to monitor. We also found that there were no differences between firms in the paternalist category and the control group in terms of the incidence of team-based production and other proxies for hard-to-monitor jobs.

There is rather more support for the agency-based perspective that sees employee ownership as a way of reducing monitoring costs by aligning employee interests with those of owners. This is especially the case with regards to the 'risk-sharing' group. Here, managers mounting management buy-outs involved employees in ownership in an attempt to secure employee support. These buy-outs were notable for the level of risk facing those organising the buy-out: in many cases, there was no prior trading history, and the success of the buy-out was dependent on securing and satisfactorily completing a small number of major contracts. In these cases, the level of employee ownership, relative to total insider ownership, was pitched at a level that was perceived to get employees 'on board' but which did not seriously dilute managerial control rights. The 'interest alignment' perspective also applies to firms in the 'representative' category to a certain extent, though here managerial interest focused on securing substantial concessions at the outset. In this respect there are many similarities between UK bus company ESOPs and US employee-owned airlines. Both were threatened by low-cost competition, and both needed to modify their cost structures to survive. Both were highly unionised and had experienced difficulties in securing union agreement to wage or employment reductions. Employee ownership expedited concessions by securing union co-operation.

Hansmann (1996) has argued that the major influence on the development of employee ownership is the 'costs of collective decision-making'. These outweigh any reductions in agency costs in most cases, and explain why employee ownership is a rare phenomenon. These costs are those of reaching agreement and the outcomes of these agreements, and these tend to be high when workforces are composed of heterogeneous interests. Only where workforces are homogenous is employee ownership a viable ownership form. Leaving aside any criticisms of the 'natural selection' and functionalist character of this model of employee ownership,[16] it has a certain degree of explanatory force for both the 'representative' and 'risk-sharing' groups. Virtually all of the firms in these categories have either highly homogeneous workforces (as in the case of stevedoring firms) or else are dominated (both numerically and in power terms) by one occupational group (such as bus drivers or miners). This tends not to be the case, however, in the 'paternalist' group but since conversion to employee ownership is not dependent on workforce mobilisation this does not present the kind of barrier outlined by Hansmann.[17] We shall consider the Hansmann case again in Chapter 6.

Finally, a unifying characteristic of the 'representative', 'risk-sharing' and 'paternalist' groups is that employee and insider ownership is a defensive strategy against changes in corporate control that would probably lead to employment reduction. Thus, a large proportion of the employee ownership firms were created during privatisation to prevent firms being taken over. In the bus industry, for instance, workforces voluntarily opted for privatisation to preclude take-overs by firms that would, in all likelihood, embark on rationalisation, asset sales, and employment contraction. Similarly, owners of paternalist firms wanted to protect their firms against take-over by competitors. In this context, it is worth noting that employees and managers in both 'representative' and 'risk-sharing' firms were so keen to protect their firms against take-over because they mainly possessed generic rather than firm-specific knowledge and skills. Thus, they possessed few or no attributes that would guarantee their employment after a take-over. Furthermore, in the case of the public sector firms, employees had acquired over the years a greater degree of wage protection against external labour market forces than their generic skills would warrant. Privatisation threatened to remove these protections and break these 'implicit contracts'. Employee and insider ownership was an attempt to protect workers and managers against this eventuality.

6 Employee participation and governance

Theory and predictions

Introduction

In this chapter we review the literature on participation and governance, as a prelude to examining structures of participation and governance in employee ownership firms in Chapter 7. By participation we mean involvement by employees in decisions which affect them as *employees*. Governance, by contrast, concerns the decision-making role of employees as *owners*. Ownership-based participation in decisions is more novel since it is based on rights that are normally attached to capital. Ownership in fact usually conveys two sets of rights. One is the right to enjoy the benefits emanating from ownership (i.e. residual earnings), the other is the right to control the use to which the asset is put, including the right to dispose of it and to exclude non-owners from using it.

Provision of a role for employees in work decisions and for employee-owners in governance decisions contrasts with the 'classic' formulation of labour in both Marxist and economic accounts, whereby labour sells its labour power and loses its independent powers to direct itself. In practice, however, employee participation is extremely common in the employment relationship because of the difficulties of specifying 'complete' labour contracts and because of the need to enlist co-operation to turn labour power into work outcomes. Certain forms of employee participation, such as direct involvement, have become more common in most advanced industrialised nations in recent years. Employee involvement in governance, by contrast, is much rarer as formal governance rights in Anglo-American systems are usually held by capital providers, with capital hiring labour rather than vice versa (Dow and Putterman 1999). There are exceptions, of course, to this generalisation, mainly in European systems of governance, where there are legally underpinned structures of co-determination. Even so, when employees became owners of the firms that employ them, we would expect that they acquire a new set of rights to determine how their companies are run and what use is made of their labour.

Our central concern is whether this expectation is translated into reality. What impact does employee ownership have, if any, on employee participation and governance? Does ownership increase, decrease, or leave untouched existing patterns of involvement? Does it lead to new forms of participation in addition to or in place of prevailing forms of participation? Are any observed changes universally found amongst employee ownership firms or are there systematic variations between sub-types of employee-owned firms. If variations in participation and governance patterns can be observed, what are the relevant causal factors? Is the level of ownership held by employees a key determinant of levels and patterns of participation, or are other factors more important?

There are a variety of means by which employee-owners may secure greater influence over decisions. They may put representatives on the board of directors of the company or may create decision-making institutions at task-unit level, or they may do both. Some institutions of participation may involve employees as employees (e.g. quality circles in the workplace) whilst others may involve employees as owners (e.g. shareholder meetings). Others still may link the two. Employee directors may be seen as representatives of employees but their presence in the boardroom may be premised on ownership stakes held by the workforce. In this context, then, board representation may be seen as a hybrid form of participation. A key empirical question is whether the forms of participation adopted in employee-owned firms give primacy to participation of employees or to participation as owners, or attach equal importance to both. A further question is whether employee and ownership participation are conjoined, or whether they are kept separate. So far the literature has not really engaged with the potential complexities of post-ownership participation and governance systems, partly because 'traditional' conceptions of the labour-managed firm have tended to see employee participation and employee-owner governance as more or less the same thing.[1] Also, recent empirical studies have tended to concentrate on providing survey data on the incidence of various forms of participation and governance, such as work teams and employee directors, rather than exploring the dynamic connections, if any, between the two.

To address the issues and questions raised above, it is necessary to examine both the employee participation and corporate governance literatures. Until recently, these have tended to be almost entirely separate. As Margaret Blair puts it, 'the tendency among economists and legal theorists has been to study the nature of the firm, as well as property rights and governance structures associated with it, separately from the structure and terms of relationships with and among employees of firms' (1999: 58). We outline the salient aspects of participation and governance 'systems' before considering how hybrid forms may be observed in employee ownership firms. We then consider the influences on the nature of participation-governance systems, and suggest that the interaction of the objectives and philosophies of those involved in creating employee ownership will have a considerable effect on the design of these systems.

Employee participation in decisions

A very large literature on employee participation has developed over the last 30 years (see Heller *et al.* 1998). One of the facets of the size of this literature has been quite a wide diversity of meanings of the term 'employee participation'. Following Marchington *et al.* (1992), we view employee participation as a generic term to refer to all forms of activity whereby employees have some involvement in either the formulation or communication of decisions about work relations, employment relations, and industrial relations (Gospel 1992).[2] 'Employee involvement' is used more specifically to describe practices initiated by management to achieve managerial goals but which provide for no *de jure* rights for employees to influence decisions. 'Industrial democracy' will refer to rights secured by employees to influence decisions. Our usage contrasts somewhat with one recent textbook in the area, which defines employee participation as state- or employee-initiated attempts to established collective representation (Hyman and Mason 1995).

Employee participation has often been justified by reference to a basic need of human beings to exercise control over their working lives.[3] Most of the recent literature, however, has taken a more instrumental form. That is, it has been concerned with the impact of participation on individual and organisational performance. As Levine and Tyson (1990) put it, there are two main types of argument in this area. One is that employee participation can counter asymmetries in work-relevant information. In complex organisations workers are likely to have knowledge about production processes and services that is not held by managers and other workers. Employee participation provides a forum for sharing this information, which can then be used to improve efficiency or the quality of goods and services. The second argument focuses more on motivation and discipline. Here it is argued that participation encourages employees to develop co-operative modes of working. Economists tend to rely on game-theory here, arguing that 'repeated games' (where a collection of individuals have the opportunity to pursue their individual goals repeatedly) may encourage co-operation as each individual comes to realise that co-operation may be the optimal strategy (Weitzman and Kruse 1990). Participation provides the forum for these repeated games to take place. Once there is this recognition of mutual interests, employees will exert peer pressure to prevent shirking by group members. Integral to both lines of argument, as expressed by economists, is the importance of incentive structures. Employees need a pay-off from participation, otherwise information-sharing and peer pressure will be underdeveloped or ineffective. The relevance of employee ownership here is clear: the provision of return rights to employees as a result of ownership offers an incentive to engage in co-operative participation.

The Sociology of Work has also generated similar sorts of observations, though from a rather different perspective. The flawed but path-breaking Hawthorne Studies in the 1930s showed the importance of peer pressure in influencing individual behaviour in settings where work groups had some discretion in allocating work tasks and determining work-flow (see Rose 1988). In this instance, peer pressure did not necessarily support managerial objectives. However, a lesson that could be drawn from the findings of Hawthorne is that participation can increase employee job satisfaction, which in turn can increase motivation and improve performance. These possibilities have been mainly explored by organisational psychologists in the last 30 years or so, and their endeavours have generated a set of findings which suggest that employee participation can increase worker commitment to the goals of the firm, generate trust, and improve job satisfaction. These may lead to reductions in absenteeism and labour turnover (e.g. Mowday *et al.* 1982).

The participation literature has identified several key dimensions of participation (see Blumberg 1968; Dachler and Wilpert 1978; Loveridge 1980; Schuller 1985; Poole 1986; Strauss 1992, Marchington *et al.* 1992; Heller *et al.* 1998). Perhaps the most important dimension is that of the nature of individual involvement in decision-making. Do individuals participate directly in decision-making and other participative institutions or do representatives participate on their behalf? This is often referred to as direct versus indirect or representative participation. Quality circles or quality improvement teams, of which all employees in a work unit are members, are a good example of the former, whilst collective bargaining between union representatives and management is a oft-cited example of the latter. Some European observers distinguish between representative participation and collective bargaining (e.g. Poutsma 2000) but UK scholars tend to conjoin these as the two are usually intertwined in practice in the UK. This contrasts with France and Germany, for instance, where collective bargaining over pay is for the most part institutionally separate from other forms of representative participation such as Works Councils.[4]

The second dimension concerns the subject matter of participation. Does participation focus on task-related issues as experienced by the individual employee or does it tend to focus on policies and strategies applying across the unit or company? Marchington *et al.* (1992) generate three categories here: strategic, operational, and task-related, though they suggest it is difficult to place particular forms of participation in any one of these as particular institutions often deal with matters of all three types. For simplicity's sake, we will divide the range of participation subjects into two: strategic issues and task-related (broadly defined) issues.

Three, what is the nature of employee rights in relation to participation institutions and practices? Do employees merely have the opportunity to have a 'say' or do they have a right to determine decisions? It is common to identify a continuum, ranging from the provision of information at one end and employee control at the other (e.g. Poole 1986; Marchington *et al.* 1992). At one extreme there may be no employee input to decisions made by others (managers or owners) but there is an attempt to communicate information about these decisions, over and above any command to employees to obey them. At the other extreme, employees may have the right to make decisions jointly with management or even to make decisions themselves. Correlating broadly with these distinctions are 'rights' to make an input or to influence decisions. In general the more advanced the nature of participation, the greater the formal rights of employees are likely to be. However, it is possible to envisage situations where employees have control of decisions through custom and practice but have no recognised rights to do so. Their capacity to exert this influence emanates from the power they possess rather than any 'constitutional' establishment of rights. A distinction between *de jure* and *de facto* systems of participation is sometimes used to refer to these possibilities.

A fourth dimension is the level of the firm at which participation takes place. Does it take place at work unit, departmental, site, business unit or company level? Different forms of participation tend to be associated with different levels. For instance, quality circles will usually take place at work unit or departmental level, whilst representational institutions tend to be found at higher levels. Most observers have drawn attention to a decentralisation of participation in recent years with, in particular, representational forms of participation being decentralised from corporate to business unit or site level (Hyman 1997). The forms of employee involvement that have become common in recent years such as team briefing, quality teams etc. necessarily occur at relatively decentralised levels. In our analysis we will mainly distinguish between forms of participation that occur at company level and those that take place at sub-company level. Work unit, departmental and site level participation will be grouped together. This can be justified given the relatively simple and undiversified organisational structures of the companies in the study.

A final dimension of employee participation concerns outcomes. Does employee participation lead to greater influence on decisions? At a simple level, an increase in employee involvement might be expected to lead to enhanced employee capacity to influence employee decisions. However, it is clear that there is a disjunction between involvement and influence, or between institutions and outcomes. At one extreme, participation might lead to no change in employee influence. This might be because participation is a 'sham' (as Marxists might claim) or because the forms of participation in use are not designed to facilitate actual participation in decisions. Communication initiatives, for instance, are not usually introduced to increase employee influence on decisions. At the other extreme, situations can be envisaged where employees have a great deal of power, possibly emanating from skill shortages in the labour market, but no formal involvement in decision-making.

Power and influence are complex issues underlying discussions of participation and representation. Power may be exercised by the capacity to prevent certain issues from coming onto decision-making or participation agendas. 'Non-decisions' may be as important as actual decisions in the exercise and distribution of power (see Lukes 1974). The corollary of this is that participation institutions and processes should be judged not merely by the extent to which employees or their representatives can influence issues that are tabled for consideration but also by the range and depth of issues that come onto the agenda. This raises methodological difficulties in that identification of issues or power contests that are not the subject of overt discussion or conflict is rather more difficult than in cases where there is a clear decision. It is therefore difficult to say when power has been exercised.

Some would argue that there is then a deeper exercise of power – the third dimension of power in Lukes' model – where power is embedded in societal structures. Extensive participation in either decisions or non-decisions in a given firm does not make a great deal of difference if there is a pronounced inequality in power between employees and owners at the societal level. This issue is relevant to employee ownership since the capacity of employees to secure control of their own firms might not mean very much if these firms are constrained by the broader structure of ownership and control in the wider economy. Turnbull and Weston (1993) advance this argument in relation to the South Wales stevedore ESOPs. They suggest that employee control of these firms is of limited significance because, as labour contractors, they are entirely dependent on resourcing decisions made by other firms. Also, as we saw in Chapter 2, critics of co-operatives have long questioned whether islands of employee ownership can survive in a sea of capitalism.

Pulling together the discussion so far, there are five dimensions to employee participation: direct vs. representative, subject matter, employee rights, levels and outcomes. From the discussion it should be apparent that it is common for certain aspects and types of participation to go together in practice. For instance, direct participation by individual employees often focuses primarily on task-related issues, takes place at work unit or departmental level, and provides employees with relatively limited rights to affect decisions. For this reason it is common to group together major types of participation, each of which tends to have a distinctive set of characteristics. Marchington *et al.*, for instance, discern four main types of participation: downward communications (team briefing, for example), upward problem-solving (e.g. quality teams), representative participation (e.g. collective bargaining), and financial involvement. A similar distinction has been used by the research group examining Employee Participation in Organisational Change (EPOC), though they classify direct participation as either *consultative participation* (where management encourages employees to make their views known) or *delegative participation* (where employees gain some discretion to take decisions)[5] (Geary and Sisson 1994).

What is the likely effect of conversion to employee ownership on employee participation? On the face of it, employee ownership should encourage more employee participation, at least of certain kinds. There may be an increase in the use of direct forms of participation, from information provision to task discretion, as employee owners seek to take more control of their working lives and to find ways of improving the performance of their firm. The act of conversion to employee ownership itself may encourage a greater climate of co-operation, participation, and information sharing. By the same token, an expansion of the range of topics of employee participation might be predicted. The capacity of employees to influence the outcomes of participation may be increased, partly as a consequence of increased employee rights. An entirely contrary thesis is that employee participation will remain unchanged by ownership. This is because employees' interests as *owners* militate against greater involvement as *employees*. The danger for them is that an increase in the number of employee decision-takers will increase monitoring costs and the transaction costs of co-ordinating participants (Jensen and Meckling 1979; Williamson 1975; Hansmann 1996).

The impact of ownership on representative forms of participation is likely to be more complicated because of fears amongst employee representatives that their role will be undermined by employees articulating new interests either as owners or as employees with new sets of interests. There may well be attempts by some to ensure that employee representation is not diminished by ownership conversion. Equally, employee owners may attach less importance to representative participation than in the past, with the result that employee representation declines post-conversion. These anxieties and possibilities tend to focus on trade union representation, and there has been a long-standing claim that employee ownership will undermine trade unionism because employees' attachment to employee representation will weaken (Webb and Webb 1914). Unions have usually not sought to counteract this by taking on ownership representation as this could lead to role conflict should there be a major conflict of interest between owners and employees (see Pendleton *et al.* 1995b).

These observations on the relationships between union representatives and employee owners, as well as the contrasting propositions outlined earlier about other forms of participation, suggest that participation structures in employee ownership firms cannot be predicted in a straightforward manner from the fact of employee ownership. The relationships between those involved in conversions to employee ownership and its aftermath are likely to affect the character and institutions of participation. The objectives of those involved in conversions is also likely to affect employee participation, as are the circumstances of conversion. Managers may well have different perspectives on participation to employees. We will return to these issues later in the chapter.

Governance participation in employee ownership firms

In employee ownership firms the issue of employee participation in decisions becomes more complex than in 'conventional' firms. Employees acquire new interests and a new set of relationships with the firm and management, deriving from their ownership of all or part of the firm. These interests may differ from those they also have as employees. For this reason, a new set of institutions and procedures for the expression of employee-owner interests may develop. Employee-owner participation in governance might be referred to as 'ownership relations' (to supplement work relations, employment relations and industrial relations, in the area of employee participation). A more widespread term, however, is 'corporate governance'.

Corporate governance is sometimes defined narrowly, sometimes more broadly. In policy discussions it tends to be perceived as the formal system of accountability of top management to shareholders (Keasey *et al.* 1997). Most academic writing, by contrast, tends to view corporate governance in a much wider way. Blair refers to it as 'the whole set of legal, cultural, and institutional arrangements that determine what publicly-traded corporations can do, who controls them, how that control is exercised, and how the risks and returns from the activities they undertake are allocated' (1995: 3). The literature on corporate governance is entirely distinct from that on employee participation. Most work is conducted in Law, Finance and Economics, rather than Human Resource Management, Industrial Relations, Sociology, and Psychology. The key concepts, issues, and underlying theory tend to differ from those discussed in the first part of the Chapter. Principal–agent perspectives are central to most writing on corporate governance and, given that agency theory permeates economic analyses of employee participation, this helps to provides a link between the two bodies of literature.[6]

The dominant view of corporate governance is an amalgam of agency theory, property rights, and contractual theory. Starting from the 'nexus of contracts' view of the firm, this perspective argues that the providers of share capital to the firm are of a different status to other bodies reaching contracts with the firm, such as employees or customers. Whereas contracts with employees, for instance, can be relatively tightly specified,[7] contracts between investors and the firm are necessarily incomplete. This is because the return rights to shareholders are residual claims i.e. shareholders receive a share of the profits after all prior claims have been met. They therefore bear the profit risk of the firm: they will receive no returns if profits have not been made. For this reason, it is argued, that residual control rights (i.e. those rights and obligations that are not specified in the initial contract) should accrue to these investors. In this view corporate governance is about how these investors control the actions of the firm's managers so that investors' interests are pursued and achieved[8] (Hart and Moore 1990; Hart 1995b).

However, in Anglo-American corporate governance systems, the formal control rights of shareholders are usually limited to the right to vote on company resolutions and the right to attend an Annual General Meeting (AGM) of shareholders. These provide share-owners with the right to elect the board of directors of the company. Although in principle these meetings may deal with any matter affecting the governance and strategic direction of the company, in practice the capacity for shareholders to raise such issues are hedged with restrictions (see Blair 1995).[9] Besides these formal limitations, the capacity for owners to exert influence on the governance of the firm tends to be constrained by dispersed ownership, the difficulties of acquiring relevant information, of co-ordinating shareholder action, and of enforcing shareholder decisions on management. Given that investment in a given firm may be just one in a portfolio of investments, the motivation for shareholders to take action may be low, especially as the benefits of closer monitoring are a public good. The possibility that greater activism may lead to reductions in share value (because of the signals it sends to financial markets) is also a profound disincentive (see Hart 1995a).

In Anglo-American systems of corporate governance, then, a preferred method of exerting influence has therefore been 'exit' (or the threat of exit) rather than 'voice', at least for many shareholders. Under-performance by managers carries the threat that shareholders will divest (thereby lowering share values), that a take-over bid will be mounted, and that incumbent management will be replaced by new owners. Corporate governance is achieved mainly through the 'market for corporate control' (Manne 1965), at least in publicly listed firms. This approach has been supplemented in recent years (the 1980s especially) by greater use of debt in corporate transactions e.g. in management buy-outs. Debt is a prior claim on cash-flow and hence constrains the freedom of action of managers. To use Jensen's words (1986), it reduces the agency costs emanating from 'free' cash flow. As Hart puts it, 'debt limits how inefficient management can be, at least if management wants to repay its debts' (1995a: 685). A further recent development in Anglo-American corporate governance systems is that the stance of major investors is now more interventionist. Major investors appear to be attempting to guide managerial behaviour by making investor preferences explicit when firms take (or do not take) major decisions. These interventions may take place publicly as in the case of major US pension funds such as CalPers, or informally and behind the scenes as tends to be the case in the UK (see Scott 1996). Ultimately, though, the source of this power resides in the threat of divestment.

It is therefore commonplace to suggest that the power and assertiveness of investors *vis-à-vis* managers has increased in recent years (Useem 1993; Cappelli *et al.* 1997; Scott 1996). The growth and increased concentration of institutional investment seems to be a major factor in this development.[10] Employee shareholders, however, do not seem to have benefited from greater investor activity and power in governance. Employee share schemes usually provide a negligible role in governance beyond formal voting rights. As employee shareholdings are relatively small and dispersed, employee shareholders have little power to affect the governance of the firm. They are unable to exert discipline on managers informally whilst divestment does not provide a credible sanction. It is possible that concerted action by all employee shareholders could make an impact in cases where they hold a relatively large proportion of stock (say 10 per cent) but UK firms do not usually have employee shareholder institutions to co-ordinate shareholder action. It seems to be the case that managers of UK firms do not encourage employee shareholder participation in corporate governance. Attendance at Annual General Meetings is rarely positively encouraged. A good case in point is the AGM of Marks and Spencer in 1999. Here employee shareholders wanting to attend the AGM had to go to a 'satellite' venue away from the AGM itself (though connected by video-link), and were required to take annual leave. There seems to be a tacit agreement between managers and major investors that employee share schemes will be restricted to the provision of remuneration benefits and that employees will not be encouraged by managers to actively participate in corporate governance. This contrasts with the US where the widespread use of supra-majority rules of corporate voting means that employee share-ownership can be used strategically by managers to block take-over bids and other actions by major investors (see Useem 1993; Useem and Gager 1996). UK experience also contrasts with some major firms in France where employee shareholders have created shareholder associations to represent their interests.

In principle, however, employee share-owners could be active and effective participants in corporate governance, especially if together they own a substantial proportion of company shares, as is the case in most of our sample firms. Employee-owners may possess several advantages relative to external owners in their capacity to monitor managers. One, they may have access to insider information – about how the firm actually works or on management capabilities and performance – which is not so readily available to outside shareholders. Two, their interests may be more homogeneous (simply by virtue that all are party to an employment relationship) than those of external owners, and hence they may be more readily able to co-ordinate their actions so as to exert discipline on management. Three, assuming that employees on the whole do not have diversified ownership holdings (and assuming that external owners do), employee owners have a relatively much greater stake in their investment, and hence a greater motivation (all other things being equal) to ensure that managers perform. The argument, then, is that employee-owners may have both a greater capacity for and interest in monitoring managers than do external shareholders with diversified portfolios.

Whether employees are able to exert some degree of control as owners will depend critically on their capacity to create institutions to exert shareholder pressure. Their capacity to do so is likely to be dependent on their cohesion as an employee group and the presence of existing mechanisms of employee 'voice'. Hansmann (1996) has argued that a critical factor in the character and success of participation, as well as the incidence and longevity of employee ownership, is the degree of homogeneity of the workforce owners. Where the workforce is heterogeneous, the free expression of conflicts of interest via participation institutions will seriously damage the performance of the firm. A further issue concerns the extent to which employees already have experience of participation. Drawing on Pateman's (1970) argument that the more participation there is the better employees (or citizens) will become at operating it, it seems likely that the extent to which new institutions of employee-owner participation are created will be influenced in part by the presence of other forms of participation. Where unions are present, for instance, there is likely to be the experience of designing and operating representative institutions desirable and possibly necessary for the creation of additional institutions. In a similar vein, Eaton and Voos (1992) have suggested that firms with an established participatory structure may find it easier (on administrative grounds if nothing else) to implement further participation schemes.

In ESOPs there is a potential instrument of collective employee-owner governance in the form of the employee benefits trusts. In the UK these vote the stock held on employees' behalf and, whilst employees cannot instruct them how to vote, their fiduciary duty to act in beneficiaries' interests means that they often cast their votes according to employee-owner preferences. There are several questions that can be asked of these trusts. One, what is the role and function of them perceived to be, and by whom? Two, do they take an active role in corporate governance or are they passive 'warehouses' for shares? Three, to what extent are employee-owners represented on trusts, and who puts them there? Four, are there any procedures for employee-owners to monitor the activities of the trust? Besides the introduction of employee benefits trusts, employee ownership might lead to other innovations in corporate governance. These mainly relate to Annual General Meetings. Are employee-owners actively encouraged to attend AGMs, and are these made 'user-friendly'? Are informal shareholder meetings held in addition to formal meetings?

Finally, employee-owners may elect representatives onto the board of directors, either as executive managers or non-executives. This provides a potentially effective means of incorporating the views and interests of employee-owners in the management and direction of the firm, and of monitoring the management team. However, the corporate governance literature shows that boards of directors are ambiguous institutions in that they are both organs of shareholder representation and the most senior tier of management within the firm (Ezzamel and Watson 1997). To some extent this ambiguity is resolved by placing non-executive directors on the board, and indeed the main component of recent corporate governance reforms in the UK has been the enhancement of the supervisory role of non-executive directors.[11] Even then, there is a possibility that non-executive directors are assimilated into management because managers take the initiative in selecting 'safe' non-executive directors, because managers control information flows, and because of the prevailing norms of consensual boardroom behaviour (Hill 1995; Pettigrew and McNulty 1995). Similar concerns were expressed in relation to employee directors in the earlier debate on industrial democracy in the late 1970s (Brannen *et al.* 1976; Towers *et al.* 1985). In an employee ownership context, there are several empirical questions about employee-owner representation in the boardroom. One, is there any explicit representation of employee-owner interests either in the form of executive or non-executive directors? Two, what are the background and attributes of employee-owner directors, and how are they selected? Three, what is the role of any employee-owner representation in the boardroom, and how does it function in practice? The questions will be addressed empirically in Chapter 7.

The conjunction of employee participation and corporate governance

In the discussion so far we have examined employee participation and corporate governance. As Blair (1999) has commented, these are generally seen as entirely separate areas of activity. In the employee ownership firm, though, it is possible that they become conjoined: employee participation in work decisions might increase because employees are owners whilst employee-owner involvement in corporate governance might operate through or in conjunction with more traditional institutions of employee representation (such as unions). In principle, employee participation could operate entirely separately from owner governance, in much the same way as occurs in the vast majority of conventional firms. For instance, employees might pursue their interests as employees via union representation, whilst operating conventional structures of corporate governance as owners. Thus, they might attend an AGM outside working hours, with an agenda limited to receiving the company accounts. Employee-owners would exercise their vote as owners, not as employees or as employee-owners.

Alternatively, the two could be inseparable, with governance and participation issues intimately bound together and little or no procedural or institutional separation between the two. For instance, employees might elect and serve on a board of directors, or management committee, which concerns itself with both major issues of strategy and day-to-day issues of work and labour organisation. The traditional concept of the 'labour-managed firm' appears to embody this view of participation and governance. It is encapsulated too in the notion of democratic worker ownership i.e. where rights emanating from ownership and employment are completely fused together. In practice, these organisational forms, which often imply also that hierarchy will be under-developed or absent (as in Williamson's (1975) 'peer group' form of organisation), are extremely rare (see Russell 1985b; Dow and Putterman 1999)[12].

There are many possible combinations in between these two extremes. These may be seen as a hybrid form of employee ownership participation. For example, board representation may be based on employees' role in ownership but the employee directors may be selected on the basis of their role as *employee* representatives and may be elected by all employees, not just owners. They may be voted onto the board on a one person, one vote system, as is usually the case in elections to employee representative bodies, even though the typical governance voting structure is based on equity shares (which may be unequal). Employee directors may have a much greater role in considering operational management issues than is the norm for non-executive directors. Another possibility is that employee councils, whose membership is based on employee constituencies, consider a wider scope of subjects than is usual for a works council, such as ownership issues and major strategic issues.

To summarise, employee ownership could have a variety of effects on participation and governance. It might lead to no change in participation and governance at all. Alternatively, it may lead to attempts to enhance employee participation but leaves pre-existing patterns of corporate governance untouched, or vice versa. Or it may lead to developments in both participation and governance. These may occur in distinct ways or may be conjoined in the ways outlined above. Our view is that the configuration of employee participation and corporate governance in each case will be a function of the circumstances of ownership conversion and the objectives of those involved in the transition to employee ownership. We will consider these propositions in more depth shortly.

Evidence on participation and governance from the United States

The evidence from the US suggests that most firms with employee ownership do not make extensive innovations in either employee participation or governance (see Rooney 1988). A recent study in Ohio found that one-quarter of ESOP companies provide no avenues for employee participation, about half make a modest effort and about one-quarter combine ownership with significant employee participation (Logue and Yates 1999: 228). In most ESOPs, these authors report, the governance and management structures are identical to those of conventional companies. In particular, there is little or no development of participation in the ownership channel or a hybrid employment-ownership channel. This finding has repeatedly emerged from studies of ESOPs. A major study in the mid-1980s found that only 4 per cent had non-managerial employee representatives on company boards (General Accounting Office 1986: 40). A later study of large firms with ESOPs found that just four out of 1,000 had non-managerial employee representation on the board (Blasi and Kruse 1991). In closely held firms the proportion seems to be higher. The Ohio study (which focused mainly on closely held firms) found that 17 per cent had non-managerial employees on the board of directors (Logue and Yates 1999: 237). The low level of employee representation is observed even in many firms with dominant or majority employee stock holdings (see also Russell 1988). As Hansmann has put it, 'one of the most striking facts about them (ESOPs) is that they generally provide for participation only in earnings, not in control' (1996: 106). The main exception seems to be in sectors such as steel, airlines, and trucking, where employee ownership has formed part of a concession bargaining package to rescue ailing firms. Employee-owner representation on boards of directors has been an integral component of these initiatives (Hunter 1998).

US law permits restrictions on employee-shareholder voting rights in closely held companies. Voting rights of shares held by trustees on employees' behalf do not have to be passed through to employees on routine matters and the selection of directors, though they do on major issues of corporate restructuring. A useful measure of ESOP firms' commitment to employee-owner participation is therefore whether they choose to pass through full voting rights. The General Accounting Office study in the mid-1980s found that this took place in only a minority of cases (in 25 per cent of private company non-leveraged ESOPs (General Accounting Office 1986)). The Ohio study found a somewhat larger proportion: 42 per cent. Even in majority employee-owned firms, full voting rights are passed through in just over a half of cases (National Center for Employee Ownership 1999; Logue and Yates 1999). Where employees do have voting powers there have been some attempts by employees or their representatives to use ownership mechanisms to influence employment issues. Blair observes that unions have become shareholder activists at several major companies, submitting resolutions on governance and social issues (1995: 317).

Overall, the evidence suggests that developments in employee participation in task-related and similar decisions are more widespread than innovations in employee governance. There are some cases where employees have gained extensive involvement in the organisation of work alongside employee ownership. Cotton (1993: 200–1) discusses the case of Quad/Graphics where employee owners work in self-directed work teams and actually run the company when the top management is absent. The Ohio study found that employee-owned firms were more likely to have introduced participatory management practices than non-employee-owned firms. The incidence of self-directed teams and problem-solving groups had more than doubled in employee ownership firms (see Leadbetter

1997; Ohio Employee Ownership Centre 1993). Overall, 75 per cent of majority ESOPs and 59 per cent of minority ESOPs had introduced some sort of shop floor team structure (Logue and Yates 1999: 239). Other studies, of publicly quoted firms, however, have found little evidence of participatory cultures being created in tandem with employee ownership. Blasi and Kruse (1991) suggest that only 5 per cent of publicly quoted firms have a participatory culture. Overall, though, innovations in employee participation appear to be more widespread than new forms of employee governance in US ESOPs.

Influences on employee participation and corporate governance

In this section we examine the influences on the patterns of participation and governance in employee-owned firms, and suggest reasons for variations between firms. We noted above that whilst many ESOPs in the US have done little to develop employee participation and governance, there are some which have an extensive range of innovations in these areas. What explains the differences between firms? One obvious explanation is that the extent of participation will be determined by the extent of ownership. The larger the ownership stake held by employees, the deeper the range and extent of participation by employees both in employment-related and ownership-related decision is likely to be. The Ohio study, for instance, found that employee participation in governance and management decisions tended to be higher in majority ESOPs than minority ones. Thirty-seven per cent of majority ESOPs had non-managerial employees on the board of directors compared with 10 per cent of minority ESOPs (Logue and Yates 1999: 238). However, the balance of the evidence indicates that the level of ownership has no necessary relationship with the level and type of participation (Young 1990). There are some firms with very low levels of employee ownership which are nevertheless highly participative in character. Equally there are firms with majority ownership which have made few attempts to develop participation by employee-owners either in governance or management decisions. A complicating factor is the varying permutations of participation. These mean that it is difficult to identify simple or linear relationships between ownership and participation. In some cases employee participation in work decisions is enhanced whilst owner participation in corporate governance is unchanged, or vice versa.

We suggest that the configuration of the institutions and mechanisms for employee participation in employee ownership firms will be an outcome of the philosophies, interests, and objectives of those involved in the conversion set in the particular context in which conversion occurs. This is a continuation of the argument about the determinants of ownership presented in Chapter 5. The relationship between levels of ownership and forms of participation is not a direct or simple causal one. Instead, ownership and participation are both outcomes of actors' aspirations and actions. Three main sets of actors may be discerned: owners, managers, and employees (and their representatives). In addition, the providers of finance may exert powerful constraints on the forms of participation and governance chosen. As we saw in Chapter 5, not all of these are necessarily actively involved in any given conversion to employee ownership. In some cases, the owner will be the sole actor in the conversion. In others, such as management-employee buy-outs during privatisation, all three may be deeply involved. Where more than one set of actors are involved we expect that participation institutions will be the bargained outcome of the interplay of the various interests and objectives.

Owners

Given the characteristics of employee ownership firms in the UK, it is possible to identify several types of owners who may have different perspectives on employee participation. The impact of these perspectives varies, however, for a variety of reasons. In some cases owners relinquish ownership rights completely upon conversion and therefore have little if any influence on the design and operation of employee participation and governance structures post-conversion. Equally there are instances where owners have retained some role in the running of firms or partnership institutions even after passing their ownership to the workforce. Some owners, such as local authorities, may wish to influence the design and operation of participative institutions prior to passing ownership to employees on the grounds that this will be in the best interests of the firms or employees.

The three sets of owners that are relevant in the UK case are public authorities (central and local government), private owners, and shareholders of publicly listed companies. In the case of public authorities, views on participation and governance seem likely to be influenced by political perspectives and philosophies. Thus, left-wing local authorities may be predicted to attach considerable importance to employee participation and governance in the firms they transfer to employee ownership. They may take positive steps to encourage certain forms of participation. By contrast, the political and managerial views of the Conservative Governments would not have been favourable to active employee-shareholder participation in governance (though this is not to suggest that these governments blocked proposals for new forms of governance where they were put forward by buy-out teams).

As for private owners, it is possible to put forward several propositions. The previous chapter has indicated that where owners of private firms pass some of their ownership stake to employees it is usually for corporate control or paternalistic reasons, or both. These objectives, coupled with the strong personal sense of ownership typically exhibited by majority owners of small and medium-sized businesses, suggest that these owners will often be hostile to the creation of institutions that facilitate employee participation in strategic decisions, either in employee or ownership matters. A strong employee voice in strategic decisions may be viewed as unnecessary (as owners may perceive themselves to be protectors of employees' best interests) and threatening to the personal prerogative of the owner. We noted in Chapter 5 that promotion of industrial democracy was not seen as an important reason for converting to employee ownership in these cases. The low take-up rate of the statutory ESOP, where there are statutory stipulations for employee representation on the employee trust, may well be viewed as confirmation of this phenomenon (Cornford 1990). Even where owners relinquish entirely ownership and control, the owner may encourage the introduction of new institutions of employee-shareholder governance, at least where the conversion embodies a broader vision of economic and industrial democracy on the part of the owner. Furthermore they may continue to play an active role after conversion to ensure that their vision is fully realised. It seems possible that they will also encourage the development of task-level institutions of employee involvement so that the broader vision can be realised at the micro-level. A further prediction is that independent forms of employee representation, based around trade unions and collective bargaining, will not be encouraged as these may inhibit or modify the realisation of the owner's vision of the new firm.

In publicly listed firms, the level of employee ownership is likely to be fairly low and hence there may be a large number of other owners. It can be predicted that these owners will be unwilling to countenance the creation of new institutions of employee-shareholder participation as this may pose the threat of weakening their own control rights. This observation is based on the experience of 'conventional' employee share schemes where attempts to expand the employee role in corporate governance rarely occur.

Managers

Turning to managers, there is substantial evidence from the US that managerial philosophies have a very important influence on the character of employee participation in employee ownership firms (Pierce *et al.* 1981). There appear to be three sorts of contexts in which to consider managerial involvement and perspectives, and which are broadly similar to those identified in relation to owners above. The first is where managers are actively involved in the conversion either as the main instigators of a management buy-out, partners in a management-employee buy-out or as lead players in an employee buy-out. In these cases managerial involvement is likely to be very high indeed and we would expect managerial perspectives on participation to have a substantial influence on institutional outcomes. The second context is privately owned firms where managers may well have very little involvement at all in the design of employee participation. The third is publicly listed firms where, given the separation of ownership and management that is typical in these firms, it is likely to be managers who take the initiative in introducing schemes for employee ownership and participation.

We expect that the objectives and orientations of managers towards employee ownership will affect their perspectives on employee-shareholder representation after the conversion. Managerial orientations to employee participation need to be seen within the contrasting imperatives of commitment and control, albeit within the relatively distinct context of employee ownership. On the one hand, managers may favour employee participation on the grounds that it promotes information- sharing, upwards problem-solving, and employee commitment (Conte and Svejnar 1990). Given that managers often have a substantial financial interest in employee-owned firms, it is in their interests to adopt these potentially performance-enhancing forms of employee participation. On the other hand, these developments in employee participation may have a number of effects that detract from managerial control (see Jensen and Meckling 1979). Work discipline may become more difficult to enforce. Decision-making will involve those who are not well qualified to make decisions. Finally, opportunities for employee participation may open up divisions within the workforce, between various occupational categories, locations etc. (Hansmann 1996). These dangers are of course always present where attempts are made to give employees a say in decisions, but they have a special resonance in an employee ownership context. Since employees may appeal to their ownership rights as a source of legitimacy, managers may find it especially difficult to resist employee demands or to place limits on the scope and breadth of employee involvement. There is therefore the possibility that employee participation could make substantial inroads into what are often seen as managerial prerogatives.

Where employees are deeply involved in buy-outs it is unlikely that managerial anxieties will preclude extensions of employee participation and governance. Instead, these concerns will colour the overall configuration of participation. It is likely that managers will want to keep employee-shareholder representation separate from employee representation so that traditional antagonisms in labour management do not contaminate potentially integrative forms of shareholder representation and involvement. Equally, managers are unlikely to want shareholder institutions to have an active involvement in operational management because of the constraints they could place on management activity. Nor is employee participation in work decisions likely to be attractive given the claims employees could make for greater *rights* in this area. The solution to these dilemmas may be to create new institutions of employee-owner participation and representation that are procedurally distinct from other forms of employee participation and representation. The main innovations may therefore be in shareholder or hybrid employee-shareholder channels rather than employee channels of participation.

It is more difficult to predict managerial influences on the design of participation institutions in firms where employee ownership comes about from owner paternalism or exits. In these cases managers might have a fairly limited role, at least in the early years, because the owner has the dominant influence. In such circumstances, managers may view employee participation as a threat because it primarily involves owners and employees. Managers may feel that they are 'stuck in the middle', especially if owners retain either partial ownership or some involvement in the direction of the firm. This is a common phenomenon in employee participation programmes: middle managers believe that passing some influence to employees or their representatives undermines their role and enables employees to bypass them by dealing directly with top management or owners (Marchington *et al.* 1992).

In publicly listed firms, where there is usually a separation between ownership and management, past experience indicates that managers rather than owners will initiate employee ownership and participation. Since governance tends to function separately and externally from internal managerial processes, employees' roles as shareholders and employees are likely to be quite separate. Unless employees acquire a very large ownership stake, it is unlikely that managers will either want or be able to enhance the organs of shareholder governance. Employee shareholders will have the same formal rights as all other shareholders but this will emanate from their role as shareholders not as employees or employee-shareholders. Nor will managers be able to design new institutions to allow participation of employees in their dual role as employees and shareholders (e.g. election of worker directors), as other shareholders will be unlikely to agree to such measures (which would in effect downgrade their control rights).

There are few grounds for suspecting that managers would want to create new institutions that could exert discipline on managers. However, since interest in share ownership may well reflect a generalised interest in integrative aspects of employee management, there may well be programmes of employee involvement in task-related issues involving downward communication or upwards problem-solving alongside share ownership. A high correlation between these and share ownership programmes in large firms continues to be found (see Pendleton 1997b).[13] What will probably not be witnessed is any attempt to enhance the involvement of employee representatives in strategic level decisions.

Employees

Employee aspirations and expectations about innovations in participation may also vary. A key issue is likely to be whether employees play an active part in the transition to employee ownership or whether they are passive recipients of shares. In general, employees obtaining shares during an employee buy-out are more likely to attempt to develop new forms of participation than those receiving shares from paternalist owners, as they are more actively engaged in the reconstruction of their firm. However, differences may be observed between employees receiving free shares as part of a high-leveraged employee buy-out and those directly subscribing to shares to part-fund conversion. The shares carry a much higher level of risk in the latter case, in so far as employees may lose capital as well as their jobs if the firm goes under. We would expect therefore the possession of control rights to be correspondingly more important. Given the risks, employees will probably attach considerable importance to the design and operation of institutions of *shareholder* participation. However, since these share subscriptions occur mainly in management buy-outs, managerial concerns may well outweigh those of employees.

An exception to these observations in relation to share subscriptions may well be observed in publicly listed firms where employees acquire shares using Sharesave mechanisms. In these cases, the level of risk is so low that employees will not require control rights to compensate them for risk, beyond those they acquire as conventional shareholders when, and if, they exercise their option. On the whole, employees participate in Sharesave to gain financial returns rather than out of any desire to exercise ownership of their firm. Baddon *et al.* found that the prospect of financial rewards at no risk, coupled with an easy method of saving and acquiring shares, were more important motives for SAYE participation than acquiring a stake in the company and its future (Baddon *et al.* 1989: 236).

A complicating factor in all this concerns the means by which employees articulate, co-ordinate, and express their objectives for participation within the firm. In all but the smallest firms it is likely that some degree of employee representation will be necessary to develop employee involvement in ownership conversion and the design of participation institutions. This may take one of three forms. Where trade unions are present, trade union representatives may act as the vehicle for the expression of employee interests. Alternatively, employees may put forward representatives to a buy-out or employee ownership committee, either because there is no system of union representation or because unions choose not to become involved. Failing that, employee interests may be marshalled by senior managers.

The role of unions is a complex one. Some unions have chosen not to become involved in employee ownership conversions for an array of reasons. These include hostility to privatisation, fears about the level of risk taken on by employees, and anxieties that the traditional role of unions as employee representatives becomes confused when employers are also the employer. A good case in point is the National Freight Corporation where the TGWU and NUR (now RMT) decided not to become involved in the employee buy-out in 1982 (see Bradley and Nejad 1989). In principle, unions are usually in favour of extensions to employee representation and participation. However, employee-shareholder institutions pose the danger that employee-shareholders will shift their allegiance to these, and union institutions will be correspondingly undermined. Where this anxiety is especially strong, unions may seek to limit the development of new institutions. Existing union-based forms of representation may continue to be the primary mode of representation and participation. However, if this is the case, employee-shareholders may attempt to express ownership interests through union institutions, and this may lead to role confusion for unions. They may have to express both owner and employee interests, which in time may detract from the unions' effectiveness.

To avoid this, unions may therefore seek to develop new institutions of participation and representation that are complementary to their own functions. The emphasis might be on the representation of employee-shareholders, with interests that are distinct from those of pay and conditions of employment. So, they may seek to create new institutions to express employee-owner interests in new areas such as investment, acquisitions, divestment etc. but from the perspective of employees. To minimise the problems of role confusion, we would expect unions to want these new forms of participation to be procedurally separate from traditional institutions of collective bargaining and consultation but nevertheless subject to some degree of union influence. Given the subject matter of new forms of participation (i.e. strategic decisions) it is likely that the type of participation will be indirect and representative in character. Innovations in task participation seem less likely since this form of participation may be feared to undermine union activities.

Where unions are absent but there is some employee-shareholder representation on the organs handling the conversion, there may be some pressure for the introduction of new forms of participation and involvement. These representatives, who may well emerge only at the point of the conversion, may be less experienced than union representatives and may therefore be less capable of expressing employee interests and views. Meanwhile, where managers or owners mobilise employees for conversion it can be anticipated that employee aspirations for participation will not be so fully articulated and may well be refracted through the perceptions and objectives of managers or owners.

Financiers

Finally, those providing finance to employee-owned firms are likely to have a strong influence on governance, if not participation. In general, financiers seem likely to be hostile to employee involvement in corporate governance on the grounds that employees are unlikely to have the level of competence for effective governance. Furthermore, employees may be thought to put employee concerns before those of efficiency and successful financial performance. Divergences of interest amongst employee-owners may add to these problems. By contrast, financiers may display less interest in systems of employee participation on the grounds that these are 'operational' and internal issues for managers.

Provision of finance capital to secure employee ownership is likely to take two main forms. One is equity finance, the other is debt. In the case of equity finance, this involves financiers sharing ownership with employees. This is not a common form of finance in ESOPs, and has been found mainly in a small number of bus companies (mainly those that were privatised in 1994) and some of the other privatised companies that were primarily management buy-outs. In these cases equity ownership has come about because institutions providing loan finance have sought equity shares to safeguard their investment. In the bus companies with investor ownership, it is usual for there to be a 'ratchet' mechanism, whereby employees' share of ownership increases at the expense of investors as loans are repaid. The main form of finance, however, for employee ownership conversions, as the foregoing suggests, is loan finance.

Given that investors of either kind are wary of employee involvement in governance, they may well attempt to limit the scope for employee governance. When there is equity investment by outside institutions, this may well be set at a level which gives investors a majority share of ownership and control. Whilst employee innovations in governance (such as worker directors) may occur, these will be subordinate to investor forms of control. In the case of loan finance, investors may insist on limitations to the extent and scope of employee involvement in corporate governance as a condition of granting loans.

The extent to which investor concerns influence systems of participation and governance is likely to be a function of the dependence of the firm on outside finance to become employee-owned, and on the leverage the firm can secure. In the case of paternalistic firms, investor influence is likely to be limited since owners typically gift their ownership shares or else finance the ownership transfer out of future earnings (as in the case of Tullis Russell). In 'technical' ESOPs in listed firms, there is generally little dependence on financial institutions to provide finance for share purchases but the dominance of investors in ownership of these firms limits the extent of ownership and control that may be passed to employees. Investor influence is likely to be most clearly in evidence in leveraged management-employee ('representative') and management buy-outs ('risk-sharing' ESOPs), where there is considerable dependence on external sources of finance. In these cases, the extent to which investors seek to influence participation and governance systems may be a function of the perceived financial prospects of the firm. In the case of bus companies, which generally have positive and stable cash-flows, limited investment requirements and stable technology (Thompson *et al.* 1990), investors may be willing to countenance innovations in employee governance (as long as employee concessions in pay and employment are forthcoming). By contrast, where the financial prospects of the employee-owned firm are uncertain, investors may take a more interventionist stance in the design of governance institutions.

Summary

In summary, the actors involved in conversions to employee ownership may have a range of different perspectives on the nature of employee participation. Given that participation structures are likely to be the outcome of the interplay of these, there are a variety of configurations of employee involvement, participation, and representation that may be observed in employee ownership firms. The logic of our comments is that there are unlikely to be similar structures of participation across the population of employee ownership firms. Nor is the nature or extent of participation likely to be determined by a single factor such as the proportion of equity owned by employees. However, we do anticipate that the configuration of involvement by the various groups of actors will be similar in similar contexts. We therefore analyse the structures of participation on the basis of the contexts identified in the previous chapter: 'representative' buy-outs with a substantial employee component, 'risk-sharing' management buy-outs, paternalistic and exit conversions, and 'technical' use of ESOP structures in publicly listed companies.

7 Employee participation and governance

Institutions, practices, and outcomes

Introduction

In this chapter we return to the empirical analysis of the employee ownership firms in our study. We examine the institutions and practices of employee participation and governance in each of the four main groups of employee ownership firms identified at the end of Chapter 5. To recap, 'representative' firms are those where employees or their representatives were deeply involved in the conversion to employee ownership. These firms were either employee buy-outs or management-employee buy-outs. This group is composed mainly of bus companies plus a small group of employee-led buy-outs of 'forced divestment' companies. 'Risk-sharing' firms are essentially management buy-outs that included an employee ownership component. All bar one member of this group were privatised firms. In these cases, managers tended to be the main initiators and developers of ownership structures. 'Paternalistic' firms are those where owners had decided to pass either partial or entire ownership to their workforces. Finally, 'technical' ESOPs are those where managers of PLCs had introduced EBT structures to prevent current and future share scheme commitments violating the rules of various regulatory agencies. Levels of employee ownership tend to differ between the four groups: the highest average level of employee ownership is found in the representative group (70 per cent), followed by the paternalist group (58 per cent). The risk-sharing group has an average level of employee ownership of 21 per cent, whilst the technical group has an average of just 5 per cent.

If, as we have argued, both ownership and participation are outcomes of actors' objectives and philosophies, it is likely that forms of participation and governance will differ between the four groups. On the basis of this argument, the least development of participation or governance is likely to be found in the 'technical group'. This is because employee ownership institutions were developed by managers for technical reasons rather than to enhance employee ownership *per se*. We suspect also that there will be limited development of participation in the 'risk-sharing' group. This is because the main actors responsible for ownership conversion are managers.

Ownership and participation institutions are likely to reflect their interests as owner-managers. Specifically, we predict that there will be little development of employee-owner governance, since this would weaken managerial control rights. Furthermore, any employee-owner involvement in governance will be kept distinct from employee participation since a conjunction of the two might threaten managerial prerogatives in day-to-day management. Control rights are important for this group since they bear the main financial risk of ownership. As these managers are concerned to share risk but not control rights with employees, we anticipate that there will be some development of forms of employee participation that enhance communication and information flows. These managers are likely to want to enhance employee alignment with the goals of the firm (as defined by owner-managers). By contrast, we think it unlikely that there will be any substantial development of representative-based forms of employee participation.

Employee participation and employee governance are likely to be well developed in the 'representative' group. In fact, employee participation will probably pre-date employee ownership since prior employee involvement provides the basis for the employee role in ownership conversion. Whether employee ownership is likely to develop employee participation further is difficult to predict. However, employee governance will be a major outcome of ownership since employees are likely to seek control rights commensurate with their ownership stakes. Governance and 'conventional' employee participation are likely to be conjoined, rather than kept separate, because employee-owners will tend to view the firm, and their ownership of it, holistically. Furthermore, as a substantial element of 'traditional' employee participation is representative-based, representatives are unlikely to promote the development of a form of separate ownership governance that undercuts their role. At the same time, the concerns of employee representatives to protect their traditional functions may mean that new forms of direct employee participation that might bypass representative structures tend not to be introduced.

It is difficult to predict developments in participation and governance in the 'paternalist' group. Given the oft-noted attachment of owners to their control rights, we might expect that paternalistic objectives to widen share ownership are not matched by corresponding developments in employee governance. At the same time, divesting owners may wish to provide means for the expression of employee-shareholder concerns and interests even though they may have a limited conception of employee-shareholder *rights*. At the same time, they may seek to discourage representative forms of employee participation on the grounds that these may impede the development of employee-shareholder philosophies and practices.

In this chapter we review the main innovations in employee representation and governance in each group, and attempt to assess to what extent these predictions have been met in practice. We also attempt, where possible, to evaluate to what extent new forms of participation and governance give employees and employee-owners a genuine 'voice'. The impact of ownership on pre-existing forms of employee participation, such as employee representation by unions, is also considered. Most of our attention is devoted to the representative group, as this is the largest of the four groups with 35 cases. Members of this group also tend to have more complex and interesting sets of innovations in participation and governance. We show that the differing interests of management and employee representatives converged on a configuration of participation and governance that emphasised employee-owner governance and employee representation but involved little innovation in direct, task-related forms of participation. We commence with the 'representative' group, before outlining participation and governance in 'risk-sharing', 'paternalist' and 'technical' firms.

Representative group

A key characteristic of the representative group was the development of novel forms of employee-shareholder governance alongside employee ownership. Furthermore, these forms of employee-shareholder governance were intertwined with other forms of employee participation, especially representative-based forms of participation. Most of the firms in this group were bus companies, and considerable similarities developed amongst these firms due to imitation effects.

Perhaps the clearest development, and one that distinguishes this group from the other three, is the widespread presence of worker directors. Non-executive directors drawn from the workforce with a remit to represent employees were placed on the board of directors in two-thirds of cases (23 firms). Five of the firms in this group had non-executive directors appointed from outside the firm to represent employee interests, and in two firms this was in lieu of employee directors. In two of these cases the outside directors were Labour Members of Parliament and in another two they were senior trade union officials.[1] In five cases, executive directors were appointed from the workforce. In fact in only one firm in the representative group were there no innovations in governance structures.

In these firms worker directors constituted between 20 and 67 per cent of board membership. In most cases employee directors did not have majority representation: there were just two cases where they exceeded 50 per cent, and both of these were employee buy-outs in 'forced divestment' situations.[2] Although they were in a minority, it was common in the bus industry for protections to be built into the Articles of Association, which in effect boosted worker directors' voting power. At West Midlands Transport and Cleveland Transport, for instance, two of the three worker directors had to vote in favour of proposals on a set of specified major issues (acquisitions, major capital expenditure, share issues and disposals, property disposals, appointment of new directors etc.) for them to be carried. In West Midlands, the approval of two employee directors was also required for any alterations to the deeds of the five trusts and to the appointment or removal of any trustees.

The function of an employee director is well described in an appendix to the Articles of Association of West Midlands Transport. In addition to the general fiduciary duties required of all directors, the Articles note that:

> an employee director will be expected to participate with all other directors in the formulation of the company's policies at a strategic level. It is not intended that Employee Directors should participate in the actual day-to-day management of the business of the Company which will be delegated by the Directors to the Management Directors.

Employee directors were also required 'to ensure that employees are systematically provided with relevant information, consulted regularly on issues likely to affect their interests and achieve a common awareness of the financial and economic factors affecting the performance of the company'. The key tasks included the following:

> actively to support and promote effective employee communication approved by the Directors including major decisions which have been taken or are being contemplated . . .;
>
> to assist in creating an environment of mutual respect in which the company can adapt to change and can best serve the needs of its customers;
>
> to liase between the Directors and employees and their representatives, meeting with them in the workplaces. . . . In doing so, Employee Directors will be informing employees of the Company's policies and acting as a channel of communication between employees and the Directors concerning matters of overall policy. It is recognised that the conduct of negotiations concerning employee relations, pay and conditions, trade union matters or any other topics concerning the day-to-day management of the company are the responsibility of the Management Directors. . . . Employee Directors should play no part in negotiations between management and employees save insofar as such matters are discussed in meetings of the Directors;
>
> to represent the company at conferences, seminars...so as to inform and answer questions concerning the Company as an employee-owned company. . . . In doing so, Employee Directors will act solely in accordance with the policies and directions of the Directors.

The role of employee directors in West Midlands, as in other bus companies, was perceived in similar terms to those in earlier experiments with worker directors (Brannen *et al.* 1976. Besides representing employee interests, and ensuring that employees were consulted, employee directors were required to communicate board decisions to the workforce and, implicitly, to work towards securing consent to these. As it was put by an ESOP trustee at one of the other bus companies, 'the worker directors had the difficult job of pointing out the realities (of running a business) to workers'. The requirement to keep out of pay and other negotiations between executive directors and union representatives was also found in the other bus companies, though employee directors would usually be party to the initial pay offer and final settlement.

To find out more about the role of employee directors we asked a set of 21 'key respondents' (top managers, union representatives, and trustees, as well as employee directors themselves) in three bus companies about the level of involvement of employee directors in a range of decision areas. For each type of decision, respondents were asked to assess how far employee directors were typically involved, on a scale of 1 to 5 where 1 is 'very great involvement' and 5 is 'little or no involvement'.[3] Table 7.1 presents the average evaluations of their involvement.

The results presented in Table 7.1 suggest that employee directors are most involved in decisions that might be viewed as key business strategy decisions, such as investment and divestment, and key governance issues such as management salaries. They tend to be less involved in labour management decisions concerned with labour deployment, staffing, and work organisation. This accords with the emphasis in these organisations on operational decision-making being the preserve of executive managers. These findings contrast with the virtually unanimous findings from earlier research on worker directors in non-employee-owned companies that worker directors tend to be most involved in labour management and industrial relations decisions (Brannen *et al.* 1976; Batstone 1976; Batstone *et al.* 1983; Towers *et al.* 1985; Hammer and Stern 1991).

Previous literature has shown that the method of selection of employee directors has an important influence on the function and effectiveness of employee directors. Batstone *et al.* (1983) suggest that selection by unions in

Table 7.1 Involvement of employee directors in decisions

Decision type	*Mean score*	*Standard deviation*
Staffing	3.33	1.33
Work organisation	3.75	1.34
Pay decisions	3.59	1.58
Labour deployment	3.88	1.31
Safety	2.30	1.38
Investment	2.35	1.63
Divestment	2.26	1.59
Product and marketing	2.78	1.56
Promotions	3.83	1.65
Management salaries	1.65	1.17
N	*20*	

the Post Office experiment at the end of the 1970s resulted in greater effectiveness of worker directors than in the earlier British Steel scheme (reported in Brannen *et al.* 1976). Similarly, Towers *et al.*'s (1985) case studies suggested that where worker directors were not selected by unions or without union involvement, management tended to have a correspondingly greater role, and this in turn weakened the power base of the worker directors. The method of selection affects the degree of legitimacy of worker directors with employees, and this legitimacy in turn affects the power resources they can marshal in their dealings with managers. In the cases in our study, the selection process provided important linkages between employee participation and employee-shareholder involvement in governance. Although the presence of employee directors was premised on share-ownership amongst employees, the selection processes were organised around employees' role as employees.

In two-thirds of cases where employee directors were present, employee directors were elected either by the workforce as a whole or by the workforce organised on an occupational constituency basis. Employees, rather than employee-owners, were entitled to vote (in all but one case). In part this was because employees were not formal owners for three years where ESOP and approved profit sharing structures were used. In part it reflected the belief that employees not currently eligible to participate in ownership indirectly (i.e. because of short job tenure) would become so in due course, and hence should have a stake in the operation of governance structures. In part, all-employee elections reflected the fundamental purpose of ESOPs to protect employees' pay, conditions and jobs, or at least to maintain employee voice in the decisions about these core aspects of employment.

Employee representatives were deeply involved in the selection process in every case. For instance, the rules governing the selection process were typically devised and operated by trade union committees. At West Midlands Transport, for instance, each of the three employee directors were appointed on the basis of rules drawn up by three employee committees organised on an occupational constituency basis. These committees were given specific powers in the Articles to appoint employee directors and to call an extraordinary general meeting to remove an employee director. The Articles notes '. . . each such committee being established to represent the interests of employees of the Group'. The Articles required that each committee member be a member of one of six negotiating committees established by the Central Negotiating Committee. It was also commonplace for those wanting to stand for employee directorships to be vetted by the trade unions in the company. At Taybus, for instance, the three worker directors were nominated by the Joint Union Liaison Committee (a committee composed of all shop stewards in the company). The purpose of this type of screening process, as described by an employee director in another company, was to ensure that candidates 'were people who knew the principle of the ESOP and knew the trade union role within it and would not be overawed by management. There is no formal requirement to be a union member but in practice you need to be.' Where employee directors were selected rather than elected, the joint trade union committee or union buy-out committee were responsible for appointment of employee directors. At Western Scottish, for instance, the employee directors were selected by the ESOP Committee though there was provision for election in the future. In every case, at least one of the worker directors had some union experience either as a lay representative within the company or as a branch official.

In three bus companies without worker directors, a shareholders' representation committee was established to represent employee-shareholder views to the board. As in those firms where employee directors were present, however, *employee* representatives were instrumental in the choice of governance structures. They also took shareholder representation upon themselves. In one case the Employee Shareholder Representation Committee (ESRC) was composed of senior shop stewards and was established by the employee buy-out committee. This alternative grew out of a coincidence of managerial and union interests. Both decided that they did not want employee directors. The unions argued that their role was to represent employees not shareholders. Ironically, the shareholders' committee was composed entirely of trade union representatives. The Managing Director commented that 'there is a culture problem with the ESRC – they to tend to talk about union issues. We say they should act as shareholders and talk about strategic issues.' Although employees were not represented on the board, there was a channel for employees' interests to be transmitted to the board. The ESRC met with the two non-executive directors (one of whom was a influential trade union movement official) monthly and with the full board every other month. Structures were similar in one of the other firms. Worker directors were not appointed because the workforce did not apparently want them and because the TGWU convenor instrumental in organising the buy-out 'felt that worker directors would become divorced from the workforce and sucked into management'. Instead, the shop stewards committee was the main instrument for employee-shareholder representation, with the TWGU convenor and deputy attending board meetings as an observer.

A further innovation in one-third of firms with employee directors was a 'shadow board', composed of directors and trade union representatives, meeting either immediately before or after a formal board meeting. In Mainline, for instance, one of the ESOP trusts (composed of shop stewards) functioned as a 'shadow board', and met monthly following the board meeting. This shadow board received all financial information prepared for the full board. As one of the employee directors explained

> they (EBT1) represent the owners, which are the shareholders, but understand that the main interests of these owners is to be workers. So

> the precise role of EBT1 members is difficult to define . . . EBT1 goes through company policies, and can ask management to go through things.

In Taybus a joint standing sub-committee of the Joint Union Liaison Committee was created, composed of worker directors, trustees, and shop stewards. As in other companies, the object of this structure focused primarily on employee representation. It was to discuss employee and company interests, act as a channel between the board and employees, and 'ensure that all employees understand their role as employee owners of the business and are adequately informed of the financial position of the business'.

The employee benefits trusts are potentially an important feature of corporate governance systems in employee ownership firms as they typically hold substantial proportions of equity on behalf of employees for considerable periods of time. Like employee directors, however, these trusts were not a vehicle for 'pure' shareholder governance. Instead they were intertwined with institutions of employee representation and participation.

Eighty-three per cent of representative firms made use of an employee benefits trust, either to hold and distribute equity or to function as a 'market maker'. Eighty-eight per cent of firms with an EBT had some employee representation on the trust. The level of representation tended to be higher than on the board: 77 per cent had a level of employee representation that was 50 per cent or more of the trust's membership. In all but four cases, employee trustees were elected by the workforce as a whole or on a constituency basis. In the remaining cases, trustees were selected by the employee buy-out committee or joint trade union committee. The important point to notice is that selection was organised on the basis of employment rather than ownership.

As voting rights legally reside in the trust until shares are appropriated to individual employees, the trusts may have an influence on key company decisions. For instance, where 75 per cent of votes are required to pass major decisions and the trust holds over 25 per cent of the equity, the agreement of the trustees is necessary. Indeed, in some of the bus companies the trusts were explicitly intended to have this 'blocking' power of last resort. Five firms planned to retain some equity permanently in trust so that the trust's votes would be needed for major resolutions to be passed. In these cases, the stated policy was that employees would be balloted on major issues and that the outcome of this would guide the trustees' voting behaviour. In these cases the trust acted in effect as the long-term custodian of employee ownership, and therefore performed a supervisory function. The clearest and perhaps most explicit instance of this was in the case of Chesterfield Transport. Here the EBT, which held a majority share of the total equity, was explicitly designed to function as a German-style 'upper board'. The Board of Directors (including one employee director) was required to report to the trust (see

Wheatcroft n.d.).[4] Even where equity was not to be retained permanently in trust, a stipulation that special resolutions secure 75 per cent of the equity meant that some of the EBT votes would usually be needed (because share distribution was typically staged over several years).

Given that EBTs had a potentially critical role in corporate governance, it is worth considering what kind of issues, if any, the EBTs tended to be involved in. We therefore asked 'key respondents' (60 in total) in eight companies about the level of involvement of the trustees in a range of decision. For each type of decision, respondents were asked to assess how far trustees were typically involved, on a scale of 1 to 5 where 1 was 'very great involvement' and 5 was 'very little or no involvement'.[5] Table 7.2 presents the average evaluations of their involvement.

As Table 7.2 shows, trustees have little involvement in labour management decisions. This is not unexpected given the conventional view that labour management decisions are operational rather than corporate governance issues. They have rather more involvement in key strategic decisions such as investment and divestment, though slightly lower involvement in these areas than employee directors (see Table 7.1). There is more variation in responses on these issues (as shown by the standard deviation), reflecting two different approaches to governance in the sample companies. In one, trustees have a mainly passive 'warehouse' role and tend not to be involved in strategy decisions. In the other, trustees have either a German-style supervisory role or else a blocking power of last resort on these key issues. In some firms, also, trustees have a fairly high pattern of involvement in managerial recruitment and setting of salary levels, in line with conventional corporate governance models, but on average their involvement is not especially high.

To summarise so far, in the bus companies there was a well-developed set of structures for representing the views of employee-shareholders in governance. On the whole employee-shareholder views were represented

Table 7.2 Involvement of trustees in decisions

Decision type	*Mean score*	*Standard deviation*
Staffing	4.71	0.68
Work organisation	4.71	0.88
Pay decisions	4.73	0.89
Labour deployment	4.60	1.01
Safety	4.39	1.04
Investment	2.42	1.58
Divestment	2.75	1.77
Product and marketing	3.27	1.16
Promotions	4.82	0.60
Managerial recruitment	2.98	1.72
Managerial salaries	3.85	1.79
N	*60*	

more through employee directors than trustees. However, though these structures were based on ownership, and whilst they tended to concentrate on the typical areas of governance, they tended to be intertwined with employees' role as employees. All employees rather than just employee shareholders were involved in the selection of directors and trustees, whilst employee representatives were deeply involved in the design, staffing, and operation of governance institutions. Furthermore, employee representatives closely monitored the functioning of these institutions through 'shadow boards' or attendance at trust meetings. The type of employee participation that these structures permitted was inevitably indirect and representative in form, and the focus of this participation tended to be strategic issues. On the whole these institutions did not become involved in the day-to-day or operational management of the company.

By contrast, there is much less evidence of developments in more 'purely' shareholder representation. Voting rights were organised on a 'conventional' basis in most cases with voting rights linked to the proportion of equity held. There were just six exceptions to this in the representative group as a whole. For instance, at Chesterfield Transport voting rights on key decisions, as identified in the Articles, were organised on a one person, one vote basis. At Taybus there was a one person, one vote system on all voting matters but, as equity was distributed equally amongst all members of the workforce, voting rights were in effect linked to the size of equity holdings.

There were few signs of attempts to develop forms of shareholder participation that would facilitate more active direct involvement in policy formulation of shareholders. Since the primary interests of employee-shareholders tended to be seen to reside in their role as employees, a need was not perceived for extensive *shareholder* activity. Unlike many workers' co-operatives, for instance, shareholder meetings were not developed much beyond the 'conventional' instruments of corporate governance. Over half of firms held just an AGM each year. In many cases employees were not legally eligible to attend this as their shares had not yet been allocated (the trustees attended in their place) but some held a shareholders' forum immediately before or after the formal AGM which employees could attend. This did not, however, have any decision-making powers and tended to function primarily as a forum for information exchange. At Peoples' Provincial Buses, for instance, a general meeting was held immediately after the formal AGM where 'employees can ask any question they like relevant to the company' (Freeman *et al.* 1989: 17). A further quarter of bus companies held an additional interim meeting after six months but this similarly did not have decision-making powers. Just two firms held more regular shareholder meetings. However, a common feature of the Articles of Association of employee owned bus companies was provision for Special General Meetings where directors proposed major strategic changes, such as divestments and acquisitions, and when there was opposition to these from worker directors or other specified parties.

Some firms did attempt to develop ways of enhancing contact between employee-owners and the directors but these were primarily organised though employment institutions rather than ownership. At Mainline, for instance, there was a monthly 'up-date' meeting of managers and unions, the content of which was then reported back to employees by union representatives. A senior manager and union official spent a day per month in the depot canteen to transmit this kind of information as well as receiving feedback from employees. Similarly, Kelvin Central and Lowland Scottish established depot meetings between all employees and board members on a regular basis but these could be viewed as employee meetings rather than shareholder meetings as such since their subject-matter often tended to be day-to-day issues arising from employment.

Turning to employee representation, there was once again a considerable degree of similarity between the bus companies within the 'representative' group. All companies were highly unionised, with an average density of 94 per cent (compared with 86 per cent in the control group of bus companies). Pay and conditions of employment were determined by collective bargaining in every company. Three-quarters had either a joint consultative committee or a works council before the ownership conversion, and just over three-quarters had a joint health and safety committee. As we have seen already, union-based employee representatives played a significant role in the design and operation of institutions of employee-shareholder governance such as trusts and employee directors.

Did these institutions of employee representation undergo any major development as a result of employee ownership? There is a variety of evidence to suggest that union-based representation was enhanced rather than diminished (as traditional critics have feared) by employee ownership (see Pendleton *et al.* 1995b). Those firms without a joint consultative committee prior to ownership conversion introduced one at conversion or shortly afterwards. Ninety per cent of firms expanded the provision of financial information to union representatives. At People's Provincial Buses, for instance, regular meetings between top management and trade union representatives added discussion of company finances and results to 'traditional' industrial relations matters. A comparison of employee-owned bus companies with the control group indicates that investment and product/marketing decisions were significantly more likely to be made jointly with employee representatives in employee-owned firms (see Pendleton *et al.* 1996: 217).[6] These findings are broadly consistent with those of Chell and Cox (1979: 27), who found that union influence on the outcomes of collective bargaining was aided by the trickle-down of information from the board via worker directors.

What impact did employee ownership have on direct participation by individual employees? There is some evidence of innovation. Seventeen per cent of firms had quality circles or similar, and 30 per cent had a Total Quality Management scheme or similar. Forty-three per cent had team briefing or similar downwards communications. Fifty-eight per cent had an employee suggestion scheme. In virtually every case these innovations were introduced after employee ownership conversion. We compared the incidence of these forms of participation in bus companies with that in the control group of companies, and found that they were slightly more widespread in the employee ownership group. In most instances these differences were not significant but TQM schemes were significantly more likely to be found in employee ownership firms (see Pendleton *et al.* 1996).[7]

There is also little difference in the provision of information to employees in employee-owned bus companies compared with the control group of firms. We asked firms in each group whether information on a range of issues was passed to union representatives and the workforce at large. Table 7.3 presents the results.

Table 7.3 indicates that in the control group of companies the incidence of transmission of information to union representatives and the workforce as a whole is more or less the same. In employee ownership firms the level of provision of information to the workforce is higher though not significantly so. By contrast, there is significantly higher provision of information to union representatives in the employee-ownership firms. These results further confirm the interpretation so far that in bus companies there was limited development of direct participation by employees (or shareholders) as a result of employee ownership. Instead, employee representatives, who played an instrumental role in the design of participation institutions and procedures, were the main beneficiaries of any expansion in participation. They also tended to have a central role in employee-shareholder governance, which was mainly representative rather than direct in nature. In this way, employee representation and employee-owner governance tended to be linked.

What are the effects of this configuration of participation and governance on employee influence? We attempted to address this issue by seeking evaluations of the role of trustees, union representatives, and employee

Table 7.3 Information provision by management to union representatives and the workforce (percentage of firms)

Issues	*Union representatives*		*Workforce as a whole*	
	EO[a]	*Control*	*EO*	*Control*
Productivity	67	15***	30	18
Labour costs	87	30***	36	28
Sales	75	28**	55	31
Company finances	81	37**	45	21

Notes
[a] EO=employee-owned.
*** Chi-square significant at 0.001.
** Chi-square significant at 0.01.

directors in nine bus companies. Sixty 'key respondents' were asked to evaluate the influence of each group across a range of issues on a 1 to 5 scale where 1 equals 'very high influence' and 5 equals 'very little or no influence'. The results are presented in Table 7.4.

The reference point for these results is the influence of top managers. As Table 7.4 shows, this group has very high influence indeed on all issues except 'operational' labour management decisions such as work organisation and labour deployment.[8] The trustees have very little influence on labour management and industrial relations issues. They have slightly more influence on strategic decisions such as investment, and also on issues connected with the recruitment and pay of top managers. To some extent this set of findings is consistent with conventional models of corporate governance – as major owners they have some impact on key strategy decisions and on top management remuneration. Union representatives have more influence over labour management decisions than over what can be viewed as typical issues of governance. They have little influence over strategic decisions, and even less on those affecting management. We cannot tell from this analysis whether employee ownership has increased the influence of union representatives over issues outside labour management but these levels of influence, albeit limited, are higher than those found in other studies. Wilson *et al.* (1982), in their study of 150 top decisions, found that in the vast majority of cases unions exercised very little or no influence at all.

Table 7.4 Influence of trustees, union representatives, employee directors, and top managers in decisions (mean scores (standard deviations))

Decision type	*Trustees*	*Union representatives*	*Employee directors*	*Top managers*
Staffing	4.61 (0.89)	2.45 (1.37)	3.00 (1.41)	1.12 (0.49)
Work organisation	4.72 (0.72)	1.64 (1.08)	3.72 (1.23)	1.84 (1.12)
Pay	4.72 (0.78)	1.59 (1.17)	2.76 (1.64)	1.03 (0.26)
Labour deployment	4.80 (0.54)	2.24 (1.41)	3.88 (1.11)	2.09 (1.29)
Safety	4.27 (1.13)	1.54 (0.99)	3.22 (1.52)	1.55 (0.97)
Investment	3.52 (1.69)	3.65 (1.29)	1.89 (1.32)	1.03 (0.18)
Divestment	3.43 (1.80)	3.38 (1.38)	1.83 (1.15)	1.08 (0.53)
Product and marketing	4.38 (1.05)	2.83 (1.31)	2.44 (1.38)	1.28 (0.63)
Promotions	4.69 (0.87)	4.62 (0.81)	3.67 (1.50)	1.14 (0.57)
Management recruitment	3.50 (1.70)	3.87 (1.39)	2.05 (1.31)	1.29 (0.91)
Management salaries	3.62 (1.71)	4.12 (1.35)	2.00 (1.37)	1.52 (1.16)
N	*60*	*60*	*20*	*60*

Worker directors display high levels of influence on issues outside labour management, especially investment, divestment, and management salaries. These findings contrast with the literature, which finds, to use Batstone's words, that 'worker directors have little affect on anything' (1976: 35). In general terms the discrepancy between our results and those found in the earlier literature on worker directors is likely to be explained by the presence of employee ownership in our firms. This provides a legitimate role for worker directors based on 'conventional' notions of property rights. The strong links to local trade union structures is also likely to be a factor in our firms, given that the literature has suggested that these linkages are a necessary if not sufficient condition for worker director influence (Batstone *et al.* 1983; Stern 1988). We believe also the convergence of management and union objectives for employee ownership is likely to be an important factor in the comparatively high levels of employee director influence. This possibility will be considered in the next section.

Before we consider the reasons for the configuration of participation and governance in bus companies, we need to outline the structures in the small number of other companies we have included in the 'representative' group. Since these other firms are rather diverse in character it is difficult to generalise about them, other than to reiterate that their workforces were deeply involved in the conversion to employee ownership. The structures of governance and participation reflect this involvement. These structures, however, are quite diverse in character. Of this group of firms, Tower Colliery is most similar to the bus companies. When Tower was acquired by its employees, two employee directors were appointed to the company board (of six directors).[9] Unusually, one of the worker directors also has an executive role (as Director responsible for Personnel), though one that is outside the main 'line of command'. Although the worker directors are in a minority, the Articles protect their role by requiring the presence of both at board meetings when major items are discussed and agreed. Like the bus companies, the worker directors came from a background of union office and activity. A further similarity with the bus companies is that the management prerogative has continued to be emphasised after the buy-out (partly for safety reasons) and there has been little change in direct employee participation. There are, however, quarterly (non-voting) employee-shareholder meetings in addition to the formal Annual General Meeting. Union membership continued unchanged after the buy-out, with the National Union of Mineworkers retaining 100 per cent membership of face-workers.[10]

The St Luke's advertising and design agency has a very different configuration of participation and governance structures from bus companies or Tower Colliery but certain core principles are more or less the same. In this case, elected trustees have a key role, especially in provision of welfare benefits. The trustees established a pension scheme for employees and a system of health checks for employees. They also review the performance of top managers and oversee the operation of the performance appraisal system (though they do not have any operational involvement in it). Meanwhile, the board (composed of one executive director and one trustee) has little operational role. The primary role of the trust differentiates St Luke's from the other firms in the representative category but the emphasis on employee-shareholder representation on key decision-making organs and the linking of employment and ownership is similar to other firms in the group. Unlike the bus companies, however, there is very considerable employee involvement in task-level decisions. Furthermore, there is no union representation at St Luke's.

The final case we mention here is that of Barry Stevedores, a stevedoring co-operative that was based in Barry, South Wales. As a firm based on co-operative principles and structures (an equal share of ownership was held by each employee-owner), governance took a different form from other 'representative' firms. Directors were elected from the workforce and could be subject to regular re-election by them. Likewise, the non-professional trustees on the QUEST were all elected from the workforce. Minutes of the monthly board meetings were published in the workplace, and regular meetings were held between all employee-owners and directors. One consequence of the system of governance at Barry was an end to active union representation. Although all employees maintained their union membership, collective bargaining over pay ceased to take place because pay levels could be determined directly by the workforce in conjunction with their elected directors. Despite the novel features of this firm, once again there was a close integration of employment and ownership in the structures of participation and governance, and an emphasis on representation of employee-owner interests.

Influences on the pattern of participation and governance in representative firms

The pattern of participation found in employee ownership firms in the bus industry tended to be primarily representative in character, and tended to occur in the employee and employee-shareholder representation channels. We suggested earlier that the design of participation structures in employee ownership firms (or indeed anywhere else) is likely to be the outcome of the interplay of the objectives and philosophies of the actors primarily involved in the conversion to employee ownership. In the bus companies' case, the two main groups of actors were those senior managers mounting the buy-out and trade union representatives. As suggested in an earlier analysis (Pendleton *et al.* 1996), the novelty of this interplay is that two apparently contradictory ideas, namely management's right to manage and employee's rights to determine company policy, have converged to generate agreement on a particular configuration of participation and governance.

Managerial objectives for participation were influenced by several important considerations. One, as we saw in Chapter 5, managerial commitment to employee participation as an integral element of the conversion to employee ownership was fairly weak. Conversion was sought for reasons other than improving the involvement of employees in decisions about their working lives. Two, the technological and operational characteristics of bus operations (a large proportion of employees spend a major proportion of their working day away from the 'workplace') placed constraints on the type of participation that could be readily developed. Three, high levels of union membership and well-developed structures of union representation meant that deep involvement of unions in the post-conversion structures of employee involvement was inevitable. Four, managers hoped that employee involvement in ownership would lead to more positive attitudes to the firm and management, and wanted to be able to harness these without their getting intertwined with more traditional collective bargaining concerns, which might dilute or pollute them.

Overall, the primary objective of managers was to retain 'conventional' structures of management and to avoid the threats to efficiency associated with workers' co-operatives. This meant a preference for representative forms of involvement rather than more direct forms. The danger of employee ownership, as expressed by managers in interviews, was that employees would exploit their ownership rights to claim a much greater say and involvement in routine management activity, especially on issues that directly affect them such as staffing and labour deployment. This problem was well described by a worker director:

> a lot of people thought that they would be able to make decisions on everyday matters that are basically the management prerogative . . . we never envisaged that they would have their say on everyday things – this is a management function. It's difficult to get people to realise it's not a co-op.

To prevent this kind of unpredictable 'interference' in management activity, managers believed it preferable to channel any employee demands for a greater say primarily through representative institutions and procedures.

In the bus industry, this inevitably meant that unions would be deeply involved in the design and operation of participation and governance institutions. Indeed, given managerial objectives, this was highly desirable for a number of reasons. Senior union representatives had substantial experience of operating institutions and procedures and could, on the whole, be relied upon to be 'responsible' and 'realistic' in the new context of employee ownership. Furthermore, union representatives were unlikely to seek an active role in management for fear of compromising their independence as defenders of *worker* interests.[11] Finally, as active participants in these buy-outs, union representatives were viewed as supportive of the principles underpinning them, and were thus seen to be committed to their success (see Pendleton *et al.* 1996).

Although managers accepted from the outset the central role of union involvement in representative participation, the separation of any innovations in participation and governance from traditional collective bargaining institutions was seen as fundamentally important. Managers wanted to avoid contaminating the potentially integrative and motivational effects of employee share ownership with the conflictual elements of 'traditional' industrial relations activity. Thus, innovations in governance were kept procedurally separate from employee representation. This concern may also explain the limited development of 'purely' shareholder forms of involvement. If shareholder involvement had been more developed, it is possible that concerns emanating from employment would have been carried over into shareholder institutions, and that this would have weakened any positive effects on employee attitudes emanating from share ownership.

There were also advantages to employee representation in the boardroom from a management point of view. If employee directors had not been present, employee-shareholders would have had to look to executive directors to carry out their wishes. But as these two groups were also in an authority relationship with each other via the employment relationship this could have set up a confusing and conflicting set of power relationships. On the one hand, directors would be answerable to employee-shareholders. On the other, employees would be responsible to directors as executive managers. Having employee directors in the boardroom focused employee-shareholder pressures in governance onto them, leaving executive directors free to manage employment and work relations in more or less traditional ways.

Given that employee directors were perhaps desirable (from a management point of view) and arguably inevitable in most cases, managerial concerns focused instead on the form that this type of representation should take. Various protections were sought by managers. In most cases, executive directors held a majority position on the board. Where employees held a majority of the equity, top managers sought protections such as 'golden shares' and restrictions on the exercise of employee voting powers. Managerial concerns also affected the role and function of employee directors. Thus, the potential role of employee directors as communicators (and supporters) of board decisions to the workforce was emphasised, and in some cases explicitly incorporated in the Articles of Association (as shown earlier in the chapter).

A critical feature of employee ownership in the bus industry was the coincidence of managerial and union objectives for participation, albeit for different reasons. Whereas managers desired to maintain 'managers' right to manage', unions sought participation structures that maintained some degree of union control whilst at the same time limiting the capacity of new institutions to compromise the traditional union role. Unions were able to achieve these objectives because they cohered at critical points with those of management and because of their deep involvement in organisational redesign.

The primary objective of union representatives for conversion to employee ownership was to protect their companies, jobs, and conditions of employment during privatisation. Employee ownership was a means to an end rather than a desired goal in itself. Unions sought to protect existing institutions of representation, both as an end in itself and as way of preserving prevailing terms and conditions of employment. A larger vision of employee involvement was notable by its absence, and indeed a recurrent anxiety was that any expansion of employee or shareholder involvement might undermine existing structures. The new institutions and procedures of involvement sought by union representatives therefore tended to dovetail with traditional industrial relations institutions.

Shop stewards played a major role in the design of participation and governance institutions. Despite the decentralised nature of this process, union approaches were similar in all cases, notwithstanding the decision taken in a minority of firms not to have employee representatives on the company board. Imitation effects were of considerable importance given the novelty of employee ownership in the industry. For instance, the buy-out committee at Chesterfield Transport visited Peoples' Provincial Buses, Yorkshire Rider and Busways for advice and information. Whilst they were mounting their buy-out they were visited by members of the buy-out committee at Merseyside Transport and South Yorkshire Transport.

Shop steward objectives were to expand the role and influence of employees in key management decisions. Union representatives believed that employee-shareholders, both as employees and owners, had *rights* to determine how their firm was run. But concerns about the possible impact of participation tended to set boundaries to new institutions. Union representatives shared the fears of managers that greater direct involvement either as employees or shareholders could interfere with management functions and the 'right to manage'. This anxiety originated from recognition of management sensitivities and the need to ensure that managers were committed to the principles of the buy-out. Union representatives also perceived that protection of employee and shareholder interests depended on the firm being managed professionally and efficiently.

A paramount consideration for local union representatives was that employee ownership should not undermine the union role by weakening employee attachment to unions or by encouraging employees to establish alternative forms of representation to unions. If such developments took place, there was always a danger that managers might manipulate these processes to undermine union representation. Unions were therefore uneasy about such institutions as shareholder forums, and this helps to explain the limited incidence of them in bus companies. Forrester (1990) reports on two seminars held for shareholders at Yorkshire Rider early on in the ESOP to report back on recent ESOP developments and to answer questions. One member of the ESOP liason committee commented,:

> it was good that so many people were interested but it was a worry at the same time. We (the TGWU) had stamped out management's team briefings a few years ago, and now, here we were with a Sunday meeting that was a bit like a mass quality circle.
>
> (quoted in Forrester 1990: 10)

A further consideration was that expansion of involvement and representation through the union itself was fraught with dangers. This derived from long-standing anxieties in the union movement about workers' co-operatives. If unions become representatives of owners, their independent role as a defender of workers' interests may be compromised. If, for instance, they are party to a strategy of retrenchment it becomes difficult for them to provide full protection against the threat of redundancy for their members as employees (Pendleton *et al.* 1995b). Research in the US has highlighted how this may damage unions' interests over time. Stern and Hammer (1986) have drawn attention to a 'yo-yo' effect, whereby union actions oscillate between co-operation with managers, based on a fusion of employee and ownership interests, and conflict, as unions return to more traditional representative functions. Over time the swings between co-operation and opposition gradually discredit the union amongst its members and potential members. Similar considerations apply to employee representation on the board, and direct union involvement in management. Unions or employee directors may be incorporated into management and lose their capacity as independent defenders of employee interests (Clegg 1960; Brannen *et al.* 1976). This was the reason why worker directors were not introduced in Clydeside Buses. In the view of our respondent, the TGWU convenor (who apparently had a very substantial influence on the design and operation of the buy-out) 'felt that if there were worker directors they would get separated from the workforce and sucked into management'.

Given these concerns and the desire to have a greater employee role in decision-making, union representatives in most of the bus companies adopted a 'third way'. They sought new forms of representation, not direct involvement, which were separate from traditional forms of employee representation but which at the same time was linked to them. The concern was to keep the institutions of collective bargaining procedurally separate from those of corporate governance so that unions' collective bargaining endeavours were not contaminated by new pressures originating from employee ownership. For instance, in all but one case, worker directors were precluded from involvement in collective bargaining. The norm was for worker directors to be asked to resign any union positions in the firm on appointment to the board. But to prevent new institutions, such as worker directors and trustees, from building an independent power-base, unions used a number of mechanisms to maintain control, such as union attendance at board and trust meetings, union selection or screening of directors and trustees, reports from directors to union branches etc. The 'shadow board' system provided for a means of unions to scrutinise board decisions and activities without actually being party to the decisions themselves. The detailed design of the new forms of employee-shareholder representation therefore reflected union concerns to exert control on the management and direction of the firm whilst at the same time maintaining some distance from the institutions of management and corporate governance.

Overall, then, there has been a convergence of union and management objectives in the design of representational structures on conversion to employee ownership, albeit from quite different starting points. The micro-political processes occurring during the transition to employee ownership led to structures of representation, participation, and governance which did not have the dire effects on union functions and representation predicted by many to result from employee ownership.

'Risk-sharing' companies

The 'risk-sharing' group is composed of nine firms that are essentially management buy-outs. The average level of employee ownership (18 per cent) is considerably lower than in the representative or paternalist groups. Given the predominance of managers in mounting these buy-outs, we predicted earlier that employee ownership would lead to few innovations in the area of governance but that there may be some innovations in direct employee participation aimed at improving employee commitment and performance. We present here the main findings concerning the presence of institutions of participation and governance. It should be borne in mind throughout that the small numbers of firms involved inhibits broader generalisations about this group.

Employee benefits trusts are less prevalent in this group of firms because of the greater difficulties of securing leverage (see Chapter 5). Of the four firms with an EBT, only one had any employee-owner representation on the trust. In this case employee trustees, who were elected by employees, constituted one third of the trustees. Employee directors were also less common than in the representative group. Two of the nine firms had an employee director, and in each case they constituted 25 per cent or less of the board. None of these firms had any external non-executive directors to represent employee-owner interests, and in none of them were any executive directors appointed from the workforce. In one case the employee director was selected by employees, and in the other by employee-shareholders. In just two cases was there a shareholder meeting or forum in addition to the AGM (in one case these were quarterly, in the other they were half-yearly). Overall, the main conclusion that emerges from this group is that there was little if any innovation in the area of employee governance. The rights of employees as owners were exercised separately from their role as employees.

Unlike the representative group, institutions of employee representation were either absent or not well developed. Unions were recognised for collective bargaining in four out of the nine firms, and a works council or joint consultative committee was present in only two. We examined the extent to which various issues (labour deployment, investment decisions etc.) were jointly determined with employee representatives in the risk-sharing group and the control group, and found that there were no significant differences between the two. Although representative participation was under developed compared with the representative group, we anticipated that direct forms of participation might be more popular. As the numbers are small it is difficult to be conclusive, but on the whole direct participation does not appear widespread. Two firms had introduced quality circles or similar quality groups, two had introduced a suggestion scheme, and three had introduced a TQM scheme. In every instance, this had taken place after the conversion to employee ownership. Some firms introduced more than one form of participation but the overall picture suggests neither that forms of participation were spread across all or more firms in this group nor that they were concentrated in a minority of firms. Downward communications mechanisms were more common, with six firms (i.e. two-thirds) having introduced team briefing. Although the incidence of this briefing appears to be more common than in the representative group, the range of information provided may have been less. Only one firm communicated information on productivity, labour costs and company finances to employees (one firm also passed information on finances to union representatives). Taking this information together it is not surprising that there are no differences between the risk-sharing group and the control group in the level of influence perceived (by management) to be possessed by employees (or their representatives) over a range of issues.[12]

The limited development of shareholder governance and employee participation in this group of firms is perhaps not surprising when the circumstances of conversion are considered. As was outlined in Chapter 5, unions or other employee representatives tended not to be involved in these conversions, even where unions were recognised. Instead, these conversions were more or less exclusively organised by managers. As we also saw in Chapter 5, belief in the desirability of employee participation was even less developed amongst these managers than amongst those in the representative group. Since many of the firms in this group were new firms without well-established trading records, securing loan finance to mount buy-outs was not easy. In the circumstances, managers took on a high level of risk. To some extent they attempted to transfer some of this to employees by inviting them to subscribe to shares. However, whilst these managers wanted to provide incentives to employees, enhancement of employee control rights posed the danger that employees might impede the effective management of the firm. For this reason, no new governance institutions were created, and employee shareholding functioned more or less entirely separately from employment. Within the employee relationship itself, managerial participation initiatives tended to concentrate on downwards information provision, such as team briefing, which might be expected to lead to improved awareness amongst employees but which did not obstruct the process of management.

'Paternalist' firms

Employee ownership in paternalist firms comes about because owners (not managers) choose to share ownership with their employees. The reasons for transferring ownership are usually a combination of philanthropy and a concern to protect the firm (and its employees) from predators. Average levels of employee ownership are high in this group: 58 per cent. The level of total insider ownership is much higher with an average of 95 per cent (higher than the representative group). The primacy of owner concerns in the transition to employee ownership tends to lead to a distinctive pattern of governance and participation. In particular, new forms of employee-shareholder participation tend to be created but these take a different form to those in the representative group. Once again, however, we need to sound a note of caution about the small numbers of firms involved.

The distinguishing feature of this group of firms is that new institutions were created for the expression of employee-shareholder concerns but few opportunities were developed for the realisation of control *rights*. In five out of the ten cases a 'partnership council' (or body with a similar title) had been created for the articulation of employee-shareholder views and interests. These bodies were designed to co-ordinate shareholder views and pass them onto management, but in most cases they had no formal role in management as such or rights to determine policy. A respondent outlined the function of the Partnership Council in his firm:

> They meet quarterly and are not a negotiating body in any way whatsoever but they do advise on the operation of the share scheme itself and are given presentations on how the company is doing. . . . It acts as a means of communication between employees and management. For example, at the annual general meeting they will be highly involved and will receive questions to be asked at the AGM if the employee doesn't wish to stand up on his own behalf and deal with that.

In a similar vein, at the Baxi Partnership prior to a set of reforms in the early 1990s, the Partnership Council primarily functioned as a body to receive information from top management.

Employee directors were present in just two cases. In one of these, the employee directors were appointed by the partnership council; in the other they were appointed by management to represent employee-shareholder interests. All ten firms in this category had an employee benefits trust, and employee representatives were present on seven of these. In four cases employees comprised more than 50 per cent of the trust's membership. Employee trustees were either elected by employees, selected by the partnership council, or selected by management. Overall, the picture in these firms is that, unlike the risk-sharing group, there are institutions that provide some degree of co-ordination for employee-shareholders, and provide a means for communicating information between shareholders and management, but their function is for the most part advisory.

In contrast to the representative group, union representatives tended not to be involved in the design and operation of these institutions. Unions were less prevalent in this group than the representative group. They were recognised for collective bargaining purposes in four of the ten firms. A joint consultative committee was present in just one of them. In fact, the forms of employee-shareholder participation and representation in these firms appeared to challenge the role and functions of union-based representation (where it existed). One of these firms had earlier derecognised unions whilst another had recently sought to remove the bargaining rights of unions, whilst emphasising the importance of the partnership council.

Whilst we predicted that employee-owners would secure a limited role in governance in paternalist firms, we anticipated that there would be extensive development of direct employee participation. We believed that the paternalist vision would encourage direct involvement of employees in task decisions, if not in major governance decisions. The results, however, are somewhat inconclusive, given the small number of firms. Seven of the ten firms (70 per cent) have a formal system of employee briefing, and four (40 per cent) had introduced a Total Quality Management scheme or similar. Just one had quality circles or similar quality teams at the time of the research. Only one had a formal suggestion scheme. None of them had a system of job rotation. In fact, there are no significant differences in the incidence of these schemes between paternalist firms and the larger control group of firms.

The limited development of shareholder and employee influence in these companies is revealed by further comparisons with the control group. There are no issues, other than share allocation decisions, that are more likely to be determined jointly with employee representatives in paternalist firms. The greater role for employee-shareholder representatives in share allocation decisions is consistent with the findings presented above concerning the activities of partnership councils. Perhaps surprisingly, however, employees (or their representatives) have significantly higher influence on decisions about working conditions and shift-work patterns despite limited direct participation, employee representation and shareholder representation. This may reflect not the presence (or absence) of institutions but paternalistic concerns amongst owners and managers about employee welfare. There is no evidence amongst paternalistic firms of greater employee involvement or influence over strategic issues such as investment decisions.

The configuration of participation and governance in paternalist firms tends to emanate from the role and objectives of former owners. In several of these firms owners had a vision of employee ownership and participation that they were reluctant to put at risk by expanding the capacity of employees to take decisions. Writing of the founders of the Scott Bader Commonwealth and John Lewis, Purkiss noted that the 'single-minded seekers of a more democratic economic order were themselves autocratic and intolerant personalities' (Purkiss 1991: 71). Bader wrote into the Constitution of the Commonwealth that both he and his son should be directors for life. However, a tension can develop in these companies between the philosophy of democracy and the actual practices of participation and governance (see Pendleton *et al.* 1995a). Periodically, an employee ownership 'crisis' developed in these companies, when some incident led employees to challenge the limited rights conferred upon them by employee ownership. This could lead to further democratisation in these firms. A good case in point here is the Baxi Partnership, where at the beginning of the 1990s the workforce appeared to be disillusioned and discontented with employee ownership. This set in motion a chain of events which led to a greater role in governance and employee representation for the Partnership Council and the introduction of employee directors to subsidiary company boards.

'Technical' ESOPs

We have outlined earlier (in Chapter 5) how the objectives behind the creation of ESOPs in this group centred on 'technical' reasons rather than a desire to extend employee ownership. Firms in this category faced the danger of infringing ABI and Stock Exchange regulations on share scheme new issues, and therefore created ESOPs to acquire their own shares on the open market. Whilst these firms were highly committed to the use of employee share schemes as a form of employee involvement and remuneration, ESOP creation in itself was not a measure to enhance employee participation.

There were therefore no innovations in employee governance in these firms. The EBTs tended to be operated by financial institutions and located offshore, with no employee representation or involvement in trustee selection. We came across just one employee trustee who had been appointed by management to forestall any union interest in trust representation. In contrast to many of the representative and paternalist firms, employee shareholders did not have any explicit rights (above their formal legal rights as shareholders) written into the company Articles, and there was no employee representation on the company board. In short, as we described it earlier:

> any rights that employees choose to exercise as shareholders are, in effect, entirely separate from their role as employees and are exercised

> through traditional institutions of corporate governance e.g. the annual general meeting. Since they comprise a very small minority of the owners they have little or no influence on the direction of the firm.
>
> Pendleton *et al.* 1995a: 52)

Summary

This chapter has uncovered substantial differences between sub-classes of ESOP and employee-owned firms in their participation and governance arrangements. The most advanced forms of employee-shareholder governance were to be found in the 'representative' category. Governance innovations were interlinked with long-standing representative forms of employee participation, and we have suggested that both benefited from its relationship with the other. By contrast, there was little development of direct employee participation in these firms after ownership conversion. There was little innovation in either employee-owner governance or employee participation in the 'risk-sharing' group. In the 'paternalist' group there was some development of shareholder representation and involvement, but little emphasis on governance rights. Finally, in the 'technical group' there was no development of either employee participation or employee-shareholder governance associated with the ESOP. The critical influence on the configuration and development of participation and governance systems was the objectives, interests, and philosophies of those involved in the creation of employee ownership

8 Ownership, participation, and employee attitudes

Introduction

Achieving change in employee attitudes and behaviour has often been an important objective of those introducing employee share ownership schemes. It is thought that share-owning employees will feel greater commitment to the firm and a greater sense of identity with its aims. This will engender a greater sense of co-operation between employees, managers, and owners. Findings presented in Chapter 5 indicated that increasing employee commitment and co-operation were important reasons (for managers at least) for becoming employee-owned, even though these were not the catalyst as such for the ownership conversion.

There has been a large number of studies investigating these questions, generated by the growing use of employee share schemes in the US and UK since the mid-1970s. Overall, the evidence is mixed. Some UK studies indicate that employees feel that employee share ownership has made a difference to their views and behaviour, whilst others indicate that levels of commitment and other job attitudes vary little between employee-shareholders and those not participating in share schemes. A common explanation for the limited impact of these schemes is that employee equity stakes are too small to bring about a pronounced sense of ownership, and that few opportunities are provided for employees to translate ownership into increased control and participation in decision-making (see Pendleton 1997b). Evidence from most US studies, which indicate that employee involvement in decision-making is critical to attitudinal change, is generally supportive of this stance. However, where employees own a large proportion of company stock and where opportunities exist for greater participation in work and strategic decisions, atttitudinal change may be more marked (Kelly and Kelly 1991). For this reason, we might expect to witness evidence of widespread and substantial attitudinal change in many of the ESOPs discussed in this book.

In this chapter we explore the relationship between share ownership, participation, and employee attitudes in firms with a sizeable level of employee ownership. Employee attitude surveys were conducted in six organisations, of which five were drawn from the 'representative' group of ESOPs and one from the 'paternalist' group. Ideally we would also have conducted surveys in firms from the 'risk-sharing' and 'technical groups' but this proved not to be possible. Since firms in the representative and paternalist groups tended to introduce more participation and governance innovations than the other groups, it may be expected that employees in these types of firms would be more likely to develop more 'positive' attitudes to their firms.

Our results are strongly supportive of earlier literature in so far as we find that perceived participation in decision-making has a strong effect on employee commitment and the extent to which employee-shareholders feel like owners of their firms. At the same time, most employees do not feel that employee ownership has led to major advances in participation. However, there are pronounced occupational differences in perceptions of participation, with managers generally believing that levels of participation are greater than do manual and clerical employee-owners. Towards the end of the chapter we suggest that the widespread perception of limited developments in participation may be explained by the particular configurations of participation and governance institutions introduced in these firms at ownership conversion. As we saw in Chapter 7, important developments in representative participation and governance occurred at the strategic level in some firms but rather less innovation can be observed in relation to task-level employee participation. Since task-level direct participation is often seen to be the most salient form by employees, it is perhaps not surprising that most employees perceive that little has changed post-ownership conversion.

Since our approach has been formulated in the context of the main findings of the employee ownership literature over the years, we provide an overview of the literature on ownership and attitudes before presenting the results of our surveys.

The effect of employee share ownership on perceptions, attitudes, and behaviour

In the literature on employee share ownership several important conclusions have emerged over the last 25 years or so. The first is that employee share ownership *per se* rarely appears to lead to major changes in either individual attitudes or in perceptions that the running of the firm has fundamentally changed (see Kruse and Blasi 1997). This conclusion has emerged from several different types of research. A popular approach has been to compare the attitudes of shareholders with non-shareholders, either within the same firm or between firms, to see whether the former have higher levels of commitment and satisfaction or whether they exhibit higher levels of 'co-operative' attitudes towards management and the firm (e.g. Baddon *et al.* 1989; Bradley and Nejad 1989; Goldstein 1978; Greenberg

1980; Long 1978b; Poole and Jenkins 1990; Russell *et al.* 1979). In general there seem to be few pronounced differences between owners and non-owners. In Baddon *et al.*'s study, for instance, SAYE participants had more sympathetic attitudes to management and the firm than non-participants but the differences were small, and the overall distribution of responses between the two groups was similar. Poole and Jenkins conclude from their attitude surveys that 'profit sharing and share ownership schemes have not fundamentally altered certain basic sets of attitudes and produce personnel who no longer consider themselves to have the status of employees' (1990: 64).

An alternative approach has been to compare the attitudes of employees over time, either at various points after share ownership schemes have commenced (e.g. Long 1982; Tucker *et al.* 1989; Kruse 1984) or before and after schemes have been introduced (e.g. Dunn *et al.* 1991; Keef 1998). The results of these studies have on the whole not been supportive of the thesis that share ownership leads to positive attitudinal changes. Kruse (1984), Long (1982), and Keef (1998) found that the attitudes of shareholders became less favourable over time rather than more so. Dunn *et al.* found little sign of attitudinal movement amongst either shareholders or non-shareholders, though those non-shareholders who had considered joining the scheme at the outset had become less favourably inclined towards the firm by the time of the second survey. Only Tucker *et al.* found that employee attitudes towards the firm improved over time.

A further approach has been to ask respondents to assess the impact of employee ownership on their own attitudes or on the state of attitudes in the company as a whole. This approach tends to generate more favourable assessments of share ownership. Bell and Hanson, in their survey of over 4,000 employees in 12 firms in the mid-1980s, found that around 50 per cent of respondents believed approved profit share schemes had improved employee loyalty to the firm, and that nearly 70 per cent believed that share schemes of this type had changed their personal view of their employer for the better (Bell and Hanson 1987: 20–9). Similarly, a Policy Studies Institute investigation of employee attitudes in four companies with approved profit sharing found that 50 per cent of respondents in each company believed that they felt more like a partner in the company because of the share scheme (Fogarty and White 1988). However, not all studies generate such findings. Poole and Jenkins, for instance, found that only small minorities of employees in financial participation firms (typically under 15 per cent) believed profit share/share schemes had improved employee commitment and identity with the firm (1990: 29–31). Most employees perceived share schemes as neither successful nor unsuccessful in changing the characteristics of the company. Similarly, Wilkinson *et al.* (1994) found only about a quarter of employees believed that share ownership had a beneficial effect on the company or employees' orientation towards it.

The small proportions of equity passing to employees in most of the firms in these studies may explain why individual attitudinal change is limited and why little appears to have changed in the firm (as perceived by employees). However, where the employee ownership stake is larger, the differences between employee-owners and non-owners might be more pronounced. Long investigated this possibility in a comparative study of three largely employee-owned firms (1980). He found that the firm with the highest degree of employee ownership had higher levels of commitment and related attitudes, and that the proportion of stock held by employees within the firm is more important that the proportion of employees holding stock (1980: 736). Earlier, he had investigated the impact of share ownership in a employee-owned trucking firm, and found that satisfaction, integration, involvement, and commitment were consistently and significantly higher amongst stockholders than non-stockholders (Long 1978b). Bradley and Nejad's study of the National Freight Corporation found significant differences between shareholders and non-shareholders in perceptions of the impact of ownership on co-operation and identification (1989: 124–5).

Given these findings, attitudes to the firm and assessments of the impact of employee ownership may well be more favourable in the employee ownership firms in our study than in the majority of UK studies, where share ownership schemes were less substantial.

The second major finding from the literature is that contingent features of share ownership have a greater effect on employee attitudes than share ownership itself. This has been most clearly expressed by Katherine Klein (1987). She identified three models of employee ownership effects, and these are now widely accepted as well-grounded approaches for distinguishing the ways employee ownership may affect attitudes. The first model, which she called the 'intrinsic effects' model, proposes that the simple fact of ownership (ownership *qua* ownership) increases employees' commitment and satisfaction with the company' (p. 320). The second model is referred to as the 'instrumental satisfaction' or 'indirect effects' model, and posits a two-stage relationship between ownership and increased commitment, mediated through the capacity of ownership to increase employee participation in decision-making. The third model is referred to as an 'extrinsic' model, and suggests that 'employee ownership increases organisational commitment if employee ownership is financially rewarding to employees . . .' (p. 320). On the basis of attitudes surveys in 37 companies with ESOPs she concludes that her

> results provide strong support for the extrinsic satisfaction model of ESOP employee ownership; money matters. At the same time, the employee ownership philosophy and ESOP communications results suggest the powerful impact of management style on employee attitudes . . . ESOP employee ownership does appear to have a positive impact

> on average employee attitudes when it is coupled with significant financial rewards or participative management practices or both.
>
> (p 329)
>
> In contrast, the data offer no support for the intrinsic satisfaction model of employee ownership.
>
> (p. 327)

Distinguishing these three different ways in which share ownership may affect attitudes helps to explain the divergent but generally downbeat assessments of the impact of share ownership schemes outlined earlier. She showed that share ownership schemes in themselves do not affect attitudes, whilst any positive effects emanating from schemes are due to the capacity of schemes to enhance employee influence or generate financial returns. Thus, those earlier studies that found positive effects of ownership may be picking up the effects of changes in employee influence, but are unable to discern these. As Klein puts it:

> much of the research suffers methodological problems stemming from the use of employee ownership status or shares as an individual-level independent variable. This measure may be confounded with employee salary, tenure, status, and pre-ownership commitment to the company.
>
> (Klein 1987: 320)

The suggestion that participation in decision-making is an essential accompaniment if share ownership is to bring about attitudinal change has been supported in study after study, especially in the US. In a comparison of an employee-owned and a conventional firm, Rhodes and Steers (1981) found that employee participation was higher in the employee-owned firm, and that the greater the feeling of participation the higher the level of organisational commitment. Long also suggested that growth in participation in decision-making occurring concurrently with ownership transfer is important in determining job attitudes (Long 1979). Recently, Buchko (1993) has tested the model developed by Klein using path analysis, and his results strongly confirm the importance of employee participation in decision-making.

Movements in decision-making participation have also been drawn upon to explain deterioration in employee job attitudes. For instance, Long (1982) suggested that the decline in employee commitment registered in his longitudinal study correlates with a decline in employee participation between the two surveys, whilst Kruse (1984) argued that disenchantment with the potential of ownership to live up to expectations about employee involvement lies behind this development. In a conclusion which also summarises the implications of several other studies, Hammer *et al.* suggest that:

> though ownership of shares seems to have some effect on work-related attitudes. . . ., the critical issue is clearly the control over the means of production and its product. Stock ownership itself does not provide this control, but it is a resource which many be used to create a greater degree of industrial democracy'.
>
> (1982: 108)

Whilst the importance of participation in decision-making is the 'conventional wisdom' in recent research into share ownership, rather fewer attempts have been mounted to test Klein's extrinsic satisfaction model. Buchko (1993) attempted to test this using a much more precise measure of financial benefits (the value of individual shareholdings) than Klein (company contributions to the ESOP). He found that financial benefits had a strong indirect effect on commitment via an intervening variable 'ESOP satisfaction'. French (1987) has also argued that the financial benefit of ownership will have a pivotal role in changes in employee attitudes because employees view ownership primarily as an investment.

Based on these findings, we expect to find that the opportunities for participation in decision-making have a substantial influence on employee attitudes. We also anticipate that the value of employees' shareholdings will affect their views. However, these earlier research findings suggest that the presence of the share ownership *per se* will not have significant effects.

The third major finding from the literature is primarily a conceptual one, and relates to the way in which employee share ownership impacts on attitudes. It is suggested that share ownership and its associated features (e.g. participation in decisions) have indirect rather than direct effects on attitudes such as commitment. There is an intermediary variable between share ownership and attitudes, which might be termed 'psychological ownership' or 'sense of ownership' (Pierce *et al.* 1991). This captures the extent of satisfaction with the ESOP arrangements themselves and the salience of ownership to employees. It is based on the supposition that share ownership is unlikely to positively affect core attitudes if employees are dissatisfied with share ownership arrangements or if share ownership is unimportant to them. If, on the other hand, employees feel a greater sense of ownership, commitment to the firm is likely to increase. This type of approach has been adopted in subsequent studies by Buchko (1993) and by Pendleton *et al.* (1998). In a causal path analysis of attitudinal effects, Buchko finds that the relationship between the financial benefits of the ESOP and organisational commitment is essentially indirect, mediated by employee satisfaction with the ESOP (1993). His results suggest also that perceived influence on decision-making resulting from ownership may have both a direct effect on organisational commitment and also an indirect one via satisfaction with employee ownership. Meanwhile, the findings of the study by Pendleton *et al.* (which utilised some of the data about to be presented here) confirmed the conceptual value of this intermediary variable. The expectation, then, is that any effects of ownership (intrinsic, extrinsic, or instrumental) may be exerted indirectly through employees' 'psychological ownership'.

Drawing on these findings from the literature, several research questions can be formulated. One, do employees feel that the characteristics of the firm have changed since the employee ownership conversion? Has it led to more co-operative relationships between employees and managers, and has it led to greater effort on the part of their colleagues? Two, do employees feel that their own attitudes and behaviour have changed as a result of employee ownership (bearing in mind the methodological problems with this line of questioning outlined earlier)? Three, does employee share ownership generate psychological feelings of ownership amongst employees and, if so, is this associated with heightened feelings of organisational commitment? Four, what is the distribution and character of views about participation in decisions, and how does this influence the answers to the other three questions? We attempt to answer these questions in the remainder of the chapter. Before we do so, we provide details of the survey and the characteristics of respondents.

Share allocations in ESOPs

We utilise data derived from six companies in our research programme who agreed to participate in an employee attitude survey. Five of these firms are bus companies ('representative' group), whilst the sixth is a catering and service organisation ('paternalist' group). The proportion of shares held (directly or in trust) by employees other than top managers (or in trust on their behalf) ranged from 12.5 per cent to 66 per cent. Three of the firms were 49 per cent owned by their employees, as was common in employee-owned bus companies at the time. At the time of the survey three of the firms were recent conversions whilst the others had been employee-owned for three to four years. Five of the firms had distributed shares to employees though at the time they remained in trust on employees' behalf. In the sixth a distribution had not yet taken place but employees had been invited to subscribe to blocks of shares. These differences may of course influence the results and we attempt to control for them where appropriate by the use of company dummies.

The questionnaires were distributed to small but representative samples in each case, stratified by occupation.[1] Comparison of respondents' occupations with the known occupational profile of each firm indicates that we secured a broadly representative pool of respondents.[2] Altogether 306 useable questionnaires were returned to us, an overall response rate of 32 per cent.

A central feature of most employee ownership firms in our study has been a widespread dispersion of share ownership. Although share scheme legislation at the time allowed firms to restrict participation to those with three years' or more employment with the firm, 80 per cent of firms in our programme had an eligibility period of one year or less. Five of the six firms here required one year's employment for participation in the scheme, with the sixth (Company B) requiring three. We would expect, then, most employees to have received a share allocation. As Table 8.1 shows, the proportion of employees eligible to participate in share ownership is above 90 per cent.[3] Eligibility is evenly spread between management, clerical, and manual occupations.

As Table 8.1 indicates, three-quarters or more employees had received shares under the ESOP arrangements in five of the six firms. We believe that these figures may understate the extent of share distribution as in all cases some shares were held in trust and some employees may not have realised that shares had been allocated to them. This is not a major problem for subsequent analysis because employee perceptions of ownership, whether accurate or not, are the cornerstones of the study. No allocations of shares had yet been made in Company F and this explains the lower proportion of share-owners in this company. Employees had been given an opportunity to purchase shares and just over half of respondents had chosen to do so. The proportion of share subscribers in the company as a whole was 68 per cent so our respondents under-represent share-owners. The presence of direct share purchase mechanisms enables us to discern whether there are any differences between shares that are allocated free of charge via ESOPs and those that are directly purchased (see Trewhitt 1999a).[4]

In all cases share distribution was a function of length of service and equality. Hence tenure is a significant influence on the number of shares allocated to each individual.[5] Table 8.2 provides summary details of the share distribution in each company.

As Table 8.2 indicates, there was considerable inequality in share distributions in each company. This is potentially important as variations in shareholdings may affect employee attitudes. The overall extent of variation in distribution appears to be greatest in Companies B and C (though Company B has a more or less normal distribution). Companies C and D

Table 8.1 Proportions of employees who had received shares (percentages)

Company	*Proportion eligible to participate in the ESOP*	*Proportion in receipt of shares from the ESOP*
A	93	84
B	92	76
C	97	90
D	98	98
E	96	88
F	91	53
N=303		

Table 8.2 Distribution of shares by company (frequencies)

Company	*Smallest shareholding*	*Largest shareholding*	*Mean (SD)*	*Median*
A	125	1,075	526 (237)	500
B	3	5,880	1,832 (1790)	1,200
C	50	6,500	1,151 (1283)	865
D	30	2,850	924 (480)	750
E	100	1,800	715 (475)	750
F	300	14,000	6,312 (3839)	6,000

tend to have more 'outliers' at the top end of the distribution:[6] this is a function of very long job tenure amongst some workers in these firms.

When we look at the companies as a whole, managers were most likely to have received shares (90 per cent), followed by manual workers (83 per cent), and then clerical workers (62 per cent). However, as there are no significant differences between these occupational groups in terms of eligibility or in tenure, we believe these differences may be attributable primarily to varying levels of comprehension about share distributions rather than differences in share allocations themselves.

For 80 per cent of respondents their shares in their employing company were their only shares. A further 10 per cent had shares in one other company. Virtually all of those with shares in other companies had obtained shares during privatisation sales, and it appears that privatisation is the main source of share ownership of other firms. There were no significant differences between occupational groupings and wider share ownership: 73 per cent of managers, 75 per cent of clerical employees and 81 per cent of manual workers did not hold any other shares.[7]

Employee perceptions of the firm

In this section we consider whether employees believe employee ownership has led to changes in company practices. Specifically, we examine perceptions of co-operation, equality, participation, and financial benefits arising from employee ownership. The questions put to employees were based on those developed by Klein (1987) and Rosen *et al.* (1986), and utilised 7-point Likert scales ranging from 'strongly disagree' (1) to 'strongly agree' (7). The structure of responses is shown in Table 8.3. For ease of presentation, 'strongly agree', 'agree' and 'slightly agree' are merged into a single category 'agree' (as are the 'disagree' categories).

As is clear from Table 8.3, most employees do not feel that employee ownership has led to improvements in co-operation, equality, or participation in decisions. Substantial majorities, ranging from just under two-thirds to nearly four-fifths of respondents, disagree with these suggestions. Small minorities (no higher than about one-fifth of respondents) perceive

Table 8.3 Employee perceptions of the effects of employee ownership on the firm (frequencies)

Item	*Disagree (%)*	*Neither agree nor disagree (%)*	*Agree (%)*	*Mean (SD)*
Employees have more say in decisions (DECISION)	70	9	21	2.64 (1.76)
It gives employees a greater share of profits (PROFITS)	49	14	37	3.58 (1.97)
Employees are treated as equals (EQUALITY)	79	7	14	2.29 (1.57)
People co-operate more (CO-OPERATION)	65	14	21	2.92 (1.66)

that employee ownership has affected these matters. These results echo those of Winther (who used the same questions as we did) who finds that 'owning stock does not increase co-operation, it does not increase employee influence in decision-making and it does not change the status of an employee in the hierarchy' (Winther 1999: 277). A much larger proportion of our respondents believe that employee share ownership has given employees a greater share of the firms' profits. This reflects the reality that employee ownership had given (most) employees a greater share of the profits as the share distributions were financed out of profits. Since this is the case, advocates of employee ownership might be rather perturbed that only half of employees perceived that employee ownership had this effect.

If the intrinsic model of employee ownership identified by Klein has any explanatory force, variations in these measures would be associated with the extent of employee share ownership. We would expect that the more ownership employees have, the more likely that they are treated as equals. Furthermore, the more equity owned by individuals, the more they might perceive positive developments in the firms. To see if this was the case, the correlations between the four measures of company developments, the proportion of equity held by the workforce, and personal share ownership (constructed as a proportion of the mean for each employee's company) were investigated. Table 8.4 presents the results.

Table 8.4 shows that the proportion of equity held by employees as a whole is negatively related (significantly so in two instances) to assessments of the impact of employee ownership on employee–management relationships within the firm. Contrary to expectations from the literature, this suggests that higher levels of equity holdings do not necessarily lead to greater changes in management–employee relationships. Individual equity holdings, by contrast, are positively related with assessments of change but the relationships are not significant except in relation to the statement that employee ownership provides employees with a greater share of the profits.

Not surprisingly, those with a higher level of share ownership tend to be more likely to agree with this statement, as their shareholdings are financed out of profits. Overall, these results suggest that high levels of personal shareholdings do not lead employees to take a 'rose-tinted' view of relationships in the firm.

Since the results presented in Table 8.4 suggest that share ownership is not sufficient to modify prevailing views of the state of management–employee relationships in the firm, it is worth enquiring what might influence these perceptions. Since there is often an association between occupation and the strength of work attitudes, we examined differences between occupational groups in the responses to these questions. The results are presented in Table 8.5.

Table 8.5 indicates that the more favourable responses to the statements about the impact of employee ownership on relationships within the firm tend to come from managers. Significant differences are observed between managers and other occupational groups in each instance. This is a potentially important finding which we will come back to at various points in the chapter.

To summarise so far, perceptions of changes in the firm post-ownership conversion do not seem to be strongly or clearly related to levels of either collective or individual shareholding, but there do seem to be clear occupa-

Table 8.4 Relationships between levels of share ownership and perceptions of the effects of employee ownership on the firm (correlations)

Share measure	*Decision*	*Profits*	*Equality*	*Co-operation*
Total employee equity	−0.038	−0.130*	−0.37	−0.188***
Individual equity	0.077	0.159*	0.061	0.035

Notes
* Significant (two-tailed) at 0.05.
** Significant (two-tailed) at 0.01.
*** Significant (two-tailed) at 0.001.

Table 8.5 Occupational differences in perceptions of the effects of employee ownership on the firm (ANOVA and means)

Occupations	*Decision*	*Profits*	*Equality*	*Co-operation*
Managers	3.16[a]	4.28[b]	2.86[b]	3.34[c]
Clerical	2.59	3.73	2.15	2.24
Manual	2.46	3.33	2.11	2.90
F	4.065*	5.910**	5.840**	5.111**

Notes
[a] Significant difference between managers and manual workers at 0.05.
[b] Significant difference between managers and manual workers at 0.01.
[c] Significant difference between managers and clerical workers at 0.01.
* Significant at 0.05.
** Significant at 0.01.

tional differences in these perceptions. The conjunction of these results suggests that 'intrinsic' theories of employee ownership have weak explanatory power whilst prior orientations and attitudes of individual employees, deriving here from occupational position, may influence perceptions of the impact of ownership on the firm.

The impact of employee ownership on personal attitudes and behaviour

Bell and Hanson found that nearly three-quarters of their respondents perceived that share ownership had improved their view of their firm (1987). Elsewhere we have sounded a note of caution about these kinds of findings because those already favourably inclined towards the firm may overstate the extent of change in their own attitudes (see Pendleton *et al.* 1998). Even so, it is worth recording our respondents' responses to this kind of question, if only for comparative purposes.

Table 8.6 shows that a substantial minority (around one-third) believe that their work behaviour has changed as a result of employee share ownership: 40 per cent suggest a reduced propensity to quit, 36 per cent indicate that they are more conscientious, and just under 30 per cent suggest that they work harder. Equally, around a third disagree with the suggestion that employee ownership has changed these work attitudes and behaviours. The main exception to these results is in relation to interest in company finances: over two-thirds say that they are now more interested in finance. This is perhaps unsurprising: the centrality of employee share ownership in these firms may well raise employees' interest in financial matters if only from the perspective of maintaining employment.

It is possible that employee perceptions of the impact of share ownership on their own attitudes and behaviour will be influenced by either their

Table 8.6 Employee perceptions of the effects of employee ownership on personal attitudes and behaviour (frequencies)

Item	*Disagree*	*Indifferent*	*Agree*	*Mean (SD)*
Owning shares makes me want to continue working here (WORK-HERE)	33	27	40	4.06 (1.91)
Share ownership makes me more interested in finance (FINANCE)	15	14	71	5.16 (1.65)
I am more conscientious because I own shares (CONSCIENTIOUS)	41	23	36	3.81 (1.90)
I work harder because I own shares (WORK HARDER)	46	25	29	3.50 (1.86)

Table 8.7 Relationships between levels of share ownership and perceived changes in personal attitudes and behaviour (correlations)

Share measure	*Work-here*	*Finance*	*Conscientious*	*Work-harder*
Total employee equity	−0.071	−0.045	0.117*	0.123*
Individual equity	0.141*	0.204***	0.232***	0.207***

Notes
* Significant (two-tailed) at 0.05.
** Significant (two-tailed) at 0.01.
*** Significant (two-tailed) at 0.001.

level of shareholding or that of employees as a whole. Alternatively, occupational differences may well be the primary influence on these perceptions. Correlations between measures of ownership and these perceptions of personal change are given in Table 8.7.

These results are quite different to those for assessments of changes in the firm after ownership conversion. There are strong correlations in three instances between the level of personal shareholding and perceptions of personal attitudinal and behavioural change. In so far as these self-perceptions can be trusted (given the methodological reservations raised earlier), the level of personal share ownership does seem to make a difference. For anyone looking for favourable effects of share ownership on performance, these results will no doubt be gratifying. The proportion of collective ownership also seems to have a positive effect, though weaker, in relation to working harder and being more conscientious. A further contrast with the earlier results for perceptions of organisational change is that there are no clear differences between occupational groups. ANOVA tests (not shown here) did not uncover any significant differences between any of the three main occupational groupings.

So far the picture seems to be that managers are more likely than other employees to perceive changes in organisational relationships as a result of employee ownership but assessments of personal change in attitudes and behaviour are more closely associated with individual levels of share ownership.

Psychological ownership and commitment

If employee ownership is to bring about major changes in attitudes and behaviour, it seems likely that employees need to feel a sense of ownership. For this reason, Pierce *et al.* (1991) suggested that it is a critical intermediary between ownership and attitudinal outcomes such as commitment. Much of the previous literature has drawn attention to a similar measure – 'ESOP satisfaction' – which also acts as an intervening variable between ESOP characteristics and attitudinal outcomes (see Klein 1987; Klein and Hall 1988; Buchko 1992, 1993). Here, we use five items from Rosen *et al.*'s (1986) ESOP satisfaction measures to measure psychological ownership, as they explicitly refer to feelings and salience of ownership. For subsequent analysis they are combined into a single scale referred to as FEEL (reliability coefficient=0.8150)

As Table 8.8 shows, the proportion of respondents displaying some feelings of ownership range from around one-third to just over half (leaving aside the negatively worded item). This is similar to the proportions found in the earlier study by Pendleton *et al.* (1998), larger than those in Poole and Jenkin's (1990) study but considerably lower than those in the research by Rosen *et al.* (1986) in the United States. Here, the value of the means indicates that the feelings of ownership displayed by those viewing employee ownership positively are not that strong, especially on the item which asks directly about feelings of ownership. In fact on this particular item the strength of feelings amongst those disagreeing with the statement about feelings of ownership is more intense. The mean for the combined FEEL scale is just slightly positive.

Although Table 8.8 indicates that positive feelings of ownership tend to be confined to a minority (albeit a substantial one) of the workforce, there are very strong relationships between feelings of ownership and the measures of perceived individual and organisational changes reported earlier, as shown in Table 8.9. The correlation coefficients are significant at 0.000 in every instance, and range from 0.496 at the lowest to 0.789 at the highest. Those who display feelings of ownership tend to perceive more equality, co-operation, and employee influence in the firm, and also are more likely to report that they have changed their own attitudes and behaviour as a result of employee ownership.

Since both earlier work and these results suggest that psychological ownership is of prime importance, it is worth addressing what makes

Table 8.8 Attitudes to ownership (frequencies)

Item	*Disagree*	*Indifferent*	*Agree*	*Mean (SD)*
Because of employee ownership my work is more satisfying	41	26	35	3.74 (1.79)
I feel like I own part of the company	52	17	31	3.34 (1.94)
It is important to me that this company has a share ownership scheme	17	31	52	4.69 (1.71)
I am proud to own hares in this company	19	36	45	4.51 (1.71)
I do not care for employee ownership at this company	63	20	17	2.99 (1.69)
FEEL (combined variable)	–	–	–	4.25 (1.34)

Table 8.9 Relationships between feelings of ownership and perceptions of individual and organisational change (correlations)

Individual change		*Organisational change*	
Work-here	0.789***	Decision	0.510***
Finance	0.602***	Profits	0.588***
Conscientious	0.554***	Equality	0.496***
Work-harder	0.579***	Co-operation	0.545***

Note
*** Significant (two-tailed) at 0.001.

employees feel like owners. As we noted earlier, Klein (1987) and Buckho (1993) identify three possible sets of determinants. These are summarised here, along with details of the type of variables used to measure them.

- *Intrinsic* – the intrinsic perspective suggests that the fact of share ownership itself should generate psychological ownership. The greater the level of employee ownership, the greater the levels of psychological ownership. Following Klein, we use the proportion of company equity held by the employees as a measure of this. An alternative measure is the extent of individual share ownership, as measured by the variation about the mean for each company, on the intuitively plausible grounds that the more of something that is possessed by someone, the more that person will feel that they possess it.
- *Instrumental* – in Klein's work this refers to the capacity of ownership to bring about desired changes in employee influence and participation in decision-making. To measure instrumental effects we use a scale (PARTICIPATION), composed of four items, which records the perceived effect of employee ownership on participation in various aspects of company policy and management (reliability coefficient=0.8694).
- *Extrinsic* – in Klein's study this refers to the financial benefits of employee share ownership. Klein used the size of the contribution made by the company to the ESOP trust to release shares for employees, and value of returns from shares. Whilst the latter displayed no clear relationship with attitudes, the former did, leading Klein to emphasise the importance of financial benefits from ownership. Other studies have used more direct measures of extrinsic benefits such as the value of personal shareholdings (French and Rosenstein 1984; Buchko 1993).

There are two ways in which extrinsic ownership could be measured here. One is employee assessments of the value of their shares. Unfortunately, over a third of employees did not know how much their shares were worth and, though this is an interesting finding in its own right, it substantially reduces the number of cases for multivariate analysis. Therefore we do not use it here. The second approach is to use actual share values, and to multiply the number of free shares allocated to each individual by the share value at the time of the survey. This measure is an imperfect one, however, as respondents may be unfamiliar with actual values, and hence it cannot be assumed that actual values will be perceived as such. It is interesting to note that the correlation between actual and perceived value is not especially high ($p=0.162$ significant at 0.048).

We assessed the relative importance of these potential determinants of psychological ownership using multiple regression analysis. In the regressions controls for personal characteristics such as age, sex, and job tenure were included as these might exert a prior influence on ownership feelings. A dummy was included for occupation of a management position, reflecting the potential importance of occupation as an influence upon psychological ownership.[8] To make explicit the contribution of each of the main variables the regression was performed in a series of steps, noting the change in fit of the model at each stage.

The findings in Table 8.10 suggest that participation and the size of individual shareholding are the most important influences on feelings of ownership. Participation is especially strong, with a coefficient of 0.370 (t-value=5.659) and a change in model fit of 0.123. This provides strong support for the instrumental satisfaction argument about employee ownership, and is entirely consistent with the findings of the previous literature. However, the significantly positive effect on the size of the shareholding (even after controlling for tenure) is a novel finding as it provides support for the intrinsic model of ownership. The more shares individuals have, the more likely they are to feel like owners. This effect is less strong than the instrumental effect, as measured by the change in model fit and beta coefficient. However, like Klein, we find that the overall proportion of company equity held by the workforce does not have a significant effect on feelings of ownership. Whilst consistent with earlier literature, this might be seen as a surprising finding since, intuitively, the larger the stake held by employees the more they might be expected to feel ownership of the firm. These results suggest though that the level of the individual's stake is much more important.

A further important difference from the findings of Klein (1987), French (1987), and Buchko (1993) is that the extrinsic measure does not have a significant effect on psychological ownership. The improvement in model fit resulting from the addition of this measure is very small. We cannot readily explain this finding but suspect that it may reside in the character of share ownership in these firms. In all cases, firms were privately owned and shares were not readily tradable. Employees could only realise the value of their shares by leaving the firm, when they could be sold back to the trusts. In any case, shares were held in trust rather than directly by their beneficial owners. So, whatever the formal value of shares, actual or perceived, it may not have been salient to employees as it could not be readily realised (see Pendleton *et al.* 1998).

Table 8.10 Determinants of 'feelings of ownership' (FEEL) (multiple regression)

Variable	*Beta coefficients (T-values) Step 1*	*Step 2*	*Step 3*	*Step 4*
Sex	0.228 (3.184)**	0.235 (3.243)***	0.160 (2.336) *	0.167 (2.433)*
Age	0.127 (1.656)	0.133 (1.770)	0.139 (1.986) *	0.143 (2.050)*
Tenure	0.053 (0.672)	−0.070 (−0.810)	−0.060 (−0.752)	−0.074 (−0.910)
Management	0.172 (2.502)*	0.154 (2.285)*	0.104 (1.650)	0.100 (1.587)
Total employee equity (%) (Intrinsic 1)	–	0.010 0.140)	0.058 (0.832)	0.023 (0.303)
Individual equity ownership (Intrinsic 2)	–	0.266 (3.453)***	0.234 (3.266)***	0.281 (3.345)***
Participation (Instrumental)	–	–	0.370 (5.6659)***	0.365 (5.570)***
Share value (Extrinsic)	–	–	–	-0.089 (−1.067)
R^2	0.099	0.154	0.277	0.281
R^2 change	0.099	0.055	0.123	0.004
F	5.219***	5.730***	10.292***	9.155
F change	5.219***	6.184**	32.025***	1.138

Notes
* Significant at 0.05.
** Significant at 0.01.
*** Significant at 0.001.

Commitment

The next step is to see whether employee ownership affects employee commitment to the firm and job satisfaction. This is not entirely straightforward as organisation commitment is a complex concept. It tends to mix together both behavioural and attitudinal components (Cooper and Hartley 1991), and also can confuse commitment to certain objects (e.g. the firm) with actions (desire to work hard) (Oliver 1990). Most studies in the employee ownership area tend to define commitment as an attitudinal construct, referring to employees' identification with and involvement in an organisation. There are usually seen to be three dimensions to this: identification with the goals of the organisation (Identification), a willingness to expend effort for the organisation (Involvement), and a desire to remain with the organisation (Loyalty). In the British Organisational Commitment

Scales (BOCS) developed by Cook and Wall (1980), these three items are measured by a six- or nine-item scale (with the latter including negatively worded items).[9]

In this study, as in Pendleton *et al.* (1998), we use slightly different measures. This is to achieve comparability with Long's studies in the late 1970s and Klein's in the mid-1980s. Thus, we have a two-item scale measuring perceptions of goal congruence with those of the firm (INTEGRATE) and a two-item scale measuring employees' sense of belonging to the firm (INVOLVE), both of which are based on Long (1978a). There is also a three-item scale measuring propensity to quit (QUIT). These are then combined together to provide an overall measure of commitment (COMMIT).[10]

As outlined earlier in the chapter, we believe that psychological ownership is likely to have an important mediating effect between ownership and these attitudes. Following Buchko (1993), we measure the direct effects of the ownership measures on these outcomes and also the additional effects of the mediating variable. In Tables 8.11 and 8.12 the first column for each dependent variable incorporates control variables relating to sex, age, tenure, and occupation, and variables for each of Klein's three types of ownership effect (intrinsic, extrinsic, and instrumental). In the second column, the second-stage results are reported. These incorporate the variable measuring psychological ownership (FEEL) in addition to those in the first stage. By approaching the analysis in this way it is possible to determine the importance of psychological ownership as an intervening factor, and also to assess to what extent the three types of ownership effect influence commitment directly.

The direct and indirect effects of employee ownership are consistent across the four measures of commitment. As with the determination of psychological ownership, the total proportion of company equity held by employees or on their behalf (Intrinsic 1) does not have a significant effect. Nor do individual shareholdings (Intrinsic 2), though this contrasts with the results in the previous section. Extrinsic effects are also notable by their absence: the share value measure is insignificant in all estimations. These results give a clear message. Employee share ownership does not directly influence employee commitment in these firms. However, individual share ownership has an indirect effect in so far as this influences feelings of ownership, which has a powerfully significant effect on the four commitment measures.

By contrast, participation in decisions is directly and significantly related to commitment in each instance. Where employee ownership is perceived to have increased employee say in decisions, there is an association with higher levels of commitment. When FEEL is included, some of these participation effects are channelled through it but significant direct effects remain, except in the case of INTEGRATE. There are some other significant relationships in these results. Age is significant in some instances, as is the occupation dummy but on the whole these are not strong or consistent results.

Table 8.11 The effects of ownership and participation on feelings of integration and involvement (multiple regression)

Variable	*INTEGRATE*		*INVOLVE*	
	Beta coefficients (T-values)			
	Step 1	*Step 2*	*Step 1*	*Step 2*
Sex	0.035	−0.050	0.044	−0.042
	(0.477)	(−0.744)	(0.609)	(−0.650)
Age	0.203	0.130	0.044	−0.030
	(2.685)**	(1.922)	(0.595)	(−0.457)
Tenure	−0.076	−0.039	−0.049	−0.011
	(−0.870)	(−0.498)	(−0.572)	(−0.147)
Management	0.147	0.096	0.183	0.131
	(2.157)*	(1.583)	(2.723)**	(2.212)*
Total employee equity (%) (Intrinsic 1)	0.028	0.016	−0.035	−0.047
	(0.341)	(0.224)	(−0.430)	(−0.661)
Individual equity ownership (Intrinsic 2)	0.053	−0.089	0.093	−0.053
	(0.590)	(−1.081)	(1.039)	(−0.657)
Participation (Instrumental)	0.295 (4.172)***	0.110 (1.623)	0.335 (4.812)***	0.146 (2.217)*
Share value (Extrinsic)	−0.057	−0.012	−0.067	−0.021
	(−0.633)	(−0.147)	(−0.755)	(−0.268)
FEEL	–	0.508	–	0.518
		(7.277)***		(7.617)***
R^2	0.162	0.348	0.188	0.381
R^2 change	0.162	0.186	0.188	0.193
F	4.532***	11.031***	5.427***	12.741***
F change		52.957***		58.012***

Notes
* Significant at 0.05.
** Significant at 0.01.
*** Significant at 0.001.

Overall the results from these two sections are very similar to those of other employee ownership studies, especially those conducted in the US Most employee-owners do not feel a strong sense of ownership but, where they do, participation in decisions is of critical importance in bringing this about. Perceived participation also has a strong effect on various measures of commitment. The proportion of company shares held by employees influences neither feelings of ownership nor commitment. In other respects, though, these results differ from previous work. Financial rewards of ownership do not seem to have a direct effect on commitment. Nor do they appear to affect feelings of ownership. The major contrast, however, is

Table 8.12 The effects of ownership and participation on propensity to quit and commitment (multiple regression)

Variable	*QUIT (reversed)*		*COMMIT*	
	Beta coefficients (T-values)			
	Step 1	*Step 2*	*Step 1*	*Step 2*
Sex	−0.022	−0.054	−0.037	−0.076
	(−0.277)	(−0.753)	(−0.475)	(−1.140)
Age	0.279	0.197	0.198	0.097
	(3.394)***	(2.575)*	(2.425)*	(1.361)
Tenure	0.068	0.142	−0.080	0.010
	(0.658)	(1.480)	(−0.774)	(0.112)
Management	−0.190	−0.086	0.141	0.060
	(−0.254)	(−1.210)	(1.857)	(0.902)
Total employee equity (%) (Intrinsic 1)	−0.065	−0.055	−0.018	−0.005
	(−0.676)	(−0.617)	(−0.189)	(−0.058)
Individual equity ownership (Intrinsic 2)	0.243	0.052	0.433	0.199
	(0.986)	(0.227)	(1.774)	(0.937)
Participation (Instrumental)	0.354	0.212	0.398	0.224
	(4.607)***	(2.826)**	(5.214)***	(3.186)**
Share value (Extrinsic)	−0.142	−0.041	−0.317	−0.194
	(−0.597)	(−0.190)	(−1.344)	(−0.953)
FEEL	–	0.419	–	0.513
		(5.288)***		(6.920)***
R^2	0.269	0.397	0.280	0.472
R^2 change	0.269	0.128	0.280	0.192
F	6.113***	9.643***	6.466***	13.095***
F change		27.966***		47.886***

Notes
* Significant at 0.05.
** Significant at 0.01.
*** Significant at 0.001.

that individual shareholdings do affect feelings of ownership, though not commitment, as we saw in the previous section.

Participation in decision-making

It is clear from the results presented in this chapter that participation in decision-making is of critical importance in determining whether employee-shareholders feel like owners of their companies. For this reason, it is worth exploring in greater depth whether employee–owners feel that the opportunities for participation have grown after ownership conversion. To do this we disaggregate the participation scale used in the multivariate analysis into its four constituent items. These are participation in task decisions, company policy decisions, pay decisions, and employment policy decisions. These correspond to the distinctions made in Chapters 6 and 7 between direct participation, governance participation, and representative participation. We then consider these items in relation to the three main occupational groupings: managers, clerical employees, and manual workers. The reason for making these occupational distinctions is that employee ownership research has repeatedly highlighted differences between occupations in perceptions of participation. Rosen *et al*'s study (1986) observed substantial differences between managers and other employees in assessments of the opportunities for involvement in decision-making. In her study of an American employee-owned airline, Wichman (1994) found that 'high status' employees such as pilots were most involved in participation programmes. Earlier in this chapter, occupational differences were correlated with perceptions of changes in company practices since ownership conversion.

Table 8.13 shows assessments of the impact of ownership on the four participation measures for each major occupational group.

Table 8.13 Occupational differences in perceptions of the impact of employee ownership on employee say in decisions (percentages)

Decisions	*Increased*	*No change*	*Decreased*	*Mean*
Job decisions				
Managers	25	61	15	3.06[a]
Clerical	12	73	15	2.91
Manual	14	58	28	2.75
F=3.579*				
Company policy decisions				
Managers	23	66	11	3.13[b]
Clerical	18	62	21	2.82
Manual	9	61	30	2.64
F=8.294***				
Pay decisions				
Managers	8	80	12	2.94[a]
Clerical	9	68	24	2.82
Manual	8	61	31	2.64
F=3.845*				
Employment decisions				
Managers	3	83	14	2.84[a]
Clerical	8	68	24	2.76
Manual	8	61	31	2.54
F=4.075*				

Notes

[a] Significant difference with manual staff at 0.05.

[b] Significant difference with manual staff at 0.001.

Table 8.13 shows that large majorities of managers, clerical workers, and manual workers believe that employee ownership had not led to any changes in opportunities for worker involvement and influence in decisions. Small proportions of employees believe that employee say had increased. However, there are significant differences between managers and manual workers in these assessments. Around a quarter of managers believed that worker say in task and company policy decisions had increased, compared with around 10 per cent of manual workers. The differences are smaller, however, in relation to pay and employment policy decisions. There are also clear differences between managers and manual workers in the proportions who believe that worker say has *declined* as a result of employee ownership. On all items, around 30 per cent of manual workers believe worker say has declined, compared with between 11 and 15 per cent of managers. Overall, the findings on the impact of ownership on participation are consistent with those findings on effects reported earlier in the chapter. Most employees feel that things have not changed but there are significant differences between managers and manual workers in these perceptions.

The largest differences between managers and manual workers are found in relation to decisions about company policy. The reason for this probably lies in the appointment of worker directors as the key institutional mechanism for employee involvement in governance. Whilst managers (especially top managers) may be acutely conscious of this innovation, rank and file employees may be relatively unaware of the impact of worker directors in decision-making. Whilst there were some attempts in some companies to make worker directors accessible to workers (by holding 'surgeries' in the canteen for instance), most of the feedback on their activities was provided to trade union branches and representative institutions, such as shop stewards' committees. Most employees did not participate directly in either of these institutions.

A critical issue in evaluating employee ownership is how much participation in decisions employee-owners actually want. If ownership fails to deliver desired increases in participation, this may have adverse effects on satisfaction with ownership or 'psychological ownership'. Several studies have suggested that a decline in job-related attitudes after employee ownership conversion may be due to this phenomenon (for example, Kruse 1984). Equally, there is evidence that employees always want more participation than they actually have, so employee ownership is not a unique phenomenon in this respect (Heller 1998). There is also considerable evidence that employee ownership does not have pronounced or clear effects on the desire for participation (see Kruse and Blasi 1997). Trewhitt (1999a), for instance, found no differences between shareholders and non-shareholders in an employee-owned bus company in levels of desire for participation.

To address the relationship between desired levels of participation and actual participation, some observers have used the notion of a 'participation gap' (e.g. Long 1979). This measures the extent to which employees' desires for participation are actually met. We calculated this measure by subtracting the score for actual participation from that of desired participation, where each was measured using a five-point scale (1=no say at all and 5=a great deal of say). Ten items were used, and on each one respondents were asked how much say or influence workers *should* have whilst the other asked how much say or influence workers *actually have*. In Table 8.14 we provide the mean scores for desired and actual participation, and for the participation gap.

Several important findings are contained in Table 8.14. One, as is usually the case, employees desire most participation in decisions that most immediately affect their day-to-day working lives (Hespe and Wall 1976; Ramsay 1976; Loveridge 1980; Heller 1998). In fact, the desire for involvement in policy decisions is significantly lower (at 0.001 in paired-sample t-tests) than that for involvement in decisions on health, safety, and working conditions. Contrary to some predictions, then, share ownership does not make involvement in policy or governance decisions more important to workers than involvement in these more immediate issues.

Two, there are high levels of correlation between each desired participation item (at 0.01 or better), indicating that the structure of responses is similar. Those seeking relatively high levels of participation on overall company issues also seek relatively high levels of participation in decisions about recruitment. Share ownership does not seem to generate a zero-sum relationship between desired involvement in governance and desired involvement in task-level decisions.

Three, as Table 8.14 clearly indicates, there is a participation 'gap' on every item. The difference between desired and actual participation is significant on each item (at 0.001 in t-tests, not shown in the table). Within this overall picture, however, there are marked differences in the structural consistency of individual responses across desired and actual participation. Although there is a significant gap between the two, actual and desired participation are significantly correlated (at 0.05 or better) for departmental

Table 8.14 Levels of desired and actual participation (means)

Decision-type	*Desired*	*Actual*	*Gap*
Company policies	3.31	1.79	1.52
Departmental issues	3.94	2.38	1.56
Own job methods	4.11	2.57	1.54
Purchase of new equipment	3.52	1.72	1.80
Changes in manning levels	3.31	1.56	1.75
Wages and bonuses	3.80	1.94	1.86
Health, safety and working conditions	4.39	2.78	1.61
Introduction of new products	3.80	2.14	1.66
Recruitment	3.00	1.52	1.48
Training	3.67	1.93	1.74

decisions, job methods, purchase of new equipment, recruitment, and training. This indicates that those who desire participation most on these items also perceive relatively high levels of actual participation. On the other items (e.g. company policy, wages etc.), actual and desired participation are less correlated. This indicates much greater variety of responses between respondents. Some of those desiring high levels of participation perceive there to be high levels of actual participation, whilst others do not. Equally, there is a split amongst those desiring lower levels of participation between some who perceive there

As it may be hypothesised that employee share ownership affects the desire for and assessment of participation, it is important to consider the influences on desired and actual participation, and the participation gap. One obvious possibility is that those with larger shareholdings will have higher desired levels of participation, especially as the earlier analysis indicated that variations in share ownership had a significant impact on feelings of ownership. Equally, earlier analysis has highlighted the association between occupational differences and perceptions of company practices. To address these issues, we selected items that corresponded to earlier survey questions on company policy, task decisions, employment policy, and pay, as well as creating combined scales out of all ten items. For each we record desired participation, actual participation, and the participation 'gap'. We then entered a range of measures into stepwise regressions to capture the strongest associations with these dependent variables. The measures chosen were personal characteristics, such as age and sex, extent of personal shareholding, dummies for each company (to capture unobserved sets of company characteristics), and occupational type.[11] We then repeated the procedure, inserting the proportion of equity held by the workforce in place of the company dummies.[12]

The findings presented in Table 8.15 are unambiguous. One, the volume of shareholding does not have a significant relationship with either the level of desire for participation or the perception of actual participation. This echoes Long's (1979) and Trewhitt's (1999b) findings that no difference could be observed between shareholders and non-shareholders in the desire for participation. Two, with just two exceptions, the management dummy has a clear and consistent relationship with desired and actual participation, and the participation gap. Managers believe that employees should have lower levels of say in decisions than do other employees. They also perceive higher levels of actual participation than do other employees, and, not surprisingly, they also perceive a smaller participation gap than do other employees.

Company characteristics are also associated with perceptions of participation, though we can only speculate as to which characteristics are relevant. The dummy for Company B is related to desired participation and negatively related to actual participation in company policy (relative to Company A). This company is the only company in the attitude survey

Table 8.15 Correlates of actual and desired participation (stepwise regressions)

Decision item (diagnostics)	*Desired participation*	*Actual participation*	*Participation 'gap'*
Company policy	Manager –** Company B *	Manager** Company F –* Company B –**	Manager –***
R^2 (adjusted)	0.046	0.057	0.072
Own job	Company C	Manager*** Company D –*	Manager –*** Company D *
R^2 (adjusted)	0.015	0.095	0.079
Manning levels	(none)	Manager*** 0.092	Manager –*** 0.068
Wages	Manager –*** Company D *	Manager *** Company D –* Company F –***	Manager –*** Company D *** Company F ***
R^2 (adjusted)	0.09	0.136	0.216
All items	Manager –**	Manager*** Company F –*** Company D –**	Manager –** Company F **
R^2 (adjusted)	0.03	0.209	0.168

Notes
In the repeated procedure, collective equity holdings are insufficiently significant to enter into any estimations.
* t-value significant at 0.05.
** t-value significant at 0.01.
*** t-value significant at 0.001.

without employee directors, and this may explain why there are higher levels of desired participation and lower perceptions of actual participation. Companies D and F record lower levels of actual participation on a number of items. It is not clear why this is so given that these companies had very similar participation and governance structures to the other bus companies in the survey. Despite these unexplained relationships, overall the results indicate that occupational position is consistently more strongly related to perceptions and desires for participation than levels of shareholding.

In the preceding analysis, perceived levels of actual participation have been used. Another way of examining this issue is to consider perceived *changes* in actual participation (i.e. the measure used in the analysis of psychological ownership) in relation to desired levels of participation. In another words, do any changes emanating from ownership conversion meet individual needs for participation. Does employee ownership help to close the 'participation gap'? This question cannot be fully addressed because ownership may increase the desire for participation (which is not measured here). With this limitation in mind, the clearest procedure seemed to be to divide the sample into two groups: those with a high desire for participation and those with a low desire, as separated at the median point. We then compare the mean scores on each of the four items measuring the extent to which employees felt that worker say had been increased as a result of employee ownership. The higher the mean score shown, the greater participation is viewed to have increased as a result of employee ownership. The results are shown in Table 8.16.

Table 8.16 provides fascinating insights. On three items (policy, pay, and employment) those with a higher desire for participation perceive smaller increases in participation as a result of employee ownership. Looking at it the other way, those with a lower desire for participation perceive a larger increase in participation. This echoes the earlier finding that those with higher assessments of actual levels of participation tend to be those who have lower levels of desired participation. These findings suggest that employee ownership appears to be imperfectly meeting the needs of employee-owners. The composition of the two desired-participation groups are consistent with the findings reported earlier. Most managers (71 per cent) and a majority of clerical workers (58 per cent) are in the low desired-participation group whilst most manual workers (58 per cent) are in the high desired-participation group.[13]

The results presented in this section provide some important findings on employee participation. Most employees do not perceive changes in worker influence emanating from employee ownership. Only a few perceive there to be an increase, whilst about a quarter of respondents suggest that employee ownership has led to a decrease in worker say. The limited impact of employee ownership on participation is consistent with the stream of results that have emanated from the US literature over the last 20 years (Kruse and Blasi 1997). The evidence presented here suggests that a large proportion of those who perceive increases in worker say are managers. When we look at perceptions of the actual level of participation, once again managers have consistently higher scores than other staff in general and manual workers in particular. Furthermore, managers believe

Table 8.16 Evaluations of increases in worker say as a result of employee ownership: comparison of those with a low and high desire for participation (means)

Item	*Low desire for participation*	*High desire for participation*	*T*
Increase in worker, say			
In company policy	2.90	2.63	2.686**
In own job decisions	2.90	2.75	1.557
In pay decisions	2.85	2.61	2.632**
In employment policy	2.76	2.52	2.602**

Note
** t-value significant at 0.01.

there should be lower levels of employee participation than do other staff. The analysis presented in Chapters 5 and 7 suggest that this arises from anxieties that worker involvement in decisions violates managerial prerogatives and impedes decision-making. The higher levels of actual involvement perceived by managers may arise from awareness of the new institutions of employee participation created alongside employee ownership, such as employee directors on the board. These results are consistent with those of Rosen *et al.* (1986: 116) who found that the presence of voting rights for employee shareholders was significantly correlated with managerial perceptions, but not worker perceptions, of worker influence.

In general, manual workers desire higher levels of worker involvement in decisions than do managers but they perceive lower actual levels and increases in involvement as a result of employee ownership. For these workers, involvement in task-related and similar decisions is clearly of most importance. The acquisition of ownership rights does not appear to have generated a set of preferences for types of participation that are different from the workforce at large, as reported in participation studies over the years. The significance of this finding has to be interpreted in the light of the advances in participation that have occurred because of employee ownership. The emphasis on developing employee-owner governance in most of the firms here is clearly at odds with what most employees actually want. It can be concluded that, as far as participation is concerned, employee ownership does not appear to meet the participation needs of employees, and furthermore it is markedly less successful in this respect for non-managerial employees. In the light of this it is not surprising that most workers do not feel a strong sense of ownership.

9 Conclusions and discussion

ESOPs and related forms of employee ownership arrived in the UK in the late 1980s and utilised structures of ownership pioneered mainly in the United States. For a while, they attracted a great deal of interest amongst politicians, business leaders, union leaders, and other opinion formers. They offered a form of organisation and governance that did not appear to suffer from the disadvantages widely thought to be associated with other types of worker ownership, such as workers' co-operatives. At the same time, they drew on approaches to financing ownership restructuring that had become common in the 1980s in both the UK and US. The highly leveraged buy-out was an especially important precursor of ESOPs. However, the number of ESOPs has remained tiny compared with the US. At the peak of their development in the mid-1990s there were probably no more than 100 or so ESOPs. Since then, the number of 'orthodox' ESOPs has declined, though this has been more than counter-balanced by the use of QUEST structures by PLCs as a 'technical' financing device to secure tax concessions for other share ownership schemes. ESOPs may well be a transitional feature of the UK economy, though employee share ownership more generally appears to be an entrenched phenomenon.

In this book we have attempted to consider why ESOPs are created, and what characteristics they have adopted. We examined the circumstances of conversion, and identified the key groups involved in transitions to employee ownership. We then outlined the forms of employee participation and governance in these firms, and attempted to assess to what extent participation and governance were interlinked. Finally, we attempted to determine the impact of employee ownership on employee attitudes to the firm, and whether employees believed that the opportunities for participation in management and governance decisions had changed as a result of ownership.

In this concluding chapter we summarise the main arguments and findings presented in the earlier chapters. Then we attempt to broaden out the discussion by considering several key issues that are found in the theoretical and empirical literature on employee ownership. The first of these concerns the nature and impact of employee participation in work decisions and governance. Then we consider the impact of employee ownership on union-based employee representation. The third section discusses the characteristics of firms with employee ownership, and how these may relate to the conversion decision. An important question here is why there are so few employee-owned firms or to use, Dow and Putterman's (1999) words, 'why capital (usually) hires labour rather than vice versa'. Are there particular characteristics or circumstances of firms that are favourable (or unfavourable) to the development of employee ownership? Finally, we assess the durability of the ESOP as a form of ownership. There is a long-established literature on producer co-operatives which suggests that they will inevitably degenerate. Here, we consider whether similar observations apply to ESOPs.

Summary of the book

In this book two key observations and arguments have permeated our analysis throughout. The first is that ESOPs display considerable diversity, even within the small group of ESOPs in the UK. The circumstances in which ESOPs are created, the reasons for their formation, the actors involved in the conversion process, the levels of employee ownership, and the institutions of participation and governance differ considerably between employee-owned firms. Similar observations have been made about the much larger group of ESOPs in the USA (Ben-Ner and Jones 1995; Kruse and Blasi 1997). The second key proposition is that the objectives, philosophies, and interests of the key actors involved in conversions to employee ownership have a critical influence on the reasons for employee ownership, the level of employee shareholding, and the forms of participation and governance adopted. These two observations are closely linked in so far as one of the main arguments of this book is that variations in ESOP structures and practices should be viewed as the outcome of the interaction of actors' intentions, philosophies, and interests.

Before we outline the main findings of the empirical research reported in earlier chapters, it is worth restating the working definitions of ESOPs and employee ownership used in this book. Any consideration of this field soon encounters terminological imprecision. There is a tendency amongst some to refer to any employee share ownership plan as an ESOP. In this book, ESOPs have been distinguished from the mass of employee share schemes (which we refer to as 'conventional' schemes). The distinguishing feature is an Employee Benefits Trust or Qualifying Employee Share Trust, holding equity collectively on behalf of the workforce. We have included a small number of firms in the study, however, who do not have an EBT or QUEST on the grounds that they passed a substantial portion of equity to employees, and that ownership conversion occurred during the same wave of conversions as ESOPs. A narrowly technical definition of an ESOP does not quite do justice to the extensive interest in new forms of employee ownership during the late 1980s/early 1990s. Equally, there are some firms who meet the strict definition of an ESOP but whose objective is a narrowly technical one focused on meeting regulatory requirements associated with 'conventional' share schemes. In fact, these are by far the largest group of ESOPs now in the UK. We have included these types of firms in the study but the evidence throughout has been that these differ in virtually every respect from the other employee ownership firms in the study. In general, the use of an ESOP in these firms does not occur as part of a major restructuring of the firm's ownership and governance. The major preoccupation in this book, however, has been restructuring of ownership to bring about a larger employee stake and, whilst they have been the most important way of doing this, ESOPs are not the only way.

We have also adopted a 'fuzzy' definition of employee ownership in the book. There is a wide diversity of employee ownership stakes in the 62 firms, ranging from just a few per cent of equity to 100 per cent. Not all employees are owners, and those that are often have unequal stakes. Most firms (51 per cent) are not employee-owned in the sense that all employees own a majority of the stock. Just under a third of firms are 100 per cent employee-owned. We have referred to all firms with some employee ownership, however large or small, as employee-owned or employee ownership firms. This usage is similar to Blasi *et al.* (1996), who define 'significant employee ownership' (in listed firms) as 5 per cent or more of total equity. In practice, virtually all of our firms are substantially owned by employees. The average level of employee ownership is 56 per cent. Only the 'technical' group of ESOPs has average employee ownership below 30 per cent. Once management stakes are taken into account, 87 per cent of our firms are majority controlled by employees. The average level of 'insider' ownership is 81 per cent, with the median point being 100 per cent.

As a form of employee ownership, ESOPs in the UK (and US) have differed in fundamental ways from workers' co-operatives. Whereas ownership is usually equally distributed amongst all employees in co-ops, in ESOPs there are usually varying levels of ownership amongst non-managerial employees. In a sizeable proportion of ESOPs, managers have ownership stakes separate from those of employees as a whole, so inequalities in ownership are even more pronounced. Idealistic philosophies of equality, self-development, and communal management that pervade many co-ops, tend to be absent or at least weakly developed amongst most ESOPs. To all intents and purposes, most are 'conventionally' organised and managed firms. Ownership is separate from employment and management in that it does not confer rights on employees to be actively involved in management or to directly control management activity on a day-to-day basis. However, there may be linkages between employee participation and employee-owner governance, though this differs between ESOPs. The different character of ESOPs compared with co-operatives reflects the differing motives behind the establishment of them. Most ESOPs are created from 'conventional' firms for defensive reasons. Cautious pragmatism has tended to be more important than idealism. In many cases, those behind ownership conversions have not even been especially ardent advocates of employee ownership.

ESOPs firms have been created in a diversity of circumstances. Nearly two-thirds, however, were created during privatisation. Of these, around two-third were bus companies. The bus industry, in fact, has been the main locus of employee ownership in recent years, though by 2000 employee ownership had virtually disappeared from the sector. A small number of firms (10 per cent) became employee-owned when their parent companies proposed to divest or shut them down. A slightly larger group (16 per cent) converted to full or employee ownership when 'paternalistic' owners wished to exit from ownership. Finally, there was a 'technical' group of ESOPs where EBT structures were utilised to obtain shares on the open market to resource commitments arising from share option schemes.

Several observations can be made about the pattern of ESOP creation. One, there are virtually no cases where ESOPs have been used by start-up firms. There was just one such firm in our study, and this firm went out of business during the course of the research. ESOPs structures are not well suited to start-ups because they can be administratively onerous (in the view of our respondents) and because the demands of acquiring external finance for physical and working capital are likely to preclude the provision of financial resources to an ESOP.

Two, the development of ESOPs has been heavily dependent on privatisation activity. ESOPs in the bus industry were created in response to government privatisation initiatives or to threats that privatisation would take place. As we saw in Chapters 3 and 4, the Thatcher Governments further assisted the creation of ESOPs by allowing closed sales and by offering price discounts to employee bids. The downturn in privatisation activity in the second half of the 1990s removed an important source of ESOP conversions. Whilst for a time in the mid-1990s it was thought that local authority direct service organisations might be suitable candidates for privatisation and employee ownership, such a development failed to materialise. Only a small number of such organisations went down this route. In fact, such organisations were not especially suitable for ESOPs since, as they usually lacked prior trading records as distinct companies, obtaining the finance to mount leveraged ESOPs was not likely to be easy. We have seen in similar firms in our study that ESOP structures tended to be used less in organisations in these circumstances, and levels of employee ownership tended to be lower than in other groups.

The development of ESOPs in the late 1980s and early 1990s took place in what Poole (1989) has called a 'favourable conjuncture'. These are sets of circumstances which arise from time to time and which provide a fertile environment for firm-level decisions in favour of financial participation. In the case of ESOPs these circumstances included a raft of share scheme legislation, an ideological emphasis on 'popular capitalism', the privatisation programme, and a context of innovation in restructuring transactions (such as leveraged management buy-outs). Once a few bus firms had formed ESOPs, there were powerful imitation effects elsewhere in the industry. Whilst privatisation was obviously not so relevant to privately owned firms adopting ESOPs, financial and organisational restructuring was an important backdrop. Awareness of the potential for damaging takeovers and rationalisation led owners to pass ownership of their firms to their workforces. Consideration of these factors highlights a unifying characteristic of most ESOPs in the UK. Most were formed as a defensive measure to protect existing patterns of employment and management in firms undergoing ownership restructuring. Unlike the US examples, ESOPs are not formed as a substitute for pay and pension benefits or as a complement to them. This is not to say that such considerations are unimportant. In 'paternalist' firms, owners used ESOPs as an additional form of reward, but this was not the primary reason for introducing employee ownership.

So, although ESOPs were formed in a diversity of circumstances, defensive and protective considerations were uppermost in most cases. Despite this, ESOPs displayed considerable variation in characteristics, and an important task in this book has been to explain this. We have argued that the philosophies, interests, and objectives of the actors involved in ownership conversions are the primary influence on the development of ESOPs. On this basis we have distinguished four categories of ESOP. The first is where employees, as well as managers, are involved in the ESOP conversions. These we have referred to as 'representative' ESOPs, because typically employee representatives are deeply involved in the conversion process and because the ESOP and its structures represent employee interests (to a certain extent). The second group we have called 'risk-sharing' ESOPs, because firms in this category are essentially management buy-outs, (though with a substantial employee ownership component). In these cases, there tends to be little involvement of employees and their representatives. In the third group, owners are the driving force for ESOP conversion. Since paternalistic concerns to protect employees are the key consideration in forming an ESOP, we have referred to these firms as 'paternalist ESOPs'. Finally, there is the 'technical' group of ESOPs, where ESOP structures are introduced by legal and financial managers to satisfy insurance and stock exchange regulations governing share option schemes. The pattern of involvement of key actors has a critical influence on the level of ownership, the form of financing, and the structures of participation and governance introduced in the ESOP.

There were clear differences in participation and governance between the four groups of firms. The basis for analysis in this area was outlined in Chapter 5. Here we suggested that it is necessary to distinguish between various forms of *employee* participation and representation, and *employee-*

owner governance. Whilst the former is concerned with employee interests as employees, the latter is concerned with their interests as owners. An interesting empirical matter is how far the two are conjoined or intertwined in practice. We found that 'representative' firms tended to introduce few innovations in direct employee participation but had well-established systems of representative participation. New structures of employee-owner governance, such as employee directors, were introduced. These tended to be closely linked with prevailing systems of *employee* representation. In the risk-sharing group there was little evidence of innovations in either employee participation or employee-owner governance, and it was argued that this reflected the emphasis on risk-sharing via participation in return rights in this group. In the paternalistic group, new forums for employee-shareholder 'voice' tended to be created but these generally lacked formal control rights. Unlike the representative group they tended to function separately from systems of employee representation. In the 'technical' group there was no evidence of any innovations in employee or owner participation associated with the ESOP, and this reflected the use of ESOP structures for 'technical' legal and financing reasons.

Finally, we investigated the impact of employee ownership on employee attitudes in six representative and paternalist firms. Here, it was proposed that employee-owners may display greater levels of commitment to the firm because of share ownership itself (*instrinsic*), the financial rewards of share ownership (*extrinsic*), and opportunities for participation provided by ownership (*instrumental*). Following Pierce *et al.* (1991), we suggested that these effects would be transmitted through 'psychological ownership'. In some respects our results echoed earlier findings, but in others they differed. Like every other study in the field, participation in decisions was a very important influence on feelings of ownership and commitment (see Kruse and Blasi 1997). However, contrary to Klein (1987) and Buchko (1992, 1993) 'extrinsic' ownership did not appear to be important. By contrast, and contrary to expectations, intrinsic ownership did affect psychological ownership. Since participation in decisions was the most important determinant of attitudes, we investigated employee desires and assessments for participation in more depth. Here, it was found that managers wanted employees to have lower levels of 'say' than did manual workers, but believed that they had higher levels of influence and involvement in practice than did other employees. Whilst this pattern of results may be typical of non-employee ownership firms as well, we suspect that the divergence in perceptions between managers and other workers may be influenced by the structures of participation and governance adopted after ownership conversion. Managers were highly conscious of new opportunities for employee 'voice' via worker directors. For workers, though, these innovations were distant from their daily working lives and, given that there were few innovations in direct participation, it is perhaps not surprising that they perceived a lesser development of participation than managers did.

In the remaining pages we extrapolate from our findings to review important issues that have arisen in the employee ownership literature.

Participation and governance

The development of participation and governance in employee-owned firms has been diverse and complex. For a large minority of firms, employee ownership has made little difference to participation and governance. In this respect our findings echo those of Blasi for the US: 'employee ownership has involved workers more in risking capital, but has not given them greater property rights or increased involvement in their firms or improved co-operation with management' (1988: 241). Hansmann too has characterised ESOPs as providing for participation in financial returns but not in decisions (1996). Yet, the majority of ESOPs in the UK (leaving aside the QUESTs that have sprung up since 1996) have led to some advances, albeit often limited, in employee participation and governance. This is especially so in the case of 'representative ESOPs', where typically employee directors or employee-shareholder committees have been introduced alongside elected trustees.

Do these new institutions make a difference? Do they give employees greater involvement and influence in decision-making? Our answer is a positive but cautious one. Our results suggest the following: in representative firms, there are greater flows of information from management to representatives, especially on financial matters; worker directors are involved in all types of board-level decisions and, in the assessments of various key actors, do seem to have some influence. This contrasts with earlier assessments of worker directors in the UK (Brannen *et al.* 1976; Batstone *et al.* 1983; Towers *et al.* 1985). There is a further contrast in that worker directors tend to be less involved in industrial relations decisions than in other areas of management.

By no means do these innovations lead to worker control, even where employees own a majority of the equity. Nor do they lead to systems of self-management, other than in exceptional cases. Managers retain the 'right' to manage, and the executive directors have the primary responsibility for leading and guiding management activities in these firms. The best way to interpret innovations in participation and governance is to view them as German-style forms of co-determination. Property rights give workers and their representatives legitimate access to information and decision-making that is rare in the UK. Whilst formal veto powers are given to worker directors in the Articles of many of these companies, these are rarely exercised. Instead, the primary importance of board or trust membership is that it provides a mechanism for the expression of employee interests at the highest level of management, and for the transmission of company information to employee representatives. These institutions create the potential for top managers to incorporate employee and employee-owner interests and concerns into top-level decisions but they do not lead to top managers making decisions at the behest of employees and their representatives. Boards of directors in these companies are best seen as coalitions of interests rather than as vehicles for translating employee-owner interests into corporate policy.

Employee ownership and unions

A long-standing question in the employee ownership literature is whether unions are damaged by employee acquisitions of sizeable ownership stakes in the companies that employ them. As we saw in Chapter 3, some unions continue to display anxieties about this possibility, and this has meant that in some cases local union representatives have had to mount ownership conversions without the active support and assistance of union organisations. The root cause of union nervousness is that employee ownership blurs and confuses the capital–labour relationship upon which trade unionism rests. Employee-owners may shift their allegiances from unions, as representatives of labour, and adopt instead the perspectives of owners. Where new institutions of participation and governance are formed, unions face a dilemma. If they do not participate in them, these new institutions may supplant union-based institutions. If, on the other hand, they do participate in them, union functions may become confused because they represent both employees and owners.

The UK experience of ESOPs, however, is moderately encouraging for unions, though much depends on the degree of involvement of unions in ownership conversion. As we have seen, union representatives have been deeply involved in the formation of 'representative' ESOPs. Although unions were typically present in 'risk-sharing' ESOPs they tended not to have an active role in conversion. There was a mixture of unionised and non-union firms in the 'paternalist' group but, where present, unions had little, if any, role in ownership conversion. In 'technical' ESOPs they had no role at all. The lesson that may be drawn from this is that unions, as an independent form of employee representation, are necessary for the creation of independent institutions of participation and/or governance in employee ownership firms.

In so doing, however, are they sowing the seeds of their own destruction? Our findings suggest that they are not. There is little evidence that employee-owners turn their back on unions once they become owners. In most cases, union membership levels were not affected by ownership, and those employees who feel ownership most do not display less favourable views towards unions. In representative firms, unions managed to gain the 'best of both worlds' by operating separately from new institutions of governance but keeping them under their control. Collective bargaining and employee representation were kept procedurally separate from employee-owner governance at the insistence of both union representatives and managers. In this way, unions could avoid being tainted by any difficult decisions taken by worker directors whilst at the same time ensuring that worker directors did not develop an independent power base. The relationship of union institutions to governance structures is similar to works council arrangements in countries like France and Germany. These structures are separate from collective bargaining and union representation but unions often influence their operation by securing representation upon them.

There are two possible exceptions to this assessment of union continuity. One is where workers become directly involved in management by electing top managers and by monitoring their work performance. In this instance union representation becomes less relevant because workers can organise their terms of employment more or less directly. The other is found in paternalist firms where institutions of shareholder representation are established entirely separately from union structures. In these cases managers may use these new structures to weaken union representation. There was one case in our study where this had occurred. Overall, though, to echo Blasi once more (1988), the transformation of management–employee relationships necessary to eliminate trade unionism (where it existed prior to conversion) simply did not occur in the firms in our study.

Characteristics of employee ownership firms

As we have seen, there is an important strand of empirical literature in the US concerned with the characteristics of firms that become employee-owned. This is linked to a more theoretical body of writing that attempts to determine why employee ownership tends to be rare in Western economies. The empirical literature is often inconclusive, probably because, as we have found, ESOPs tend to be created in distinct sets of circumstances and with varying objectives. The theoretical literature is often of little help because it incorporates unreal assumptions about the characteristics and behaviour of employee-owned and labour-managed firms. The assumption that labour-managed firms have no hierarchy or that worker effort is constant (as in Ward 1958) tends to inhibit the development of well-grounded empirically testable propositions to guide research into the incidence of employee ownership (Bonin *et al.* 1993; Dow and Putterman 1999; Blair 1999). It may also be argued that functionalism tends to pervade the Theoretical Economics literature: it is assumed that employee ownership rarely occurs because of the (theoretically derived) limitations of this form of ownership and organisation. It is also implicit in these approaches that financial markets generate first-best corporate forms over time. If employee ownership did not have the severe limitations identified in the theoretical literature, then markets would ensure that it became a more common organisational form (Jensen and Meckling 1979).

Whilst the arguments from the literature provide many illuminating insights, a basic problem with them is that they do not fully incorporate the objectives and philosophies of the actors involved, or the interaction of these actors, as causal variables. For instance, in the UK bus industry one important influence on the formation of employee-owned firms was the political complexion of local authorities. Also in the bus industry, the interaction of managerial and union concerns about employee participation led to an emphasis on forms of employee-owner governance which might not be predicted from that strand of the literature concerned with the problems of dilution of control rights (e.g. Jensen and Meckling 1976). The key point is that the strengths and weaknesses of employee ownership, as identified in the theoretical literature, are not necessarily causal factors in themselves. Instead they may be translated into such by the actors involved in developing (or preventing) employee ownership. Different considerations may be relevant in different circumstances.

With these reservations in mind, it is worth considering whether there are distinctive characteristics of our firms and how these might have impinged on the decision to become employee-owned. Focusing on the bus industry initially, there are several core features of bus firms that make them suitable candidates for employee ownership and leveraged buy-outs. These include stable cash-flow, stable if slowly declining markets, stable technology, limited research and development needs, and limited investment requirements (Thompson *et al.* 1990). Furthermore, physical capital (i.e. buses) takes a fairly generic form so that sunk costs are potentially limited. Williamson has argued that debt is an appropriate form of finance when capital is generic (1988). Overall, the risks for those providing debt finance to established bus companies seem to be relatively limited.

Yet why should management-employee or employee buy-outs rather than management buy-outs take place when owners choose to divest? Chaplinksy *et al.* (1998) suggest that employee buy-outs will be chosen in preference to management buy-outs amongst more poorly performing firms. In the US, ESOPs can provide access to pension fund assets and facilitate concession bargaining, thereby reducing the costs of leverage. The situation is not quite the same in the UK because share ownership and pensions are not so closely intertwined (though two of the bus companies paid for their acquisition by taking on pension fund liabilities). However, we saw in Chapter 5 that bus companies becoming employee-owned had lower levels of profitability and higher wage costs than other firms in the industry. Employee ownership certainly facilitated restructuring of pay and conditions. As in the US steel and airline industries, the bus industry had experienced an influx of low-cost competitors. Unlike these American examples, however, employee ownership was not a bargaining counter in an otherwise stalemated bargaining situation. The direction of causality was more or less reversed in the bus industry. Once the bus industry became employee-owned, it was in the interests of employee-owners to restructure pay and conditions to ensure competitive survival and repayment of the main loan. Employee ownership certainly eased concessions but it did not come about for these reasons. That said, securing concessions may have been a motive for managerial involvement. Our evidence on this score is not clear-cut. Whilst securing employee co-operation was viewed as very important by bus managers as a reason for employee ownership, constraining wage claims was not. In future research, questions to managers should be reformulated to capture these possible motivations more precisely.

Performance considerations also help to illuminate why the MBOs in the 'risk-sharing' group had an employee ownership component. Many of the firms in this category had no prior trading records and hence found it difficult to raise loan finance. Offering equity to employees helped to raise finance and demonstrated to loan-providers that managers mounting the buy-out had secured employee commitment to the new business. The picture is very different in paternalist firms, however, as there tends not to be a significant requirement for external finance to achieve employee ownership. In fact, firms in the paternalist category tended to be good performers, though ones facing relatively high competition in product markets. In these cases, the choice to become employee-owned is not constrained by finance providers to the same extent as in the 'representative' and 'risk-sharing' groups.

An influential set of arguments suggests that decisions to become employee-owned may be relatively more likely in contexts where monitoring of worker activities is costly and where employees have transferable skills, knowledge, and reputation (Russell 1985b). Drawing on the work of Alchian and Demsetz (1972), it is suggested that provision of ownership rights to workers engenders work effort and peer pressure by aligning employee and owner interests. Meanwhile, Williamson's work on asset specificity (1979) is used to show how ownership can be used to 'lock-in' workers with skills that are valuable to the firm or where costly investments have been made in skill development (Blair 1995). Although these arguments appear to be useful for explaining the incidence of share-based remuneration in high technology and knowledge-based companies, they do not appear very powerful in relation to our firms. On the face of it, monitoring the work of bus drivers, coal miners, stevedores, and local authority service workers does not appear to present especially insuperable difficulties. Nor do these types of occupations usually require especially large investments in skills development. It has been noted that workforces in co-operatives tend to be relatively unskilled (Bonin *et al.* 1993), and whilst we do not make these claims for UK ESOPs nor would we claim that their employees tend to be unusually skilled. Furthermore, it is difficult to perceive extensive labour market opportunities for many of these employees. Indeed, employee ownership is attractive because of its apparent job preservation capacities. However, the logic of our core argument that employee ownership comes about because actors want it to, rather than because of theory-derived strengths and weaknesses of employee ownership, implies that actor perceptions of monitoring costs, skills, and labour mobility are more important than their actual levels. Future research investigating these factors should attempt to use actors' assessments of these rather than proxy measures (such as the proportion of white or blue-collar workers).

A recent analysis by Hansmann (1996) suggests that the main impediment to employee ownership is the costs of collective ownership. When employees acquire control rights of the firms that employ them, the costs of co-ordinating a multitude of claimants are high if the workforce is heterogeneous. These costs arise from the 'technical' problems of co-ordination and from reconciling divergent and conflicting interests. Employee-owned firms, therefore, tend to have relatively homogeneous workforces. Hansmann's case is broadly supported by the evidence from our study. Most of the firms have relatively undiversified workforces with a small number of major occupational groupings. However, observation of bus companies, mining companies, and the like suggests that employee-owned firms have a dominant occupational group (e.g. bus drivers, face-workers etc.) in terms of numbers, status, and power, even if they do not have a homogeneous workforce as such. This is similar to employee-owned airlines, where pilots tend to be the driving force behind employee ownership (see Wichman 1994; Gordon 1998). One possibility, which we have not been able to investigate in our study, is that this dominant group is able to transfer most of the costs of employee ownership, such as employment reductions or pay concessions, onto minority occupational groups. It may be worth pursuing this line of enquiry in future research.

Finally, a significant influence on the development of employee ownership is the possibility of changes in control that may lead to high costs for incumbent workforces. Evidence from the US has repeatedly shown that ESOPs in public companies help to preserve firms from take-overs, and that ESOPs tend to be formed in companies facing take-over pressures (Useem and Gager 1996; Chaplinsky *et al.* 1998). We have shown that defensive protection from adverse consequences of changes in control has been an important objective for workers in firms becoming employee-owned in a large proportion of cases. One possibility, which we have not been able to explore fully, is that this reason is especially important for managers. The management roles in most of the firms in our study do not appear to require firm-specific or even especially advanced skills and knowledge. For this reason, managers may be judged to have been especially at risk (more so than most manual workers) from changes in control. They may therefore have been unusually sympathetic to employee ownership because it entrenched their own position and employment. We have shown how 'insider' control was 100 per cent in many of the 'representative' and 'paternalist' firms, and often substantially exceeded the employee ownership component. Chaplinsky *et al.* (1998) have shown that managerial ownership tends to be higher in management-employee buy-outs than in 'orthodox' management buy-outs, and they suggest that MEBOs may be preferred to MBOs by managers because they pass more control to them. It is noticeable that the 'risk-sharing' MBOs in our study not only have lower levels of employee ownership but lower levels of management ownership as well, with external financiers making up the difference. Given what we know about the stringent performance conditions imposed by venture capitalists on MBOs (Thompson and Wright 1987; Kaplan and Stromberg 2000), the exercise of control rights by worker directors may well be preferred by managers to those exerted by external financiers.

Life cycle and viability of ESOPs

Finally, we reflect on the viability of ESOPs as an organisational form. Are ESOPs a durable form of ownership or do they tend to be a temporary phenomenon? As discussed in Chapter 2, there is an extensive literature dating back to the Webbs (Webb and Webb 1918) concerning the survival of workers' co-operatives. This literature suggests that co-operatives will have a higher than average failure rate because of under-investment, lack of commercial acumen amongst members, difficulties in co-ordinating members, and perverse forms of firm behaviour (e.g. expansion of output during recessions). Those that survive will degenerate into conventional organisations owing to the need to hire professional managers and to create organisational hierarchies. Furthermore, as co-operative members are believed to want to maximise net revenues per member, the tendency will be to hire non-member employees to meet expansions of demand or replace departing members. In time there will be one member left and a set of paid employees (Bonin *et al.* 1993). As Ben-Ner (1988) has described it, co-operatives are not a viable long-term form of ownership because they go out of business during recessions and convert into conventional firms during up-turns of the business cycle. These arguments have been contested, however, on the basis of empirical evidence indicating organisational longevity and vitality (Estrin and Jones 1992; Perotin 1987; Whyte and Whyte 1988), and also on the grounds that they incorporate unrealistic assumptions about how co-ops and their members actually behave (Dow and Putterman 1999; Blair 1995).

ESOPs are not likely to be subject to degeneration in the same way as there is less to degenerate from. Management hierarchies are present from the outset, and equity ownership is often unequal anyway. It is possible that worker say in governance and employment matters might be reduced as management priorities change or enthusiasm for employee ownership wanes (as in Wilkinson *et al.* 1994) but it must be remembered that in many ESOPs there were relatively few opportunities for direct participation by individual employees anyway. Even so, the life cycle of employee participation and governance is an issue worth exploring further in future research.

There is some evidence of ESOPs going out of business. In our data-set of 62 firms five firms failed during the research. However, on the whole

ESOPs may help to prevent failures because they can facilitate restructuring of pay and employment conditions in contexts where the survival of the firm is threatened by low-cost competition. Transformation of ESOPs into 'conventionally owned' organisations as a result of acquisitions has been a much more widespread phenomenon. Many of the early UK ESOPs (not in our study) were acquired by other companies within a couple of years of becoming employee-owned (see Wright and Robbie 1992). In our study the most notable development has been the demise of employee ownership in the bus industry. At the time of writing there are only two employee-owned firms remaining, one with direct ownership, the other with ESOP mechanisms. All of the others have been acquired by the major firms in the bus industry (Stagecoach, First Group, National Express etc.).

The average duration of employee ownership in the bus industry is 3.7 years with the longest period of employee ownership being eight years and the shortest under one year. Was the demise of employee ownership inevitable, and did aspects of employee ownership contribute to its downfall? To some extent, other factors, such as the concentration of the industry that occurred during the 1990s, were responsible though employee ownership may have weakened the capacity of firms to ward off predators. Given the restructuring that was going on in the industry the following features of employee-owned firms rendered them susceptible to take-over bids. The first, as we saw in Chapter 8, was that most workers in these firms did not feel a strong sense of ownership. The limited opportunities for direct participation was an important contributory factor here, and for many workers employment by an employee-owned firm did not seem to differ much, if at all, from that by other firms. The second was that the non-payment of dividends by these firms (so as to divert profits into share allocations and loan repayment) meant that there were no clear financial rewards of ownership. Also at the same time, repayment of loans in these highly leveraged firms led to rapid growth in share values. At the same time, the emphasis on loan repayment led to under-investment in many ESOP firms, so that they were unable to respond to competitive threats posed by predators. In the circumstances, it is not surprising that employee-owners accepted take-over bids. The rewards from divestment seemed to far exceed the financial and psychological rewards of ownership. The employee-owners of Tyne and Wear based Busways, for example, were offered £4.58 for each 5p share.

As far as we know, four of the nine 'risk-sharing' MBOs have been sold on. The weakness of firms in this group is that they tended to be dependent on a small number of major contracts. Failure to renew or secure critical contracts left these firms vulnerable to take-over, especially where the market was dominated by larger firms (as in local authority services). Since employees held minority shares in these companies, exit decisions were anyway outside their control. By contrast, employee ownership in paternalistic firms appears to be a more stable phenomenon. The only exit that we know of is that of Roadchef in 1998, which was sold to the Japanese firm Nomura after 11 years of partial employee ownership.

The conclusions we draw from these patterns of events is that employee ownership achieved via highly leveraged buy-outs is probably unlikely to be durable. This form of transaction is oriented towards early realisation of value, and the escalation of share values as debt is repaid presents strong temptations to employee-owners to sell their share. Looking at the bus industry, employee ownership may be viewed as a transitional event (Gordon 1988). It facilitated restructuring of pay, benefits, and employment in a comparatively painless way for workers, and provided them with a pay-off for these concessions fairly shortly afterwards. By contrast, employee ownership in paternalist firms appears to have better long-term prospects. Since there is typically little use of external finance to facilitate ownership transfers, the value of the firm is more stable than in the case of the bus firms. Sizeable proportions of equity are often retained in trust for a considerable period – sometimes in perpetuity – so that workers may have little say in divestment decisions. In some cases equity is passed gradually to the trusts by owners with the result that they retain substantial control rights for a considerable period of time. Some owners are able to maintain involvement in the trusts even after divestment. Since the primary objective of these owners was to prevent take-over, they have an interest in maintaining employee ownership. The problem with the paternalist form is that conversion to employee ownership occurs at the whim of paternalist owners, and there do not seem to be many of them.

What, then, are the prospects for employee ownership and ESOPs in the UK? Whilst there will probably always be occasional conversions by paternalist owners, the wave of ESOPs and other forms of equity-based employee ownership seen in the late 1980s/early 1990s may well be a transient phenomenon. As we have seen, ESOP creation was closely associated with privatisation. Whilst other forms of restructuring transactions, such as MBOs, continue to take place in significant numbers, the level of control sought by venture capitalists is generally not supportive of substantial employee ownership and control rights. Meanwhile, the government has recently sought to extend the incidence of employee share ownership schemes, and new institutional arrangements seem likely to simplify conversions to employee ownership. Whether this leads to a new wave of employee-owned firms will need to be addressed by future studies.

Appendix 1 Do employee-owners co-operate with management and exert peer pressure?

A recurrent theme in the employee ownership literature is that providing employees with a stake in ownership should lead to greater willingness to co-operate with management, to work harder, and to exert peer pressure on under-performing fellow workers (see Conte and Svejnar 1990). The argument here is that employee-owners have an interest in improving work performance because they receive a material pay-off from it. In so far as employee participation in decisions accompanies ownership this may provide the forum for co-operation and information-sharing. These arguments are commonly expressed in econometric analyses of the performance effects of share ownership and profit-sharing, and they are said to provide the link between financial participation and company performance (e.g. Fitzroy and Kraft 1987). Prior to financial participation, employees attempt to appropriate surplus by withholding effort. Share ownership allows them to participate directly in this surplus. Since shirking and free-riding imposes costs on all workers, social sanctions (peer pressure) will be exerted on those workers who deviate from a new work norm of greater effort. A somewhat different view, expressed by Cable and Wilson (1989), is that positive economic effects of financial participation will be achieved through advances in technology and organisation facilitated by employee ownership rather than by greater effort or monitoring.

Despite the importance of the possible link between ownership and outcomes, there has been little empirical investigation of whether share ownership induces these behavioural effects amongst workers. Bradley and Gelb, in an early study of the Mondragon co-operatives (1981), found some evidence to confirm that horizontal monitoring takes place but this line of enquiry has not been followed up in subsequent studies. To investigate behavioural impacts of share ownership we asked a number of questions about peer pressure, work effort, co-operation, and information-sharing in the employee surveys in six firms (see Chapter 8). These items are

- *Horizontal monitoring:* a three-item scale (alpha coefficient=0.5450) measuring beliefs that peer pressure is important;

- *Effort*: a two-item scale (alpha=0.5936) measuring the extent to which respondents believed their work effort had changed as a result of employee ownership;
- *Prerogative:* a two-item scale (alpha=0.7400) measuring individuals' acceptance of management's right to manage;
- *Like-change:* a two-item scale (alpha=0.6420) measuring individual receptiveness to change at work.

To see whether employee ownership influences employee views and behaviour on these issues, we assess the extent of correlation of these variables with psychological ownership (FEEL). The proposition is that the more employees feel like owners, the more they are likely to co-operate with management and exert pressure on their colleagues. The correlation coefficients are shown in Table A1.1.

The coefficients presented in Table A1.1 are supportive of the arguments commonly found in the Economics literature on employee ownership. Those employee-owners who most feel like owners are most likely to believe in the value of peer pressure, to exert greater effort because of ownership, to accept management's right to run the company, and to be receptive to change.

Table A1.1 The relationship between feelings of ownership, co-operation, and peer pressure (correlation coefficients)

	Horizontal monitoring	*Effort*	*prerogative*	*Like-change*
Feel	0.2834***	0.4514***	0.2786***	0.2760***
Horizontal monitoring		0.2884***	0.1425*	0.0023
Effort			0.1359*	0.0145
Prerogative				0.2936***

Notes
* Significant at 0.05.
*** Significant at 0.001.

Appendix 2 Do employee share-owners have weaker attachment to trade union representation?

We noted in Chapters 6 and 7 that a recurrent fear of unions about employee ownership is that it will weaken employee support for unions. The argument is that employees who acquire shares will take on the perspectives of capital rather than labour, and hence will withdraw support from unions. Furthermore, if employee remuneration becomes more dependent on company performance (and stock price performance) collective bargaining over basic pay rates will decline in importance to employees. The evidence presented in Chapter 7 suggests that in most cases the union role has not been institutionally threatened by employee ownership. Quite the reverse in fact, as far as bus companies are concerned. However, institutional strength of union structures in the short term may mask a decline of support amongst employee-owners. To see whether such a development had occurred we asked a number of questions about support for unions. These were taken from Long's investigations at the end of the 1970s (Long 1978c), and subsequently also used by Poole and Jenkins (1990). They are not ideal questions as they tend to conflate orientations to unions with descriptive assessments of union role and power in the company. For this reason we do not report findings from all of the questions here. Those that are reported here are:

> 'In a dispute with your company, how much sympathy would you have with the union?' (DISPUTE);
> 'A union is not really necessary in this company at this time' (UNNECESSARY).

To test whether share ownership has any relation to these orientations to unions, we correlate them with the variable measuring feelings of ownership (see Chapter 8). The correlation coefficient with DISPUTE is 0.1257 ($p=0.040$) and that with UNNECESSARY is -0.0936 ($p=0.116$). These results suggest that greater feelings of ownership are not associated with a decline in support for union representation. In fact, the correlation between psychological ownership and sympathy for unions is positively significant though weakly so. It could perhaps be argued, however, that the companies from which these results are derived are special cases as union representatives had an important role in bringing about ownership and supporting employee-owner governance after conversion. Even so, they indicate that a decline in support for unions is not an inevitable consequence of share ownership.

Notes

1 Introduction

1 86 per cent of the workforce subscribed £800 to buy a combination of preference (£750) and ordinary voting shares (£50).
2 Most of the information in this account is taken from papers written by Dave Wheatcroft, the Employee Director of Chesterfield Transport.
3 There is a sizeable UK literature showing how co-operatives in practice often do not live up to the co-operative ideal. See Chapter 2. These features of most UK co-operatives may be in large part a consequence of their small size. In France, Italy, and the Mondragon area of Spain many co-operatives are substantially larger and have management structures and hierarchies.
4 This is not to say that governance issues are absent or that such firms do not have extensive employee participation. It is simply that these employee share schemes tend to be self-contained and are not usually part of a large-scale attempt to restructure ownership, governance, and participation.
5 Estimates were made by lobbying and consultancy organisations, and were mainly based on personal contact with firms, word of mouth, newspaper reports etc.
6 These are defined contribution rather than defined benefit pension plans. Employees subscribe on a regular basis to purchase shares either in their own company or in others. Typically, the company matches the employee contributions by adding its own shares to the employee accounts.
7 In defined contribution schemes, the final pension settlement to the employee is unknown at the time of making the contributions. Much depends on the performance of the stock held in the plan during its lifetime. Employer contributions are limited to the matching stock offered during the course of the plan. This contrasts with defined benefit pension plans. Here, a pension is guaranteed at the outset (often expressed as a percentage of final salary). The employer makes good any shortfall in employer and employee contributions when the employee retires so that the defined benefit can be paid. The employer therefore faces an unquantifiable risk when it offers defined benefit pensions to employees when they join the firm.
8 Principal–agency approaches are common in discussions of owner-manager relationships (corporate governance) and of management–worker relations (in writing on share ownership). When the focus is workers, there is a tendency to conflate the firm, owners, and managers (i.e. to assume there is no agency problem between owners and managers).
9 This line of argument is now commonly expressed in the UK, reflecting the recent and highly publicised emergence of so-called 'dot.com' companies. Some recent dot.com entrants to the FTSE 100 have tiny income streams compared with the more long-standing members of this elite.

10 A keynote conceptual paper on corporate governance at the American Finance Association conference in January 2000 by Luigi Zingales argued that the problem of corporate governance should now be viewed as how to hold network-based and human capital-based firms together rather than how to exert discipline on managers (as contract and property rights theory had suggested) (see Zingales 2000).

11 Alchian and Demsetz were, however, hostile to self-management by employees because they believed that employees would 'sweat' physical equipment to meet output goals (see Blair 1999).

2 The development of employee ownership

1 The conversion to employee ownership at Baxi Partnership in 1983 could well be seen as the first ESOP. In this conversion the vast majority of the company's equity, held by just two individuals, was sold at a highly reduced price to a pre-existing Employee Benefits Trust, which held 2 per cent of the firm's equity, using finance from the firm's profits. The equity thereby purchased was cancelled on receipt in the EBT so that the 2 per cent of equity already held became 100 per cent of the equity. Some of the shares were then distributed to individual employees using a combination of approved profit sharing and Save As You Earn share schemes (see Best 1999).

2 This argument has been advanced by Ackers *et al.* (1992). Ramsay has argued in response that employee involvement initiatives of the 1980s, of which share ownership is one, reflected managerial dominance. The decline of interest in industrial democracy in this decade reflected the changed balance of power in the workplace, and hence is consistent with the 'cycles of control' approach.

3 That co-operatives tend not to be found in large or complex businesses may be seen as proof of this.

4 Because workers maximise revenues rather than profits in co-operatives, when revenues fall (possibly because of a recession) workers will want to expand production. This will lead to new members joining the co-operative and a dilution of revenue per member.

5 Hansmann (1996) argues that a key influence on formation of employee-owned firms is the heterogeneity of the workforce. Worker ownership is most likely to succeed, and hence most likely to develop (for natural selection reasons), in firms with homogeneous workforces.

6 Perotin's study of French co-operatives found that failing co-operatives had a shorter supply of capital (1987).

7 This industry in this area has long been characterised by a substantial level of co-operatives.

8 A feature of French co-operatives is that they may employee sizeable numbers of employees who are not owners. Russell (1985a) found a similar phenomenon in his study of San Francisco refuse collectors. This employment dualism may occur in successful employee-owned firms, where the existing employee-owners are reluctant to dilute their rights to future returns when they require to hire additional labour.

9 In 1999 some employees (or 'Partners') raised the possibility of selling the company, which was thought to be worth around £3.5 billion at the time. They were clearly inspired by the building society demutualisations and it was speculated that John Lewis employees would receive around £100,000 each. This campaign was vehemently resisted by the top management of the company. The likelihood of a sale of John Lewis is very low because the trust deed requires that the trustees pursue the interests of current and future. Even if current

employees voted to sell the company the trustees could refuse to sell on the grounds that it would not be respecting the interests of future employees. The only way such a refusal could be overridden is by a private parliamentary Bill to change the trust deed.

10 Individual ownership of shares had been in decline for many years, mainly because institutional and professional investors have 'soaked up' most of the massive expansion of equity that has occurred in recent years. The proportion of total equity owned by individuals fell from 54 per cent in 1963 to 37 per cent in 1975. In fact this proportion fell by a further eight percentage points in the 1980s, and the significance of the Thatcher programme of 'popular capitalism' is that by the end of her period in office the 'free-fall' had been halted. Individual ownership stabilised at around 20 per cent of total equity (see Central Statistical Office 1995).

11 At the time of writing the draft legislation had not passed into law so the details here are provisional.

12 Changes to the capital gains tax regime in the 2000 Budget mean that employees in Sharesave schemes will pay little or no CGT. A CGT taper was introduced whereby employees holding shares for four years will benefit from a 10 per cent CGT rate.

13 The schemes introduced in the 1970s and 1980s require that ordinary voting shares be used. The requirement was relaxed in the new schemes introduced in 2000.

14 The situation is very different in the US where unions are now the most active institutional investors through their involvement in pension funds (O'Sullivan 2000).

15 Discretionary option schemes in the UK could be used to provide substantial lump sums towards the end of senior managers' careers but the reduction in the limits on discretionary options post-1996 and the increasing insistence of investors that executive rewards be linked to individual performance have tended to curtail this somewhat.

3 Employee ownership and politics

1 The TUC, however, tends to be sceptical of these links.

2 Criticism of privatisation was starting to emerge at the time that ESOPs 'took off' based on public perceptions that uncontrolled private monopolies had been created. Thus it was seen as important in the privatisation of the electricity generation industry, for instance, to create more than one company.

3 A Conservative advocate of ESOPs has argued that these governments missed a 'golden opportunity' by not including ESOPs in the principal privatisations of the 1980s and 1990s. The preferential employee share schemes in these firms were a one-off phenomenon and represented only a small proportion of equity. Employee share ownership was widened but not deepened (Taylor 1992). Much of it was 'precarious' in that it did not transform employee attitudes to ownership or act as a catalyst for further involvement in capital markets by individual shareholders (Taylor 1988: 6).

4 The 1979 Thatcher Government terminated the worker director experiment in the Post Office shortly after gaining office.

5 A 'poison pill' is a device adopted by firms to prevent take-overs. Typically they give current shareholders rights to purchase further discounted shares in the company or of those of an acquiring company in the event of a take-over bid.

6 It is noticeable that there was no reference to workers' co-operatives in the Employment Department booklet *The Competitive Edge: Employee Involvement in*

Britain (1994) despite its emphasis that employee involvement can take many shapes and forms.

7 This facility has been a central feature of New Labour's All-Employee Share Plan.

8 The ascendancy of the left in the early 1980s has been attributed to the weakened state of the trade unions (normally supportive of centrist economic and industrial policies), the exit of key members of the centre-right to form the Social Democratic Party (SDP), and abhorrence of the policies of the right-wing Thatcher Government (Thompson 1996).

9 It is worth noting that the current New Labour Government is currently in the vanguard of opposition to a draft European Directive on the provision of information and consultation rights to employees.

10 Approved profit sharing has been particularly prevalent in the finance sector for some time (see Poole 1989 and Gonzalez-Menendez *et al.* 2000)

11 The TUC's interest in ESOPs is shown by the recent appointment of an officer at TUC headquarters to provide specialist expertise on ESOPs.

12 Gavin Laird became the Chairman of the Greater Manchester North bus company after the buy-out.

13 In highly leveraged employee buy-outs, the finance for the main loan to buy the company has normally been obtained from 'High Street' banks. Where Unity Trust has been involved, it has typically provided a small loan to the trust to purchase equity in the new company.

4 The structures of employee ownership

1 Accounting regulations, as expressed in UITF 13 *Accounting for ESOP Trusts*, distinguish between ESOPs designed primarily as a means of remunerating employees from those where ESOPs are used to bring about 'partnership'. Partnership is defined as 50 per cent or higher employee ownership. In the former case the ESOP trust is viewed as being under the *de facto* control of the sponsoring company, and hence ESOP transactions and assets/liabilities should be incorporated into the main company accounts.

2 In principle, distribution could also be achieved using the new All-Employee Share Plan introduced in the 2000 Budget. However, there would be little point in establishing both structures from new as the flexibility in the 2000 scheme, coupled with the reclassification of employee share schemes as 'business assets' (and hence subject to capital gains tax taper relief), would probably render an EBT redundant in most cases.

3 In practice it has usually been necessary to create an EBT for each 25 per cent of the equity to be held in trust (though it is common to use the same trustees for each EBT).

4 Given that tax deductions are secured via the PST it may be wondered why firms set up EBTs at all. The reason is that PSTs have a capital gains tax liability on shares that are not appropriated within 18 months. This requirement is in the 1978 legislation to ensure that companies distribute shares as intended by the scheme. The benefit of an EBT is that equity may be held for a longer period, and hence use of an EBT facilitates a one-off acquisition transaction rather than repeated acquisitions as would be necessary with a PST. This is clearly relevant in the case of employee buy-outs.

5 Given the average size of APS share allocations, there would have to be substantial increases in share value before CGT is payable. Higher-paid employees, where allocations are linked to salary, are most likely to encounter taxable capital gains. However, the reclassification of employee share schemes as

business assets in the 2000 Budget, coupled with reductions in the time period of business assets taper relief, is likely to mean that fewer participants become subject to capital gains tax. Where they do, the marginal rate of CGT is likely to be low (i.e. significantly less than the marginal rate of income tax), given the reductions in the tax rate for each year of the taper.

6 The functions of the trustees were defined in statute as to receive sums of money to purchase shares in the founding company, to acquire shares in the company, to distribute them (or cash) to employees, and to manage their investments (Reid 1992: 38; Pett 1998).

7 Chargeable assets include quoted company shares, works of art, unit trusts, commercial property etc.

8 It is thought that most companies with QUESTs have used a standing committee of employee representatives, perhaps already selected as pension fund trustees, to select trustees so that an election need not be held each time a trustee retires (Pett 1998).

9 Previously ESOPs were thought to be exempt from this but the situation was unclear.

10 The 2000 Budget proposes that shares held in a QUEST at the time of the budget may be transferred into a new trust formed to operate the new All-Employee Share Plan without any tax clawbacks. Since there are no statutory requirements governing the composition of the new trusts this can make existing QUESTs more flexible in practice.

11 Information kindly provided by the Inland Revenue.

12 Conservative MP Ian Taylor has argued that whilst these opportunities widened share ownership they did not 'deepen' it (1988).

13 The management-employee buy-outs in both companies were assisted financially by Luton

14 The balance of the purchase was funded by a loan from Barclays Bank (£540,000) and Unity Trust (£46,750) (Freeman *et al.* 1989).

5 Contexts and reasons for employee ownership

1 The kurtosis statistic is −1.684 (S.E=0.604) and the skewness statistics is 0.032 (S.E.=0.306).

2 Although we asked respondents to assess the main reasons for the conversion taking place, it is inevitable that the responses will be biased somewhat by managerial preferences.

3 The differences between groups are greater than those within groups for the item 'create business awareness', as shown by an F-test.

4 In firms where unions were not present, we scored the answers to these questions as 'little or no involvement'.

5 Commercial services were those mounted by bus operators as they saw fit whilst tendered services were commissioned by local authorities to fill gaps in commercial services. The evidence suggests that many new entrants concentrated their activities on securing contracts for tendered services rather than engaging in 'on the road' competition with incumbent firms. However, there was considerable variation between areas: in the metropolitan areas, Manchester and Strathclyde experienced considerable market entry to commercial services whilst the West Midlands and West Yorkshire had very little (see Stokes *et al.* 1990).

6 This analysis does not include all SBG firms in the database, as restructuring of subsidiaries immediately prior to or after privatisation meant that relevant trading information is not available. These excluded firms were very poor performers.

7 Some metropolitan authorities, such as South Yorkshire and Strathclyde, were highly opposed to privatisation and, although the workforces in their companies had started to consider employee ownership, they delayed agreement to such sales on the basis that Labour might win the 1992 election and halt the privatisation programme. When Labour lost this election these authorities came to the view that employee ownership buy-outs were the best option.
8 Significant at 0.05 in a rank-sum test. The presence of competition was significant at 0.01.
9 Competition since deregulation often led to reduction of services outside peak hours and on less popular routes (Stokes *et al.* 1990).
10 None of the other stated reasons in Table 5.4 were significantly correlated with the extent of union involvement.
11 The difference was statistically significant for the 1991 group (Z-statistic significant at 0.006) but not for the 1993 group (Z-statistic significant at 0.078).
12 Z-statistic significant at 0.002.
13 The firm was sold in 1992 and employee and insider ownership ceased.
14 Initially employees at Tower had attempted to save their mine from closure by British Coal by voting to put the pit through the independent colliery review closure. However, when British Coal offered to increase the size of redundancy payments in return for workers voting to accept closure, the workforce eventually voted to accept the closure of the pit. Subsequently, they mounted the successful bid to purchase the pit.
15 This is a slight misnomer in so far as many of the firms in this category do not use an ESOP to effect the initial buy-out transaction.
16 The Hansmann model can be viewed as functionalist in so far as it conflates the reasons for the development of employee ownership with the costs and benefits of employee ownership.
17 To some extent, Hansmann's case depends on a very narrow definition of employee ownership. He excludes ESOPs on the grounds that, whilst they give employees the returns rights of ownership, they tend not to provide the set of control rights normally associated with ownership.

6 Employee participation and governance: theory and prediction

1 The paper by Ben-Ner and Jones (1995) is an exception to this generalisation.
2 Work relations covers the way work is organised and the deployment of workers around technologies and production processes. Employment relations deals with the arrangements governing such aspects of employment as recruitment, training, job tenure, promotion, and the reward of employees. Industrial relations is defined to cover the representational and collective aspirations of employees and the resulting institutional arrangements which may exist, such as joint consultation, works councils, and collective bargaining (see Gospel 1992).
3 Marx argued that the capacity for 'free conscious activity' distinguished humans from other beings. The pattern of authority relations and work organisation in capitalist firms separated or alienated human beings from their essential human attributes.
4 In Germany, for instance, pay determination has traditionally been determined by collective bargaining at sectoral level, i.e. outside the firm. Works Councils are firm-level institutions, and are legally precluded from formal collective bargaining (though informal determination of pay supplements often occurs).
5 These studies were commissioned by the European Foundation for the Improvement of Living and Working Conditions, based in Dublin.

6 Furthermore, there is currently a new strand of thinking emerging in Financial Economics which redefines corporate governance in a way which elevates employee participation to a similar status to that of shareholder rights (see Blair 1999; Rajan and Zingales 1998).
7 Labour process theory would dispute this claim because employers purchase only the capacity to provide labour, not specific units of labour as such.
8 There have been a series of major criticisms of the conceptual foundations of this model of ownership and governance. One strand, associated especially with Margaret Blair (1995), argues that employees are also risk-bearers, and hence should benefit from return and control rights. Another strand, developed by Kay and Silberston (1995), argues that share ownership provides ownership not of the firm but of the shares themselves. Share ownership is a financial contract that specifies certain (variable) financial returns. Once this is recognised, the claim to control rights that are superior to those of other contractors evaporates.
9 In the US, for instance, the number of issues that must be submitted to shareholder votes is usually limited to changes that are not part of the ordinary business of the company. In many states, directors only have to submit proposals to shareholders once they have already approved them (see Blair 1995: 69). In other words, shareholders have little come-back on proposals that have already been rejected by directors.
10 Over 60 per cent of equity investment is undertaken by financial institutions in the UK. In the US around half of all corporate equities are held by institutional investors. Since 1960 shareholdings by institutional investors have grown from just over $50 billion to around $3,000 billion (see Blair 1995: 46).
11 The Cadbury Code requires that remuneration committees, composed mainly of non-executive directors, set the pay of senior managers, and that non-executive directors be selected by nomination committees.
12 Dow and Putterman (1999) define the labour-managed firm as one where labour elects the board of directors. This provides symmetry with the more conventional capital-managed firm in terms of governance. It is a more restricted definition, however, than the traditional one, which tends to suggest the absence of hierarchy.
13 Preliminary analysis of the Workplace Employee Relations Survey suggests these relationships still hold (see Gonzalez-Menendez *et al.* 2000).

7 Employee participation and governance: institutions, practices, and outcomes

1 In Mainline there were also two directors appointed with special reference to community interests.
2 In the case of Mainline, employee directors had parity with management directors, with community directors making up the rest of the board.
3 This approach to assessing involvement in decision-making is known as the 'reputational' approach. It was pioneered by Tannenbaum in a study which measured the distribution of power in unions (1957). A shortcoming of our approach is that, unlike Hickson *et al.* (1986), the questions do not refer to specific decisions. The less specific the question, the more likely respondents are to give idealised rather than well-grounded assessments of involvement and influence.
4 However, as there was minority employee representation on this trust (three out of seven trustees) there were complaints early on that the trust, whilst having a critical role in the governance of the firm, was not responsive to employee-shareholder interests. For this reason regular meetings were instigated between employees and the trustees.

5 See note 3.
6 T-statistics were significant at 0.05 in both cases. There were no significant differences between employee-owned companies and other companies in respect of labour management decisions.
7 Chi-square=9.496, significant at 0.002
8 On these issues other managers achieve higher influence scores.
9 The banks funding the buy-out insisted that worker directors should be in a minority on the board.
10 One clerical union was de-recognised after the buy-out due to very low numbers of members. A management union, which had been closely allied with NCB management during the 1984–5 miners' strike, was also denied representation rights.
11 We did come across one case where a senior trade union representative did have an active role in management and it may well be significant that this firm had few new institutions of employee-shareholder representation such as worker directors.
12 These issues included staffing numbers, working conditions, hours of work, rates of pay, staff deployment, recruitment levels, investment decisions, product and marketing decisions, introduction of new technology, introduction of new work methods, and selection of managers.

8 Ownership, participation, and employee attitudes

1 Sample sizes/number of respondents/response rate are Company A – 300, 87, 29 per cent; Company B – 100, 37, 37 per cent; Company C – 100, 49, 49 per cent; Company D – 100, 33, 33 per cent; Company E – 150, 65, 43 per cent; Company F – 100, 35, 35 per cent.
2 Clerical/administrative workers were under-represented in the sample from company F.
3 The high proportion of eligible employees in the firm with a three-year eligibility period may be due to a bias amongst respondents towards those participating in the scheme rather than a high proportion of employees with three years or more tenure in the workforce as a whole. It may also be due to lack of awareness of eligibility requirements. The lower rates of actual participation than most of the other companies may be a better reflection of the eligibility requirements.
4 We do not pursue this line of analysis here due to constraints on space. However, statistical comparisons of direct share purchasers and ESOP beneficiaries uncover no significant differences. These findings echo the more substantial analysis of Trewhitt (1999a).
5 The correlation coefficients between tenure and share allocations are significant at 0.000 for Companies A-E.
6 As shown by kurtosis and skewness statistics
7 Managers had a higher level of involvement in privatisation offers (31 per cent) compared with clerical workers (16 per cent) and manual workers (20 per cent) but this difference was not statistically significant.
8 Ideally, company dummies should have been included too but the variable measuring the proportion of equity held by workers was rejected when these were inserted (because of multi-collinearity).
9 Some studies have shown that the 6 item set of scales is more robust (Peccei and Guest 1993). These items are also added together to form a single measure of commitment.
10 Scale reliability coefficients are 0.6949, 0.7851, 0.8196 respectively. These scales have neither the conceptual underpinning nor the proven empirical validity of

the Mowday *et al.* (1979) or Cook and Wall (1980) scales. However, they do provide continuity with previous employee ownership research.

11 Normally, it would be appropriate to include union membership in such an analysis but as union membership was so high in these companies it was not expected to be an influence. Test results confirmed this supposition.

12 Multicollinearity precluded the presence of both company dummies and measures of total employee ownership in a single estimation

13 Chi-square=16.574, significant at 0.000.

Bibliography

Abell, P. (1983) 'The viability of industrial producer co-operation', in C. Crouch and F. Heller (eds) *International Yearbook of Organisational Democracy*, London: Wiley.

Ackers, A., Marchington, M., Wilkinson, A. and Goodman, J. (1992) 'The use of cycles? Explaining employee involvement in the 1990s', *Industrial Relations Journal* 23(4): 268–84.

Alchian, A. and Demsetz, H. (1972) 'Production, information costs and economic organisation', *American Economic Review* 62: 777–95.

Argyris, C. (1957) *Personality and Organisation*, New York: Harper and Row.

Arrowsmith, C. and Anderson, M. (1992) 'Taxation and accounting for ESOPs', in N. Wilson (ed.) *ESOPs: Their Role in Corporate Finance and Performance*, London: Macmillan.

Baddon, L., Hunter, L., Hyman, J., Leopold, J. and Ramsay, H. (1989) *People's Capitalism? A Critical Analysis of Profit-sharing and Employee Share Ownership*, London: Routledge.

Barry, A. (1989) 'Esops on the move', *Industrial Participation*, Spring: 12–15.

Batstone, E. (1976). 'Industrial democracy and worker representation at Board level: a review of European experience' in E. Batstone and P. Davies (eds) *Industrial Democracy: European Experience*, London: HMSO.

—— (1983) 'Organization and orientation: a life cycle model of French co-operatives', *Economic and Industrial Democracy* 4: 139–61.

Batstone, E., Ferner, A. and Terry, M. (1983) *Unions on the Board: An Experiment in Industrial Democracy*, Oxford: Blackwell.

Beatty, A. (1994) 'An empirical analysis of the corporate control, tax and incentive motivations for adopting leveraged employee stock ownership plans', *Managerial and Decision Economics* 15: 299–315.

Beaumont, P. and Harris, R. (1995) 'The pattern of diffusion of employee share-ownership schemes in Britain: some key findings', *International Journal of Human Resource Management* 6(2): 391–410.

Bell, W. and Hanson, C. (1987) *Profit Sharing and Profitability: How Profit Sharing Promotes Business Success*, London: Kogan Page.

Ben-Ner, A. (1988) 'The life cycle of worker-owned firms in market economies', *Journal of Economic Behaviour and Organisation* 10: 287–313.

Ben-Ner, A. and Jones, D. (1995) 'Employee participation, ownership and productivity: a theoretical framework', *Industrial Relations* 34(4): 532–53.

Berle, A. and Means, G. (1932) *The Modern Corporation and Private Property*, New York: Commerce Clearing House.

Best, J. (1999) *Owning Your Own Job: Employee Ownership in Action*, London: Partnership Research Limited.

Bharvava, S. (1994) 'Profit sharing and the financial performance of companies: evidence from UK panel data', *Economic Journal* 104: 1044–56.

Blagburn, R. (1992) 'Financing ESOPs: the company's wider perspective', in N. Wilson (ed.) *ESOPs: Their Role in Corporate Finance and Performance*, London: Macmillan.

Blair, M. (1995) *Ownership and Control: Rethinking Corporate Governance for the Twenty-First Century*, Washington DC: Brookings Institution.

—— (1999) 'Firm-specific human capital and theories of the firm', in M. Blair and M. Roe (eds) *Employees and Corporate Governance*, Washington DC: Brookings Institution.

Blasi, J. (1988) *Employee Ownership: Revolution or Ripoff?*, New York: Ballinger.

Blasi, J. and Kruse, D. (1991) *The New Owners: The Mass Emergence of Employee Ownership in Public Companies and What it Means to American Business*, New York: Harper Collins.

Blasi, J., Conte, M. and Kruse, D. (1996) 'Employee stock ownership and corporate performance among public companies', *Industrial and Labor Relations Review* 50(1): 60–80.

Blasi, J., Kruse, D. and Sesil, J. (1999) 'Critical issues in understanding the spread and the impact of financial participation', paper presented to University of Nijmegen Business School and European Foundation for the Improvement of Living and Working Conditions conference on The Nature and Extent of Financial Participation in the European Union, Leiden, September.

Blumberg, P. (1968) *Industrial Democracy: The Sociology of Participation*, London: Constable.

Bonin, J., Jones, D. and Putterman, L. (1993) 'Theoretical and empirical studies of producer co-operatives: will ever the twain meet?', *Journal of Economic Literature* 31: 1290–1320.

Bradley, K. and Gelb, A. (1981) 'Motivation and control in the Mondragon experiment', *British Journal of Industrial Relations* 19(2): 211–19.

—— (1983) *Worker Capitalism: The New Industrial Relations*, London: Heinemann.

Bradley, K. and Nejad, A. (1989) *Managing Owners: The National Freight Company Buy-out in Perspective*, Cambridge: Cambridge University Press.

Bradley, K., Estrin, S. and Taylor, S. (1990) 'Employee ownership and company performance', *Industrial Relations* 29(3): 385–402.

Brannen, P. (1983) *Authority and Participation in Industry*, London: Batsford.

Brannen, P., Batstone, E., Fatchett, D. and White, P. (1976) *The Worker Directors: A Sociology of Participation*, London: Hutchinson.

Braverman, H. (1974) *Labor and Monopoly Capital*, New York: Monthly Review Press.

Brickley, J. and Hevert, K. (1991) 'Direct employee stock ownership: an empirical investigation', *Financial Management* (Summer): 70–84.

Buchko, A (1992) 'Effects of employee ownership on employee attitudes – a test of three theoretical perspectives', *Work and Occupations* 19(1): 59–78.

—— (1993) 'The effects of employee ownership on employee attitudes: an integrated causal model and path analysis', *Journal of Management Studies* 30(4): 633–57.

Buckley, N. (1995) 'Employees to get £43 million as John Lewis rises 25%' *Financial Times*, 10 March.

Bullock, A. (1977) *Report of the Committee of Inquiry on Industrial Democracy*, Cmnd. 6706, London, HMSO.

Buxton, J. (1995) 'Dignified exit plan – how does a family-owned company remove its capital without harming the business', *Financial Times* 17 January.
Cable, J. and Wilson, N. (1989) 'Profit-sharing and productivity: an analysis of UK engineering firms', *Economic Journal* 99(396): 366–75.
Callaghan, B. (no date) 'Industrial and economic democracy; trade union issues for the future', TUC seminar on ESOPs and Other Forms of Financial Participation.
Cappelli, P., Bassie, L., Katz, H., Knoke, D., Osterman, P. and Useem, M. (1997) *Change at Work*, Oxford: Oxford University Press.
Carnell, D. (1992) 'ESOPs in listed and unquoted companies compared', in N. Wilson (ed.) *ESOPs: Their Role in Corporate Finance and Performance*, London: Macmillan.
—— (1998) 'How accountancy issues help and hinder employees' share plans', at ESOP Centre Tenth Anniversary Conference, London, June.
Carstensen, V., Gerlach, K. and Hubler, O. (1995) 'Profit sharing in German firms', in F. Buttler, W. Franz, R. Schettkatt and D. Soskice (eds) *Institutional Frameworks and Labour Market Performance: Comparative Views on US and German Economies*, London: Routledge.
Carter, N. (1990) 'Changing ownership: meaning, culture and control in the construction of a co-operative organisation', in G. Jenkins and M. Poole (eds) *New Forms of Ownership, Management and Employment*, London: Routledge.
Central Statistical Office (1995) *Share Ownership: a Report on the Ownership of Shares at 31st of December 1994*, London: CSO.
Chang, S. (1990) 'Employee stock ownership plans and shareholder wealth: an empirical investigation', *Financial Management* (Summer): 48–58.
Chaplinksy, S. and Niehaus, G. (1994) 'The role of ESOPs in takeover contests', *Journal of Finance* 49: 1451–71.
Chaplinsky, S., Niehaus, G. and Van de Gucht, L. (1998) 'Employee buy-outs: causes, structure and consequences', *Journal of Financial Economics* 48: 283–332.
Cheadle, A. (1989) 'Explaining patterns of profit sharing', *Industrial Relations* 28(3): 387–400.
Chell, E. (1983) 'Political perspectives and worker participation at Board level: the British experience', in C. Crouch and F. Heller (eds) *Organizational Democracy and Political Processes*, New York: John Wiley.
Chell, E. and Cox, D. (1979) 'Worker directors and collective bargaining', *Industrial Relations Journal* 10(3): 25–31.
Church, R. (1971), 'Profit-sharing and labour relations in England in the nineteenth century', *International Review of Social History* 26, Part 1.
Clegg, H. (1951) *Industrial Democracy*, London: Blackwell.
—— (1960) *A New Approach to Industrial Democracy*, Oxford: Blackwell.
Commission of the European Communities (1996) *Report from the Commission: Pepper II, Promotion of Participation by Employed Persons in Profits and Enterprise Results (including Equity Participation) in Member States*, Brussels: Commission of the European Communities, COM (96) 697 final.
Commission on Social Justice (1994) *Social Justice: Strategies for National Renewal*, London: Commission on Social Justice/Institute for Public Policy Research.
Conservative Party (1997) *You Can Only be Sure with the Conservatives*, London: Conservative Party.
Conte, M. and Svejnar, J. (1990) 'The performance effects of employee share ownership plans', in A. Blinder (ed.) *Paying for Productivity: A Look at the Evidence*, Washington DC: Brookings Institution.

Cook, J. and Wall, T. (1980) 'New work attitude measures of trust, organizational commitment and personal need non-fulfilment', *Journal of Occupational Psychology* 53: 39–52.

Cooper, J. and Hartley, J. (1991) 'Reconsidering the case for organisational commitment', *Human Resource Management Journal* 1(3): 18–31.

Copeman, G. (1958) *The Challenge of Employee Shareholding,* London: Business Publications.

Cornford, J. (1990) *A Stake in the Company. Shareholding, Ownership and ESOPs*, London: Institute of Public Policy Research.

Cornforth, C. (1982) 'Trade unions and producer co-operatives', *Economic and Industrial Democracy* 3: 17–30.

—— (1995) 'Patterns of co-operative management: beyond the degeneration thesis', *Economic and Industrial Democracy* 16: 487–523.

Cornforth, C., Thomas, A., Lewis, J. and Spear, R. (1988) *Developing Successful Worker Co-operatives,* London: Sage.

Cotton, J. (1993) *Employee Involvement: Methods for Improving Performance and Work Attitudes*, London: Sage.

Craig, B. and Pencavel, J. (1992) 'The behaviour of worker cooperatives: the plywood companies of the Pacific Northwest', *American Economic Review* 82(5): 1083–105.

Cully, M., O'Reilly, A., Millward, N., Forth, J., Woodland, S., Dix, G. and Bryson, A. (1998) *The 1998 Workplace Employee Relations Survey: First Findings*, London: Department of Trade and Industry.

Dachler, P. and Wilpert, B. (1978) 'Conceptual dimensions and boundaries of participation in organisations: a critical evaluation', *Administrative Science Quarterly* 23: 1–38.

Darling, A. (1997) 'A political perspective', in G. Kelly, D. Kelly and A. Gamble (eds) *Stakeholder Capitalism,* Basingstoke: Macmillan.

D'Art, D. (1992) *Economic Democracy and Financial Participation: A Comparative Study*, London: Routledge.

Dilts, D. and Paul, R. (1990) 'Employee ownership of unionized firms: collective bargaining or codetermination', *Business and Society* 29: 19–27.

Donaldson, G. (1994) *Corporate Restructuring: Managing the Change Process*, Cambridge, Mass.: Harvard University Press.

Dow, G. and Putterman, L. (1999) 'Why capital (usually) hires labour: an assessment of proposed explanations', in M. Blair and M. Roe (eds) *Employees and Corporate Governance*, Washington DC: Brookings Institution.

Drago, R. and Heywood, J. (1995) 'The choice of payment schemes: Australian establishment data', *Industrial Relations* 34(4): 507–31.

Drago, R. and Turnbull, G. (1996) 'On the incidence of profit sharing', *Journal of Economic Behaviour and Organisation* 31: 129–38.

Dunn, S. (1993) 'From Donovan to . . . wherever', *British Journal of Industrial Relations* 31(2): 169–88.

Dunn, S., Richardson, R and Dewe, P. (1991) 'The impact of employee share ownership on worker attitudes: a longitudinal case study', *Human Resource Management Journal* 1(1): 1–17.

Eaton, A. and Voos, P. (1992) 'Unions and contemporary innovations in work organisation, compensation and employee participation', in L. Mishal and P. Voos (eds) *Unions and Economic Competitiveness,* New York: Sharpe.

Eccles, T. (1981) *Under New Management*, London: Pan.

Economist (1988) 'Many more fares, please', *The Economist* 309 (12 November): 90–1.

Edwards, C. and Heery, E. (1989) *Management Control and Union Power: A Study of Labour Relations in Coal-Mining*, Oxford: Clarendon.

Elliott, J. (1978) *Conflict or Co-operation? The Growth of Industrial Democracy*, London: Kogan Page.

Employment Department Group (1994) *The Competitive Edge: Employee Involvement in Britain*, London: Employment Department Group.

Estrin, S. and Jones, D. (1992) 'The viability of employee-owned firms: evidence from France', *Industrial and Labor Relations Review* 45(2): 323–38.

Estrin, S. and Wilson, N. (1986) 'The micro-economic effects of profit sharing', *Centre for Labour Economics Discussion Paper 864*, London: London School of Economics.

Evans, A. (1990) 'Competition and the structure of local bus markets', *Journal of Transport Economics and Policy* 24(3): 255–81.

Ezzamel, M. and Watson, R. (1997) 'Wearing two hats: the conflicting control and management roles of non-executive directors' in K. Keasey, S. Thompson, and M. Wright (eds) *Corporate Governance: Economic, Management and Financial Issues*, Oxford: Oxford University Press.

Fitzroy, F. and Kraft, K. (1987) 'Co-operation, productivity, and profit sharing', *Quarterly Journal of Economics* 102(1): 23–35.

Flanders, A., Pomeranz, R. and Woodward, J. (1968) *Experiment in Industrial Democracy: A Study of the John Lewis Partnership*, London: Faber and Faber.

Fogarty, M. and White, M. (1988) *Share Schemes – As Workers See Them*, London: Policy Studies Institute.

Forrester, K. (1990) 'Owning a bus company. Yorkshire Rider busworkers and the Employee Share Ownership Plan', presented to Employment Research Unit Annual Conference, Cardiff Business School, September.

—— (1993) 'Buses', in A. Pendleton and J. Winterton (eds) *Public Enterprise in Transition. Industrial Relations in State and Privatized Corporations*, London: Routledge.

Freeman, J., Gee, R. and Atkinson, A. (1989) 'Employee buy-out takes to the road', *Industrial Participation* (Winter): 16–19.

French, L. (1987) 'Employee perspectives on stock ownership: financial investment or mechanism of control?', *Academy of Management Review* 12(3): 427–35.

French, L. and Rosenstein, J. (1984) 'Employee ownership, work attitudes, and power relationships', *Academy of Management Journal* 27(4): 861–69.

Gamble, A. (1992) 'Labour's Policy Review', in M. Smith and J. Spear (eds) *The Changing Labour Party*, London: Routledge.

Gamble, J. (1998) 'ESOPS: Financial performance and federal tax incentives', *Journal of Labour Research* 19: 529–41.

Gates, J. (1998) *The Ownership Solution: Towards a Shared Capitalism for the Twenty-First Century*, Harmondsworth: Penguin.

Geary, J. and Sisson, K. (1994) *Conceptualising Direct Participation in Organisational Change: The EPOC Project*, Dublin: European Foundation for the Improvement of Living and Working Conditions.

General Accounting Office (1986) *Employee Stock Ownership Plans: Benefits and Costs of ESOP Tax Incentives for Broadening Stock Ownership* (GAO/PEMD-87-88), Washington DC: Government Printing Office.

—— (1987) *Employee Stock Ownership Plans: Little Evidence of Effects on Corporate Performance* (GAO/PEMD-88–1).
Goldstein, S. (1978) 'Employee share ownership and motivation', *Journal of Industrial Relations* (September): 311–30.
Gonzalez-Menendez, M., Pendleton, A. and Robinson, A. (2000) 'Profit sharing in the UK', in A. Pendleton and V. Perotin (eds) *Profit Sharing in Europe*, Cheltenham: Edward Elgar.
Gordon, J. (1998) 'Employee stock ownership in economic transitions', in K.Hopt, H. Kanda, M. Roe, E. Wymeersch and S. Prigge (eds) *Comparative Corporate Governance: the State of the Art and Emerging Research*, Oxford: Clarendon Press.
Gordon, L. and Pound, J. (1990) 'ESOPs and corporate control', *Journal of Financial Economics* 27: 525–55.
Gospel, H. (1992) *Markets, Firms and the Management of Labour in Modern Britain*, Cambridge: Cambridge University Press.
Gould, B. (1989) *A Future for Socialism*, London: Jonathan Cape.
Gourlay, R. (1995) 'Spreading the Esop message – Richard Gourlay meets an engineering group which believes employee ownership makes sense', *Financial Times* 2 (May).
Green, S. (1992) 'The impact of ownership and capital structure on managerial motivation and strategy in management buy-outs: a cultural analysis', *Journal of Management Studies* 29(4): 513–36.
Greenberg, S. (1980) 'Participation in industrial decision-making and worker satisfaction: the case of producer cooperatives', *Social Science Quarterly* 60(3): 551–69.
Gregg, P. and Machin, S. (1988) 'Unions and the incidence of performance-linked pay in Britain', *International Journal of Industrial Organisation* 6(1): 91–109.
Grossman, S. and Hart, O. (1986) 'The costs and benefits of ownership: a theory of vertical and lateral integration', *Journal of Political Economy* 94: 691–719.
Grout, P. (1994) 'Popular capitalism', in M. Bishop, J. Kay and C. Mayer (eds) *Privatisation and Economic Performance*, Oxford: Oxford University Press.
Hadley, R. and Goldsmith, M. (1995) 'Development or convergence? Change and stability in a common ownership firm over three decades: 1960–89', *Economic and Industrial Democracy* 16: 167–99.
Hall, M. (1992) 'Behind the European Works Council Directive: the European Commission's legislative strategy', *British Journal of Industrial Relations* 30(4): 547–66.
Hammer T. and Stern R. N. (1980) 'Employee ownership: implications for the organisational distribution of power', *Academy of Management Journal* 23: 78–100.
Hammer, T. and Stern, R. (1986). 'A yo-yo model of co-operation: union participation at the Rath Packing Company', *Industrial and Labor Relations Review* 39: 337–49.
—— (1991) 'Worker representation on boards of directors: a study of competing roles', *Industrial and Labor Relations Review* 44(4): 661–80.
Hammer, T., Stern, R. and Gurdon, M. (1982) 'Workers' ownership and attitudes towards participation', in F. Lindenfield and J. Rothschild-Whitt (eds) *Workplace Democracy and Social Change*, Boston, MA: Porter Sargent.
Hanford, T. and Grasso, P. (1991) 'Participation and performance in ESOPs', in R. Russell and V. Rus (eds) *International Handbook of Participation in Organizations, Volume 3, Ownership and Participation*, Oxford: Oxford University Press.
Hansmann, H. (1996) *The Ownership of Enterprise*, Cambridge, MA and London: Belknap.

Hart, O. (1995a) 'Corporate governance: some theory and implications', *Economic Journal* 105: 678–89.

—— (1995b) *Firms, Contracts and Financial Structure*, Oxford: Clarendon.

Hart, O. and Moore, J. (1990) 'Property rights and the nature of the firm', *Journal of Political Economy* 98: 1119–58.

Hattersley, R. (1987) *Choose Freedom: the Future of Democratic Socialism*, Harmondsworth: Penguin.

Hatton, T. (1988), 'Profit sharing in British industry, 1865–1913', *International Journal of Industrial Organization* 6: 69–90.

Heald, D. and Steel, D. (1986) 'Privatisating public enterprises: an analysis of the government's case', in J. Kay, C. Mayer and D. Thompson (eds) *Privatisation and Regulation: The UK Experience*, Oxford: Clarendon.

Heller, F. (1998) 'Influence at work: a 25 year programme of research', *Human Relations* 51(12): 1425–6

Heller, F., Pusic, E., Strauss, G. and Wilpert, B. (1998) *Organizational Participation: Myth and Reality*, Oxford: Oxford University Press.

Herman, E. (1981) *Corporate Control, Corporate Power*, Cambridge: Cambridge University Press.

Heseltine, P. and Silcock, D. (1990) 'The effects of bus deregulation on costs', *Journal of Transport Economics and Policy* 24: 239–54.

Hespe, G. and Wall, T. (1976) 'The demand for participation among employees', *Human Relations* 29(5): 471–505.

Hickson, D., Butler, R., Cray, D., Mallory, G. and Wilson, D. (1986) *Top Decisions: Strategic Decision-making in Organisations*, Oxford: Blackwell.

Hill, S. (1995) 'The social organisation of boards of directors', *British Journal of Sociology* 46(2): 245–78.

Hobbs, P. and Jefferis, K. (1990) 'So how many co-operatives are there? – a critical note on co-operative studies' in G. Jenkins and M. Poole (eds) *New Forms of Ownership, Management and Employment*, London: Routledge.

Hochner, A. (1983) 'Worker ownership, community ownership, and labor unions: two examples', *Economic and Industrial Democracy* 4: 345–69.

Holland, S. (1975) *The Socialist Challenge*, London: Quartet.

Hunter, L. (1998) 'Can strategic participation be institutionalised? Union representation on American corporate boards', *Industrial and Labor Relations Review* 51(4): 557–78.

Hurlston, M. (1998) 'Speech to tenth anniversary conference', at ESOP Centre Tenth Anniversary Conference, London, June.

Hutton, W. (1995) *The State We're In*, London: Jonathan Cape.

Hyman, J. and Mason, R. (1995) *Managing Employee Involvement and Participation*, London: Sage.

Hyman, R. (1997) 'The future of employee representation', *British Journal of Industrial Relations* 35(3): 309–31.

Incomes Data Services (1986) *Profit Sharing and Employee Share Options*, London: IDS.

Industrial Democracy in Europe Research Group (1981) *Industrial Democracy in Europe*, Oxford: Clarendon.

Inland Revenue (1999a) *A New All-Employee Share Plan*, London: Inland Revenue.

—— (1999b) *Enterprise Management Incentives*, London: Inland Revenue.

—— (1999c) *Inland Revenue Statistics 1999*, London: HMSO.

IRS Management Review (1998) 'Financial participation', *IRS Management Review*.

James, N., Rubra, N. and Silcock, D. (1985) *Working Practices in the British Bus Industry and Their Implications for Operating Costs*, Newcastle: University of Newcastle Upon Tyne Transport Operations Research Group (Report 60).

Jenkinson, T. and Mayer, C. (1992) 'The assessment: corporate governance and corporate control', *Oxford Review of Economic Policy* 8(3): 1–10.

Jensen, M. (1986) 'Agency costs of free cash-flow, corporate finance and takeovers', *American Economic Review* 76: 323–9.

—— (1993) 'The modern industrial revolution, exit and the failure of internal control systems', *Journal of Finance* 48: 831–80.

Jensen, M. and Meckling, W. (1976) 'Theory of the firm: managerial behaviour, agency costs and ownership structure', *Journal of Financial Economics* 3: 305–60.

—— (1979) 'Rights and production functions: an application to labor-managed firms and co-determination', *Journal of Business* 52: 469–506.

Jones, D. (1975) 'Producer co-operatives and the view of the Webbs on participation and the ability to survive', *Annals of Public and Co-operative Economics* 46(1): 23–44.

Jones, D. and Kato, T. (1995) 'The productivity effects of Japanese employee stock ownership plans: evidence from Japanese panel data', *American Economic Review* 85(3): 391–414.

Jones, T. (1996) *Remaking the Labour Party*, London: Routledge.

Kaplan, S. and Stromberg, P. (2000) 'Financial contracting theory meets the real world: evidence from venture capital contracts', paper at American Finance Association conference, Boston, January.

Kaufman, R. and Russell, R. (1995) 'Government support for profit sharing, gainsharing, ESOPs and TQM', *Contemporary Economic Policy* 13: 38–48.

Kay, J. (1997) 'The stakeholder corporation', in G. Kelly, D. Kelly and A. Gamble (eds) *Stakeholder Capitalism*, London: Macmillan.

Kay, J. and Silberston, A. (1995) 'Corporate governance', *National Institute Economic Review* (153): 84–97.

Keasey, K., Thompson, S. and Wright, M. (1997) *Corporate Governance*, Oxford: Oxford University Press.

Keef, S. (1998) 'The causal association between employee share ownership and attitudes: a study based on the Long framework', *British Journal of Industrial Relations* 36(1): 73–82

Kelly, G., Kelly, D. and Gamble, A. (1997) *Stakeholder Capitalism*, Basingstoke: Macmillan.

Kelly, J. and Kelly, C. (1991) '"Them and us": social psychology and the new industrial relations', *British Journal of Industrial Relations* 29(1): 25–48.

Kelso, L. and Adler, M. (1958) *The Capitalist Manifesto*, New York: Random House.

Kelso, L. and Hetter, P. (1967) *How to Turn Eighty Million Workers into Capitalists*, New York: Random House.

Kenner Thompson, J. (1993) 'Promotion of employee ownership through public policy: the British example', *Journal of Economic Issues* 27(3): 825–47.

Klein, K. (1987) 'Employee stock ownership and employee attitudes: a test of three models', *Journal of Applied Psychology* 72(2): 319–32.

Klein, K. and Hall, R. (1988) 'Correlates of employee satisfaction with stock ownership: who likes an ESOP most?', *Journal of Applied Psychology* 73(4): 630–8.

Klein, K. and Rosen, C. (1986) 'Employee stock ownership in the United States', in R. Stern and S. McCarthy (eds) *The Organizational Practice of Democracy*, New York: John Wiley.

Kovenock, D. and Sparks, R. (1990) 'An implicit contract approach to employee stock ownership plans', *Journal of Comparative Economics* 14: 425–51.

Kruse, D. (1984) *Employee Ownership and Employee Attitudes: Two Case Studies,* Norwood, PA: Norwood Editions.

—— (1993) *Profit Sharing: Does it Make a Difference?,* Kalamazoo, Michigan: Upjohn Institute for Employment Research.

—— (1996) 'Why do firms adopt profit sharing and ownership plans?', *British Journal of Industrial Relations* 34: 515–38.

—— (1999) 'Economic democracy or just another risk for workers? Reviewing the evidence on employee ownership and profit sharing', paper presented at the Democracy, Participation and Development conference, Columbia University, April.

Kruse, D. and Blasi, J. (1997) 'Employee ownership, employee attitudes, and firm performance: a review of the evidence', in D. Lewin, D. Mitchell and M. Zaidi (eds) *The Human Resource Management Handbook,* London: JAI Press.

Labour Party (1982) *Labour's Programme 1992,* London: Labour Party.

—— (1983) *The New Hope for Britain,* London: Labour Party.

—— (1986) *Social Ownership,* London: Labour Party.

—— (1987) *Britain Will Win,* London: Labour Party.

—— (1989) *Meet the Challenge, Make the Change: a New Agenda for Britain. Final Report of the Labour Policy Review for the 1990s,* London: Labour Party.

—— (1992) *It's Time to Get Britain Working Again,* London: Labour Party.

—— (1997) *New Labour Because Britain Deserves Better,* London: Labour Party.

Leadbetter, C. (1997) *A Piece of the Action: Employee Ownership, Equity pay and the Rise of the Knowledge Economy,* London: DEMOS.

Levine, D. and Tyson, D. (1990) 'Participation, productivity and the firm's environment', in A. Blinder (ed.) *Paying for Productivity: A Look at the Evidence,* Washington DC: Brookings Institution.

Liberal Democrat Party (1997) *Make the Difference,* London: Liberal Democrat Party.

Liberal Party (1992) *Changing Britain for Good,* London: Liberal Party.

Likert, R. (1970) 'New patterns of management', in V. Vroom and E. Deci (eds) *Management and Motivation,* Harmondsworth: Penguin.

Logue, J. and Yates, J. (1999) 'Worker ownership American style: pluralism, participation and performance', *Economic and Industrial Democracy* 20(2): 225–51.

Long, R. (1978a) 'The effects of employee ownership on organisational identification, employee job attitudes and organisational performance – a tentative framework and empirical findings', *Human Relations* 31(1): 29–48.

—— (1978b) 'The relative effects of share ownership versus control on job attitudes in an employee owned company', *Human Relations* 31(3): 753–63.

—— (1978c) 'Employee ownership and attitudes towards the union: an empirical study', *Relations Industrielles* 33(2): 237–53.

—— (1979) 'Desires for and patterns of worker participation in decision-making after conversion to employee ownership, *Academy of Management Journal* 22(3): 611–17.

—— (1980) 'Job attitudes and organizational performance under employee ownership', *Academy of Management Journal* 23(4): 726–37.

—— (1981) 'The effects of formal employee participation in ownership and decision-making on perceived and desired patterns of organisational influence: a longitudinal study', *Human Relations* 34(10): 847–76.

—— (1982). 'Worker ownership and job attitudes: a field study', *Industrial Relations* 21(2): 196–215.

Loveridge, R. (1980) 'What is participation? A review of the literature and some methodological problems', *British Journal of Industrial Relations* 18(3): 297–317.

Lukes, S. (1974) *Power: A Radical View*, London: Macmillan.

Lynch, M. (1990) *ESOPs, ECOPs and Employee Ownership*, London: Transport and General Workers' Union.

McCarthy, W. (1988) *The Future of Industrial Democracy*, Fabian Tract 526, London: Fabian Society.

McElrath, R. and Rowan, R. (1992) 'The American labor movement and employee ownership: objections to and uses of employee stock ownership plans', *Journal of Labor Research* 13: 99–119.

McNabb, R. and Whitfield, K. (1998) 'The impact of financial participation and employee involvement on financial performance', *Scottish Journal of Political Economy* 45(2): 171–89.

Manne, J. (1965) 'Mergers and the market for corporate control', *Journal of Political Economy* 73: 110–20.

Marchington, M., Goodman, J., Wilkinson, A. and Ackers, P. (1992) *New Developments in Employee Involvement*, Sheffield: Research Management Branch, Employment Department Group.

Mason, N. (1992) 'ESOPs and co-operative enterprise: the employee common ownership plan (ECOP)', in N. Wilson (ed.) *ESOPs: Their Role in Corporate Finance and Performance*, London: Macmillan.

—— (1998) 'ESOPs as an exit route', at ESOP Centre Tenth Anniversary Conference, London, June.

Meade, J. (1972) 'The theory of labour-managed firms and of profit sharing', *Economic Journal* 82: 402–28.

Meister, A. (1984) *Participation, Associations, Development and Change*, New Brunswick, NJ: Transaction Books.

Millward, N., Stevens, M., Smart, D. and Hawes, W. (1992) *Workplace Industrial Relations in Transition: the ED/ESRC/PSI/ACAS Surveys*, Aldershot: Dartmouth.

Milne, K. (1996) 'The certainty man', *New Statesman and Society* 9(393): 24–5.

Mitchell, D. (1995) 'Profit sharing and employee ownership: policy implications', *Contemporary Economic Policy* 13: 16–25.

Monopolies and Mergers Commission (1996) *Stagecoach Holdings PLC and Chesterfield Transport (1989) Ltd: A Report on the Merger Situation*, London: HMSO, Cm. 3086.

Mowday, R., Porter, L. and Steers, R. (1982) *Employee–Organisation Linkages: The Psychology of Commitment, Absenteeism, and Turnover*, New York: Academic Press.

Mowday, R., Steers, R. and Porter, L. (1979) 'The measurement of organizational commitment', *Journal of Vocational Behaviour* 14: 224–47.

Moye, M. (1993) 'Mondragon: adapting co-operative structures to meet the demands of a changing environment', *Economic and Industrial Democracy* 14(2): 251–76.

National Center for Employee Ownership (1998) *Combining ESOPs and 401 (k) Plans*. Online. Available HTTP://www.nceo.org/library/combine.html.

—— (1999) *A Statistical Profile of Employee Ownership*. Online. Available HTTP://www.nceo.org/library/eo_stat.html (3 February 2000).

Nichols, T. and O'Connell Davidson, J. (1992) 'Employee shareholders in two privatized utilities', *Industrial Relations Journal* 23: 107–19.

Ogden, S. (1982) 'Trade unions, industrial democracy and collective bargaining', *Sociology* 16(4): 544–63.

Ohio Employee Ownership Centre (1993) *Employee Ownership in Ohio's Economy: Effects on Job Growth, Corporate Performance and Employee Involvement*, Kent, Ohio: Ohio Employee Ownership Centre.

Oliver, N. (1984) 'An examination of organizational commitment in six workers' co-operatives in Scotland', *Human Relations* 37(1): 29–46.

—— (1990) 'Work rewards, work values, and organizational commitment in an employee-owned firm: evidence from the UK', *Human Relations* 43: 513–26.

Oliver, N. and Thomas, A. (1990) 'Ownership, commitment and control: the case of producer co-operatives', in G. Jenkins and M. Poole (eds) *New Forms of Ownership: Management and Employment*, London: Routledge.

Organisation for Economic Cooperation and Development (1995) 'Profit sharing in OECD countries', *Employment Outlook* (July).

O'Sullivan, M. (2000) 'Shareholder value, financial theory, and economic performance', paper presented to 52nd Annual Meeting of the Industrial Relations Research Association, Boston, MA.

Parkinson, J. (1997) 'Company law and stakeholder governance', in G. Kelly, D. Kelly and A. Gamble (eds) *Stakeholder Capitalism*, London: Macmillan.

Pateman, C. (1970) *Participation and Democratic Theory*, Cambridge: Cambridge University Press.

Peccei, R. and Guest, D. (1993) *The Dimensionality and Stability of Organizational Commitment*, London School of Economics: Centre for Economic Performance, Discussion Paper 149.

Pendleton, A. (1992) 'ESOPs and employee relations', in N. Wilson (ed.) *ESOPs: Their Role in Corporate Finance and Performance*, London: Macmillan.

—— (1997a) 'Stakeholders as shareholders: the role of employee share ownership', in G. Kelly, D. Kelly and A. Gamble (eds) *Stakeholder Capitalism*, Basingstoke: Macmillan.

—— (1997b) 'Characteristics of workplaces with financial participation: evidence from the WIRS', *Industrial Relations Journal* 28(3): 103–19.

—— (1999) 'Ownership or competition? An evaluation of the effects of privatisation on industrial relations institutions, processes and outcomes', *Public Administration* 77(4): 769–92.

Pendleton, A., Robinson, A. and Wilson, N. (1994) 'Worker directors: their influence on strategic decisions', Bradford University Management Centre, mimeo.

Pendleton, A., McDonald, J., Robinson, A. and Wilson, N. (1995a) 'The impact of employee share ownership plans on employee participation and industrial democracy', *Human Resource Management Journal* 5(4): 44–60.

—— (1996) 'Employee participation and corporate governance in employee-owned firms', *Work, Employment and Society* 10(2): 205–26.

Pendleton, A., Robinson, A., and Wilson, N. (1995b) 'Does economic democracy weaken trade unions? Recent evidence from the UK bus industry', *Economic and Industrial Democracy* 16(4): 577–604.

Pendleton, A., Wilson, N. and Wright, M. (1998) 'The perception and effects of share ownership: empirical evidence from employee buy-outs', *British Journal of Industrial Relations* 36(1): 99–124.

Perotin, V. (1987) 'Conditions of survival and closure of French worker cooperatives', *Advances in the Economic Analysis of Participatory and Labor-Managed Firms* 2: 201–24.

—— (1997) 'Entry, exit and the business cycle: are coops different?', paper presented at the Eighth Conference of the International Association for the Economics of Participation, Prague, August.

Pett, D. (1998) 'Statutory ESOPs', at ESOP Centre Tenth Anniversary Conference, London, June.

Pettigrew, A. and McNulty, T. (1995) 'Power and influence in and around the boardroom', *Human Relations* 48(8): 845–73.

Pierce, J.L, Rubenfeld, S.A. and Morgan, S. (1991), 'Employee ownership: a conceptual model of process and effects', *Academy of Management Review* 16(1): 121–44.

Poole, M. (1986) *Towards a New Industrial Democracy: Workers' Participation in Industry*, London: Routledge.

—— (1988) 'Factors affecting the development of employee financial participation in contemporary Britain: evidence from a national survey', *British Journal of Industrial Relations* 26(1): 21–36.

—— (1989) *The Origins of Economic Democracy: Profit-Sharing and Employee-Shareholding Schemes*, London: Routledge.

Poole, M. and Jenkins, G. (1990) *The Impact of Economic Democracy: Profit-Sharing and Employee-shareholding Schemes*, London: Routledge.

Poole, M. and Whitfield, K. (1994) 'Theories and evidence on the growth and distribution of profit sharing and employee shareholding schemes', *Human Systems Management* 13(3): 209–20.

Portillo, M. (1995) 'The competitive edge', *Department of Employment Gazette* (July): 271.

Poutsma, E. (2000) *Recent Developments in Financial Participation within the European Union*, Report for the European Foundation for the Improvement of Living and Working Conditions, Dublin.

Poutsma, E., Nijs, W. and Doorewaard, H. (1999) 'Promotion of employee ownership and profit sharing in Europe', *Economic and Industrial Democracy* 20: 171–96.

Proshare (1998) *Employee Share Ownership Research*, London: Proshare.

Purkiss, A. (1991) 'The death of the democratic dream?', *Director* (November): 66–71.

—— (1992) 'ESOP Fables', *Director* (July): 32–6.

Rajan, R. and Zingales, L. (1998) 'Power in the theory of the firm', *Quarterly Journal of Economics* 113(2): 387–432.

Ramsay, H. (1976) 'Participation: the shop floor view', *British Journal of Industrial Relations* 14(2): 128–41.

—— (1977) 'Cycles of control', *Sociology* 11: 486–506.

—— (1983) 'Evolution or cycle? Worker participation in the 1970s and 1980s', in C. Crouch and F. Heller (eds) *International Yearbook of Organizational Democracy*, vol. 1, Chichester: Wiley.

—— (1993) 'Recycled waste? Debating the analysis of worker participation: a response to Ackers et al.', *Industrial Relations Journal* 24(1): 76–81.

Reid, D. (1992) 'ESOPs: legal complexities unravelled', in N. Wilson (ed.) *ESOPs: Their Role in Corporate Finance and Performance*, London: Macmillan.

Rhodes, S. and Steers, R. (1981). 'Conventional vs worker-owned organizations', *Human Relations* 34(12): 1013–35.

Richardson, R. and Nejad, A. (1986), 'Employee ownership schemes in the UK – an evaluation', *British Journal of Industrial Relations* 24(2): 233–44.

Robinson, A. and Wilson, N. (1993) 'Co-operative vs private firms: an empirical comparison of co-operative and private small firms in Britain', *International Business Review* 2(3): 281–96.

Roche, B. (1999) 'Employee share ownership', Adjournment debate, *Hansard*, 14 July.

Rooney, P. (1988) 'Worker participation in employee-owned firms', *Journal of Economic Issues* 22(2): 451–8.

Rose, M. (1988) *Industrial Behaviour*, 2nd edition, Harmondsworth: Penguin.

Rose, M. and Jones, B. (1985) 'Managerial strategy and trade union responses in work reorganization schemes at plant level', in D. Knights, H. Willmott and D. Collinson (eds) *Job Re-design: Critical Perspectives on the Labour Process*, Aldershot: Gower.

Rosen, C., Klein, K. and Young, K. (1986) *Employee ownership in the United States: The Equity Solution*, Lexington, MA: Lexington Books.

Russell, R. (1984) 'Using ownership to control: making owners workers in the contemporary United States', *Politics and Society* 13(3): 253–94.

—— (1985a) *Sharing Ownership in the Services*, Albany: State University of New York Press.

—— (1985b) 'Employee ownership and internal governance', *Journal of Economic Behaviour and Governance* 6: 217–41.

—— (1988) 'Forms and extent of employee participation in the contemporary United States', *Work and Occupations* 15(4): 374–95.

Russell, R., Hochner, A. and Perry, S. (1979) 'Participation, influence and worker ownership', *Industrial Relations* 18(3): 330–41.

Saunders, P. and Harris, C. (1990) 'Privatisation and the consumer', *Sociology* 24(1): 57–76.

Schleifer, A. and Summers, L. (1988) 'Breach of trust in hostile takeovers', in A. Auerbach (ed.) *Corporate Takeovers: Causes and Consequences*, Chicago: National Bureau of Economic Research.

Scholes, M. and Wolfson, M. (1990) 'Employee stock ownership plans and corporate restructuring: myths and realities', *Financial Management* 19: 12–28.

Schuller, T. (1985) *Democracy at Work*, Oxford: Oxford University Press.

Scott, J. (1996) *Corporate Business and Capitalist Classes*, Oxford: Oxford University Press.

Smith, G. (1993) 'Employee share schemes in Britain', *Employment Gazette* (April): 149–54.

Smith, M. (1992a) 'The Labour Party in opposition', in M. Smith and J. Spear (eds) *The Changing Labour Party*, London: Routledge.

—— (1992b) 'A return to revisionism? The Labour Party Policy Review', in M. Smith and J. Spear (eds) *The Changing Labour Party*, London: Routledge.

Sockell, D. (1985) 'Attitudes, behaviour, and employee ownership: some preliminary data', *Industrial Relations* 24: 130–8.

Stern, R. (1988) 'Participation by representation: workers on boards of directors in the United States and abroad', *Work and Occupations* 15(4): 396–422.

Stern, R., Whyte, W., Hammer, T. and Meek, C. (1983) 'The union and the transition to employee ownership', in W. Whyte, T. Hammer, C. Meek and R. Stern (eds) *Worker Participation and Ownership*, Cornell University: ILR Press.

Stokes, G., Pickup, L., Meadowcroft, S., Kenny, F. and Goodwin, P. (1990) *Bus Deregulation: The Metropolitan Experience*, London: Association of Metropolitan Authorities/Passenger Transport Executive Group.

Strauss, G. (1992) 'Worker participation', in J. Hartley and G. Stephenson (eds) *Employment Relations*, Oxford: Blackwell.

Tannenbaum, A. (1957) 'Control structure and union functions', *American Journal of Sociology* 61(2): 127–40.

—— (1968) *Control in Organizations*, New York: McGraw-Hill.

Taylor, Ian, MP (1988) *Fair Shares for all the Workers*, London: House of Commons Library.

—— (1992) *A Community of Employee Shareholders*, London: Bow Group.

Thompson, N. (1996) *Political Economy and the Labour Party*, London: University College of London Press.

Thompson, S. and Wright, M. (1987) 'Markets to hierarchies and back again: the implications of management buy-outs for factor supply', *Journal of Economic Studies* 14(3): 3–24.

Thompson, S., Wright, M. and Robbie, K. (1990) 'Management buy-outs from the public sector: ownership form and incentive issues', *Fiscal Studies* 11(3): 71–88.

Thornley, J. (1983) 'Workers' co-operatives and trade unions: the Italian experience', *Economic and Industrial Democracy* 4: 321–44.

Toscano, D. (1984) 'Employee ownership and its effects on attitudes towards trade unions', *Labor Studies Journal* (Spring): 80–7.

Towers, B., Cox, D. and Chell, E. (1985) *Worker Directors in Private Manufacturing Industry in Great Britain*, London: Department of Employment, Research Paper 29.

Trades Union Congress (1974) *Industrial Democracy*, London: Trades Union Congress.

—— (1987) *Annual Congress 1987*, London: TUC.

—— (1990) *TUC Note to the CBI Wider Share Ownership Task Force*, London: Trades Union Congress.

—— (1999a) *Response to Consultation on Employee Share Ownership*, London: Trades Union Congress.

—— (1999b) *Share Ownership, Productivity and Company Performance*, London: Trades Union Congress.

Treasury (1998) *Consultation on Employee Share Ownership*, London: HM Treasury.

Trewhitt, L. (1999a) 'A tale of two bus companies: identifying forms of employee share ownership and implications for employee attitudes, behaviours and effects', paper presented at the British Academy of Management conference, Manchester Metropolitan University, September.

—— (1999b) 'Employee involvement and employee share ownership: never the twain shall meet', paper presented at the British Academy of Management conference, Manchester Metropolitan University, September.

Tucker, J, Nock, S. and Toscano, D. (1989) 'Employee ownership and perceptions of work', *Work and Occupations* 16(1): 26–42.

Turberville, S. (1999) 'Mapping employee financial participation in Australia: evidence from AWIRS 90 and 95', paper presented at the British Academy of Management conference, Manchester Metropolitan University, September.

Turnbull, P. (1993) 'Docks', in A. Pendleton and J. Winterton (eds) *Public Enterprise in Transition: Industrial Relations in State and Privatised Corporations*, London: Routledge.

Turnbull, P. and Weston, S. (1993) 'Co-operation or control? Capital restructuring and labour relations on the docks', *British Journal of Industrial Relations* 31(1): 115–34.

Useem, M. (1993) *Executive Defense: Shareholder Power and Corporate Reorganization*, Cambridge, MA: Harvard University Press.

Useem, M. and Gager, C. (1996) 'Employee shareholders or institutional investors? When corporate managers replace their stockholders', *Journal of Management Studies* 33(5): 613–31.

Uvalic, M. (1991) *Social Europe: The PEPPER Report*, Brussels and Florence: European Commission.

Vanek, J. (1977) 'The basic theory of financing of participatory firms', in J. Vanek (ed.) *The Labor-Managed Economy: Essays by Jaroslav Vanek*, Ithaca: Cornell University Press.

Vaughan-Whitehead, D. (1995) *Workers' Financial Participation: East–West Experiences*, Geneva: International Labour Office.

Wadhwani, S. and Wall, M. (1990) 'The effects of profit-sharing on employment, wages, stock returns and productivity: evidence from micro-data', *Economic Journal* 100(399): 1–17.

Walley, K. and Wilson, N. (1992) 'Employee share ownership plans in the UK: a preliminary survey', in N. Wilson (ed.) *ESOPs: Their Role in Corporate Finance and Performance*, London: Macmillan.

Ward, B. (1958) 'The firm in Illyria', *American Economic Review* 48(4): 566–89.

Watts, J. (1998) 'Running an ESOP – trusteeship and other issues', at ESOP Centre Tenth Anniversary Conference, London, June.

Webb, S. and Webb, B. (1914) *Co-operative Production and Profit Sharing*, London: *New Statesman* Special Supplement.

Weitzman, M. and Kruse, D. (1990) 'Profit sharing and productivity', in A. Blinder (ed.) *Paying for Productivity: A Look at the Evidence*, Washington DC: Brookings Institution.

Welford, R. (1990) 'The organisation and behaviour of UK worker co-operatives: an empirical investigation', in G. Jenkins and M. Poole (eds) *New Forms of Ownership: Management and Employment*, London: Routledge.

Wheatcroft, D. (no date) 'From public to private hands via the employee ownership model: the Chesterfield Transport model', mimeo.

Whyte, W. and Whyte, K. (1988) *Making Mondragon: the Growth and Dynamics of the Worker Cooperative Complex*, Ithaca: ILR Press.

Wichman, A. (1994) 'Occupational differences in involvement in ownership in an airline employee ownership program', *Human Relations* 47(7): 829–46.

Wilkinson, A., Marchington, M., Ackers, P. and Goodman, J. (1994) 'ESOPs Fables – a tale of a machine tool company', *International Journal of Human Resource Management* 5(1): 121–43.

Williamson, J. (1997) 'Your stake at work: the TUC's agenda', in G. Kelly, D. Kelly and A. Gamble (eds) *Stakeholder Capitalism*, Basingstoke: Macmillan.

Williamson, O. (1964) *The Economics of Discretionary Behaviour: Managerial Objectives in a Theory of the Firm*, New York: Prentice-Hall.

—— (1975) *Markets and Hierarchies: Analysis and Antitrust Implications*, New York: Free Press.

—— (1979) 'Transaction–cost economics: the governance of contractual relations', *Journal of Law and Economics* 22: 233–61.

—— (1988) 'Corporate finance and corporate governance', *Journal of Finance* 43: 567–91.

Wilson, D., Butler, R., Cray, D., Hickson, D. and Mallory, G. (1982) 'The limits of trade union power in organization decision-making', *British Journal of Industrial Relations* 20: 322–41.

Wilson, N. (1992) *ESOPs: Their Role in Corporate Finance and Performance*, London: Macmillan.

Wilson, N. and Peel, M. (1991) 'The impact on absenteeism and quits of profit-sharing and other forms of employee participation', *Industrial and Labor Relations Review* 44(3): 454–68.

Winkler, J. (1974) 'The ghost at the bargaining table; directors and industrial relations', *British Journal of Industrial Relations* 12(2): 191–213.

Winther, G. (1999) 'Theory O – is the case closed?', *Economic and Industrial Democracy* 20: 269–93.

Wright, M. and Robbie, K. (1992) 'Employee buy-outs in the UK', in N. Wilson (ed.) *ESOPs: Their Role in Corporate Finance and Performance*, London: Macmillan.

Wright, M., Chiplin, B., Thompson, S., and Robbie, K. (1990) 'Management buy-outs, trade unions and employee ownership', *Industrial Relations Journal* 21: 136–46.

Wright, M., Dobson, P., Thompson, S. and Robbie, K. (1992) 'How well does privatisation achieve government objectives? The case of bus buy-outs', *International Journal of Transport Economics* 19: 259–85.

Wright, M., Pendleton, A. and Robbie, K. (2000) 'Employee ownership in enterprises in Africa and Asia', *International Journal of Human Resource Management* 11(1): 90–111.

Wright, M., Thompson, S. and Robbie, K. (1989) 'Privatisation via management and employee buyouts: analysis and UK experience' *Annals of Public and Co-operative Economy* 60(4): 399–429.

Young, K. (1990) 'Managing and employee-owned company', in K. Young (ed.) *The Expanding Role of ESOPs in Public Companies*, Westport, CT: Quorum Books.

Zingales, L. (2000) 'The next 2000 years', paper presented at the American Finance Association conference, Boston, January.

Index